IMAGES
of America

# RIVERSIDE PARK

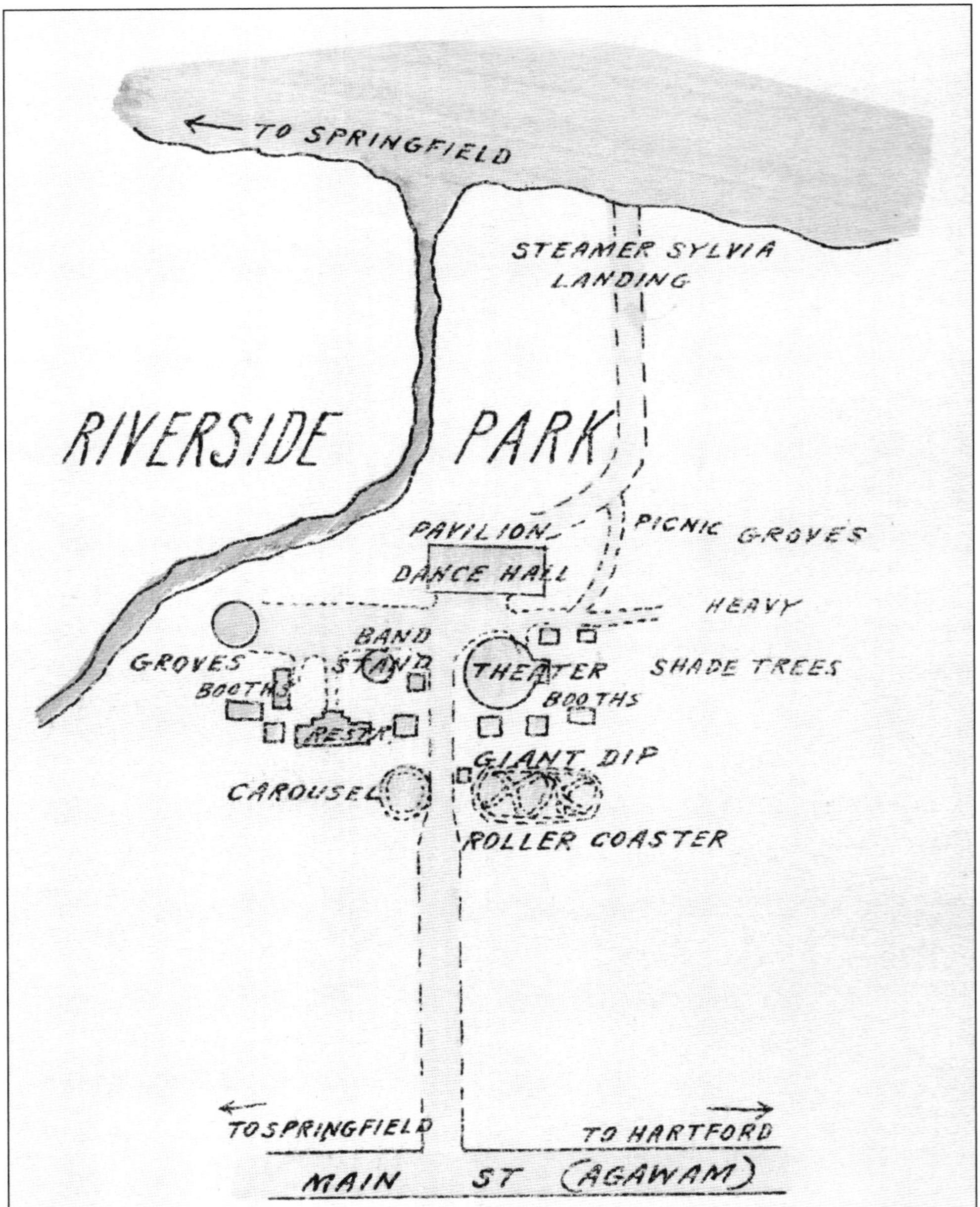


This detail from a 1912 Richards Map Company map of Agawam, Massachusetts, shows the layout of Riverside Park as it appeared that year under the new ownership of Henry J. Perkins, which marked the birth of Riverside as a true amusement park. The Connecticut River is at top, with Three Mile Brook extending downward from top left. The park has grown over the years, expanding westward toward Main Street. (Collection of the author.)

**On the Cover:** Riverside Park opened for the 1919 season on May 17 to larger than expected crowds, despite heavy showers. All buildings on the grounds had been painted green with white trim, and according to a newspaper account, they looked "very pretty in the setting of trees that surrounds them." The next day, another large crowd enjoyed good weather and a concert by the 104th Regiment Band. (Collection of the author.)

IMAGES
*of America*

# RIVERSIDE PARK

David Cecchi

ARCADIA
PUBLISHING

ISBN 978-0-7385-7504-9

Published by Arcadia Publishing
Charleston, South Carolina

Printed in the United States of America

Library of Congress Control Number: 2010939351

For all general information, please contact Arcadia Publishing:
Telephone 843-853-2070
Fax 843-853-0044
E-mail sales@arcadiapublishing.com
For customer service and orders:
Toll-Free 1-888-313-2665

Visit us on the Internet at www.arcadiapublishing.com

*For my parents, Robert and Emily Cecchi, who always worked so hard to provide my brothers and me with everything we needed and nearly everything we wanted. Thank you.*

# CONTENTS

# ACKNOWLEDGMENTS

The seed for this book was planted while working on the first of two books chronicling my hometown, *Agawam and Feeding Hills.* The chapter on Riverside Park could have taken up the whole book, but I wasn't ready for that project at that time. In the decade since, I have continued to collect Riverside artifacts, much to the consternation of my wife, especially as I bid higher and higher at a Monson, Massachusetts, auction on an early album that contained numerous photographs and postcards of Riverside, including the incredible panoramic image from July 1919 (pages 56 and 57). I have attempted to present the history of the park as accurately as possible but have found that the showbiz aspect of the industry sometimes obscures the real story. Newspaper articles often contradict earlier accounts. Planned new rides are almost always heralded when introduced, but not always built, and many older attractions are renovated, renamed, or removed without fanfare, causing some confusion as to exactly what happened to them and when. I also found several inaccuracies that are presented as fact on multiple websites—one downfall of the digital age. At any rate, I take responsibility for any erroneous information presented here and welcome any and all corrections.

I am indebted to those who generously loaned me photographs and shared their experiences and memories of the park. I was contacted by people from around New England and as far away as Minnesota, Las Vegas, and North Carolina. Those who opened their archives and collections made it possible to portray the story of Riverside in a way never before seen.

Conversations and e-mail correspondence with David Barden, Jaqueline Chapdelaine, Florence Frasco, Ann LaPalme, the late Raymond Lord, Mary Jane Murat, Yvonne Pomeroy, and Jim Roche provided interesting background information regarding the park, the grove, and the rollaway. The extensive stock-car racing collection of Bob Balise was a treasure trove of information regarding the speedway from its earliest days until the last race there in 1999—more of which I wish I could have included in this book. Mike Donahue's aerial photographs of the park provided a perfect visual ending to the Riverside story.

My sincere thanks also go to the Agawam Historical Association; the late Jim Birchall; Edward J. Carroll Jr.; Dick Chapman; Virginia Craig; Marilyn Curry; Tom DeNardo; James S. Gleason, library services manager at *The Republican*; David Kruger; Susan and David Maiolo; Cliff McCarthy, archivist at the Lyman and Merrie Wood Museum of Springfield History; Cynthia Simison, managing editor of *The Republican*; and Karl Stieg, whose generous gift of nearly a decade's-worth of newspaper clippings was invaluable in chronicling the park's recent history. Unless otherwise noted, all images are from the collection of the author.

Enjoy!

—David Cecchi
Agawam, Massachusetts
November 2010

# INTRODUCTION

On the western bank of the Connecticut River, at the south end of Main Street in the town of Agawam, between Three Mile Brook and the Massachusetts-Connecticut state line, are situated more than 200 acres dedicated for more than a century to the recreation of area residents.

I wondered why my young sons gave me quizzical looks when I spoke of Riverside Park, until I realized that they really had no idea what I was talking about. Although I still refer to the park as Riverside, Joe and Bailey never knew it as anything other than Six Flags New England, as the park has been known since they were toddlers.

Although younger generations will presumably flock to Six Flags for years to come, the Riverside Park of years gone by has left an indelible mark on the region. More than just a collection of rides and concessions, Riverside Park, at various points in its existence, truly had something for everyone—a giant swimming pool, dancing to the most popular bands of the day, a picnic grove, delicious clambakes, roller-skating, appearances by the biggest entertainers, stock-car racing, and bigger, faster, and more thrilling roller coasters. Some amusement parks had one or two of these features, but none had them all for so long or presented them so well. In addition, Riverside provided employment for hundreds of concessionaires, and later thousands of high school and college students, for whom a summer job meant a summer at Riverside.

Riverside Park grew into the largest amusement park in New England very quickly and never looked back. It suffered dearly during the Depression, but a white knight arrived from Boston and rebuilt a new and improved Riverside. He and his son developed the park as far as one family could, and looking to the future, they realized the survival of Riverside demanded its sale. The transaction eventually cost the park its name, but its underlying soul remains intact. To the throngs of visitors who arrive from New England and beyond, the park remains the summer-fun destination, regardless of what it is called.

Six Flags New England, Riverside Park, Riverside Grove, Gallup's Grove: this pleasure ground was not always so carefree. One of the earliest cotton mills in Massachusetts was erected on the part of the site known as Factory Ground in 1810. That mill closed in 1825, reopened in 1832, and operated until 1834 as a woolen mill. In 1851, it was converted to manufacture wallpaper by Lewis and Lyman Whitman. Harvey Porter later purchased an interest in the business and operated it under the name Whitman & Porter until 1867. By 1882, the three-story mill was in ruins. A boardinghouse and 8 to 10 small homes were also situated on the property, including one said to have sheltered Daniel Shays after his 1786 rebellion (see page 12).

Just south of the mill was a popular picnic area—a grove of white pines with a fine meadow between it and the river. The 54 acres were purchased in 1857 by John Gallup from Anson Cook. In 1870, Gallup built several pavilions and simple amusements and opened Gallup's Grove. Previously a freighter on the Hudson River, Gallup launched the steamboat *Mayflower* that year to transport guests to the grove. Later, as the crowds grew, he launched a larger steamboat, the *River Belle*.

In 1881, Gallup sold the grove and *River Belle* to Harvey Porter, who, in 1887, sold the property to Henry Smith and his son Elmer, who renamed it Riverside Grove. The Smiths operated another popular camping and picnic area, Calla Shasta, and built the 50-foot steamboat *Calla*, and later *Calla II*, to transport patrons to their property, located just north of Gallup's Grove. *Calla II* proved inadequate for the crowds at Riverside, and Smith constructed the 78-foot double-deck *Mascot* in 1885. By 1900, an even larger boat was needed, and the 92-foot, 350-passenger *Sylvia* was launched.

In 1900, the Springfield Street Railway constructed a trolley line along Agawam's Main Street to the Connecticut state line. Soon enough, up to a dozen trolley cars could be seen travelling back and forth, loaded with picnickers headed for Riverside on hot summer days, causing the railway to add several sections of double track to ease congestion. Despite the fact that Riverside was located at the end of a trolley line, and contrary to several published reports, it was not built by or ever owned by the Springfield Street Railway, and therefore is not considered a true trolley park.

Elmer Smith sold the grove and the *Sylvia* to Henry J. Perkins in July 1911, but he continued to captain the *Sylvia* until his retirement in 1918. An article in the July 20, 1911, *Springfield Daily Republican* titled "The New Riverside Grove—What H.J. Perkins Plans To Do" concludes, "Riverside Grove has been in existence as a resort some 40 years. Capt. Smith has had it for about 20 years, and before that his father controlled it. Capt. Gallup, who now lives in Connecticut, had the grove before that, and under its several owners it has always been a moneymaker."

Perkins, a prominent Springfield businessman and civic leader, had big plans. As president of the Riverside Park Amusement Company, he proceeded to transform the property into a "first-class recreation resort" with an initial expenditure of $50,000, which he used to build an open-air dance hall, erect the giant "dip" coaster and merry-go-round, and construct a new entrance and parking lot. The grove section of the park was improved, and the famous clambakes could now accommodate 3,000 diners at one sitting. The park opened for the 1912 season as Riverside Park. In years to come, Perkins would add a roller-skating rink and an enormous swimming pool, both of which were immensely popular. The dance hall was rebuilt, enlarged, and enclosed. A succession of new attractions was introduced with each opening season, a practice still followed to this day. The advertising slogan "Let's Go" was introduced and appeared in all Riverside promotions.

Perkins, who owned controlling interest in the park, died on February 16, 1927, at age 67, and the directors of the Riverside Park Amusement Company voted to sell the park in order to settle his estate. Despite rumors of million dollar–plus offers by New York and Boston syndicates and "Cincinnati capital," the park was bought in 1928 by a local concern headed by Perkins's brother Frank after "an error in the date of the auction" resulted in him being the only interested party to attend. The Agawam Amusement Corporation was formed with Michael J. Daley as president, Frank B. Perkins as treasurer, and D.B. Woodgate as clerk. George Bernert was named manager of Riverside Park for the 1928 season, and many changes were announced, including the creation of a second main entrance and additional automobile parking.

The stock market crash of 1929 and the ensuing economic crisis took their toll on the park. By September 1931, it was announced that Riverside was going into foreclosure. The 1930s would prove to be a decade of turmoil and uncertainty at the park. The Riverside Park Corporation was formed in April 1932 by Michael J. Daley, D.B. Woodgate, and Leon J. Zipf. The park was open only Wednesday through Sunday during the 1932 season and was open just three Mondays that year—Memorial Day, July Fourth, and Labor Day.

As the Depression worsened, so did the situation at Riverside. In 1934, the Town of Agawam's April 1932 assessment of the value of the property was contested by Michael J. Daley. He testified that the park had not been operated since 1932, that neither the officers nor the directors of the company ever drew a salary, that the corporation lost $30,000 annually, and that the swimming pool and other structures at the park were in very poor condition.

By 1935, a total of $16,000 in back taxes was owed. It was rumored that the year's opening was dependent on a favorable town vote regarding horse racing at the former Bowles Airport in Agawam. Days later, it was announced that a New York amusement company was interested in opening the park if a satisfactory agreement could be worked out with Daley and the Town of Agawam regarding back taxes. In late June, it was reported that Daley, holder of two mortgages on the property, "was the single bidder at a foreclosure sale" and bought the park for $45,000. New York amusement interests were then said to be interested in purchasing the property from Daley, who in addition to being owner of the park was the Emergency Relief and Construction Act administrator for Hampden County. July 1 newspaper reports stated that New Yorkers Samuel Moskowitz and Paul Pierce would be taking over the park, and that a crew of 75 workers was busy making renovations in preparation of a July 3 opening. More than 1,000 people turned out the night of July 3, only to find the gates shut and Agawam police officers posted to turn people away. Negotiations between concerned parties had broken down over the terms of the contract, and no permits would be issued until payment of the now $17,000 tax bill was resolved. Now referred to as a white elephant in the press, Riverside sat idle for the rest of the 1935 season as negotiations wore on. That fall, the would-be owners fought extradition to Massachusetts from New York on charges of larceny. It was alleged that they had represented themselves as owners of the park, engaged workmen in its renovation, and received money from concessionaires before vacating the area, leaving wages unpaid. In December, in connection with action by the Town of Agawam to seize the property for nonpayment of taxes, a sheriff's sale was announced to dispose of equipment, office furniture, and other personal property at Riverside Park.

The situation continued to worsen. In March 1936, the ballroom, on the bank of the Connecticut River, received considerable damage due to extensive flooding. In May, the Town of Agawam began foreclosure proceedings on the property. A July 23, 1936, news article reads, "All hope of opening Riverside Park, old-time amusement resort, this year has been abandoned. It was learned yesterday from Michael J. Daley, owner, who said he would sell the place 'cheap.' " In December, Daley squared the $24,000 real estate tax bill with a payment of $15,000.

Although the park itself was not open for much of the 1930s, picnics were still occasionally held in the grove area for groups such as the local bartenders union and newspaper carriers. Dances were also held in the ballroom.

Things began to turn around in 1937, when it was announced that Joseph P. McMahon of Springfield would open the Riverside parking lot on the evening of July 24 as an "outdoor moving picture show." Opened as the Riverside Park-In Outdoor Theater, it was the first drive-in theater in western Massachusetts, offering a double-feature program with newsreel.

July 1939 witnessed the announcement by Michael J. Daley that the park would reopen in August 1939 as the New Riverside Park. A crew of 50 men was reported to be clearing hurricane debris from the midway. A July 12 news article ends, "In the past five years nothing has been taken care of, the grass has been allowed to grow anywhere and the buildings have been neglected. Several pieces of equipment such as the Ferris wheel have been sold. On the property is the open-air theater which has been severely criticized by townspeople and church people." The park did not open that year.

Edward J. Carroll arrived from Boston in 1938 to manage the Park-In Theater and became intrigued with the nearby ruins of Riverside. His company, Stuart Amusement Company, purchased the park for $31,000 in October 1939. The following February, Carroll held a luncheon for more than 20 newspapermen at the Highland Hotel in Springfield, after which a tour of Riverside Park was given and planned improvements presented. A new emphasis on quality of product at the Park-In Theater was announced, as was the rebuilding of the roller-skating rink and dance pavilion. Carroll promised to have "number one name bands" booked for the dancing season and stated that Riverside Park would be "the public's park."

A crowd running into five figures joined state, city, and town officials at the dedication ceremonies of the reopened Riverside Park on Wednesday night, May 29, 1940. By 8:30 p.m., traffic was backed up almost four miles on Main Street, from the park to the Agawam–West Springfield Bridge, and three miles on River Road to the South End Bridge.

Attractions on opening night included dancing from 9:00 p.m. to 1:00 a.m. to Horace Heidt & His Musical Knights and Frankie Carle in the renovated Riverside Ballroom, which boasted 2,500 seats and 18,000 square feet of new Michigan maple flooring. Also featured were the Flying Allens' death-defying balloon cannon parachute jump, a Loop-the-Loop, 12 dodgem cars, a Ferris wheel, food stands, a fun house, and a 1909 M.C. Illions carousel purchased with 300 pairs of roller skates. Olga the Headless Wonder, the Gang Busters Show, and Yazoo the elephant, centerpiece of Carroll's 12-acre Animal Kingdom, appeared straight from the 1939 World's Fair in New York.

There was no roller coaster at Riverside that opening season, but Carroll had made arrangements to purchase the plans, cars, and tracks from the World's Fair for what was to open as the Cyclone in 1941 and later be named the Thunderbolt roller coaster, as it is still known.

By the end of the decade, as the big-band era was winding down, Carroll made the decision to close the famed dance hall, the largest in New England. In its place would be built the Riverside

Speedway. Opened as a one-fifth-mile track and later enlarged to a quarter mile, stock-car races at the speedway would become a huge part of Riverside's popularity in the coming years.

Carroll continued the practice begun by Henry Perkins of opening each season with a new attraction or "spectacular," rebuilding Riverside into the largest amusement park in New England. Carroll operated Riverside until his death in 1979, when his son Edward J. Carroll Jr. assumed ownership.

Carroll Jr. continued the legacy his father had begun, building New England's first loop coaster (the Loop, later known as the Black Widow) in 1977 and the William L. Cobb–designed Cyclone roller coaster in 1983. In 1987, the 150-foot-high Colossus Ferris wheel was added, and in 1989, a water park called Wild River Falls was opened. A proposal to open a riverboat casino and high-rise hotel was soundly defeated at the polls in 1994 by nearly 70 percent of Agawam voters.

By the mid-1990s, the Carroll family had determined that they had taken the park as far as one family was able. Lacking access to major capital, funding for construction of ever larger attractions such as $10 million–plus roller coasters was unlikely, leaving them at a serious disadvantage in the highly competitive amusement park industry. In December 1996, the park was sold to Premier Parks, Inc., of Oklahoma City for a reported $22.5 million.

The park opened for the 1997 season as Riverside The Great Escape, with nearly $30 million of renovations and new attractions, including the Mind Eraser roller coaster and Shipwreck Falls water ride. The following year, Premier Parks purchased the Six Flags theme park chain.

By 2000, when Riverside was rebranded as Six Flags New England, Premier had invested $100 million in the park. That same year, the Superman Ride of Steel roller coaster was opened. Over 200 feet high, the coaster was the tallest on the East Coast and has since been reworked as Bizarro. The coaster has won *Amusement Today*'s coveted Golden Ticket Award for Best Steel Coaster five times—in 2003, 2006, 2007, 2008, and 2009. A huge water park, Hurricane Harbor, has also been developed on the property.

As of this writing, Six Flags New England boasts over 60 rides, including 10 roller coasters, the most recent of which, Gotham City Gauntlet Escape from Arkham Asylum, opened at the start of the 2011 season.

# *One*

# The Grove

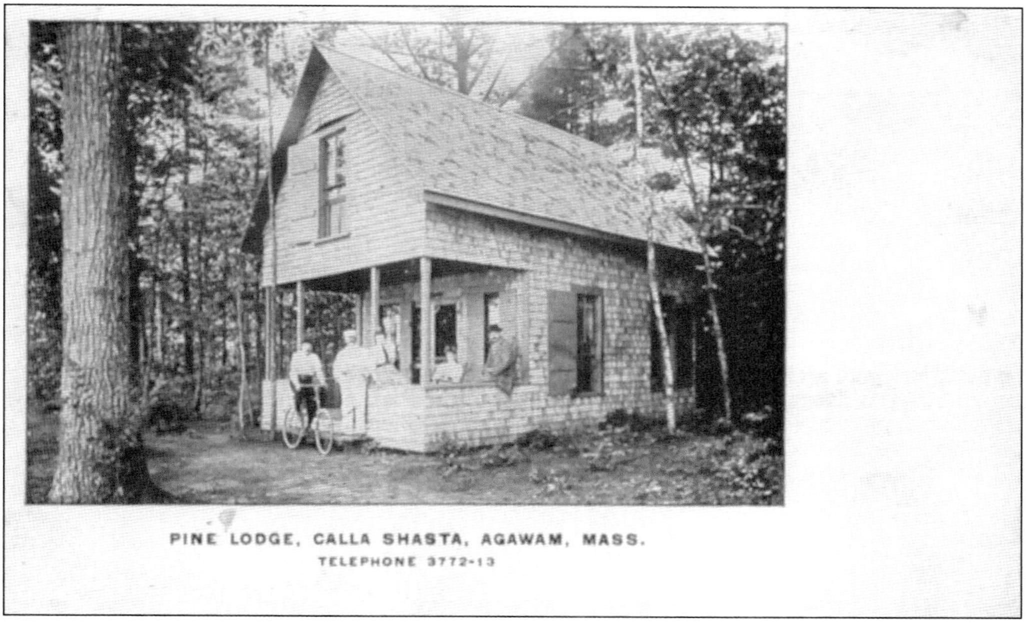


In 1887, Henry Smith and his son Elmer purchased Riverside Grove from Harvey Porter after having leased the property for the previous three years. The Smiths also operated the steamer *Mascot* and the Calla Shasta campground, just north of Riverside. Planned improvements at Riverside included a 300-seat restaurant, rowboats available for rental, and the creation of Lover's Bowers, which would be "plenty and attractive."

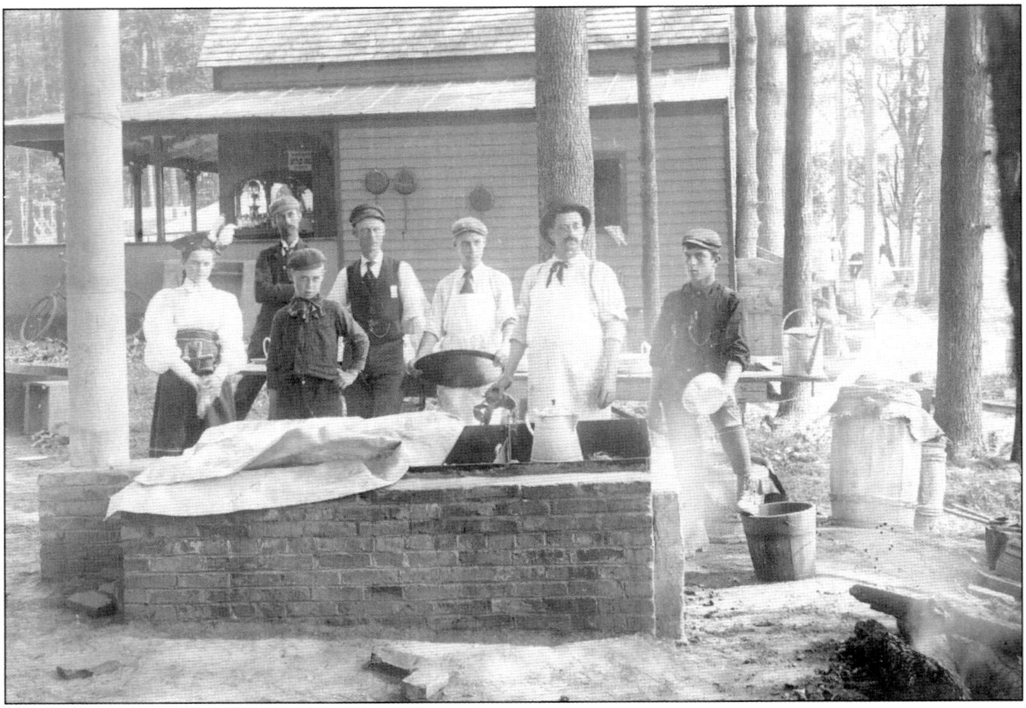

Riverside Grove became famous for its clambakes. An account in the July 26, 1895, *Springfield Daily Republican* describes the annual Company A clambake as a "delightful entertainment," where even the "staidest of businessmen . . . gambol like schoolboys." It further stated that "no one whose good fortune leads him to Riverside Grove would be likely to make the complaint so often heard that Americans do not know how to enjoy themselves." (Courtesy of the Agawam Historical Association.)

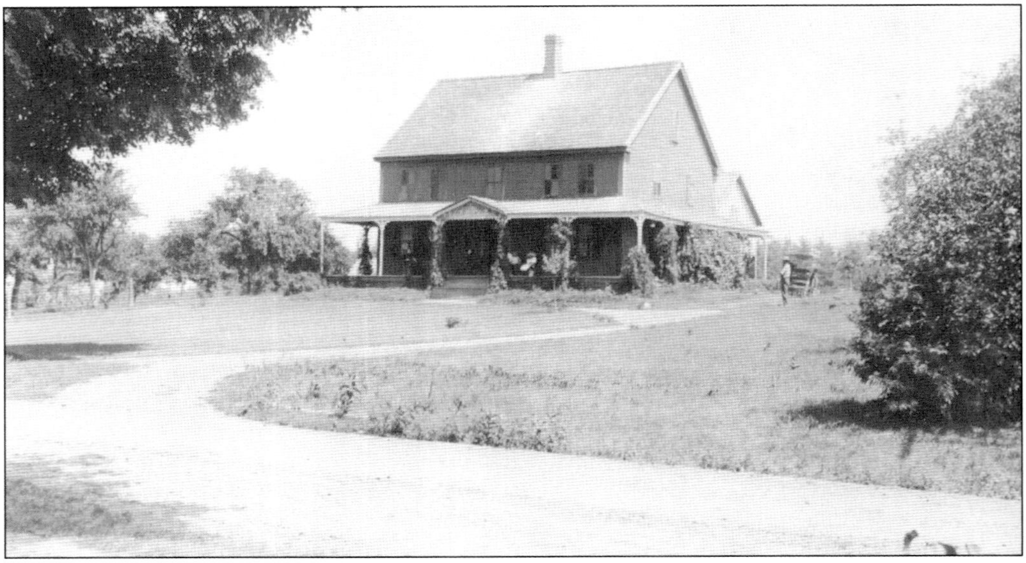

Charles Palmer Davis (founder of *Current Events* magazine) and Minerva Davis lived in the old Gallup House at 1615 Main Street. Pictured in 1896, the property was sold to Henry J. Perkins in 1911. The house was said to have been the refuge of Daniel Shays after his 1786 rebellion and later housed Riverside's Let's Go Inn, Green Gables, and Parkview restaurants.

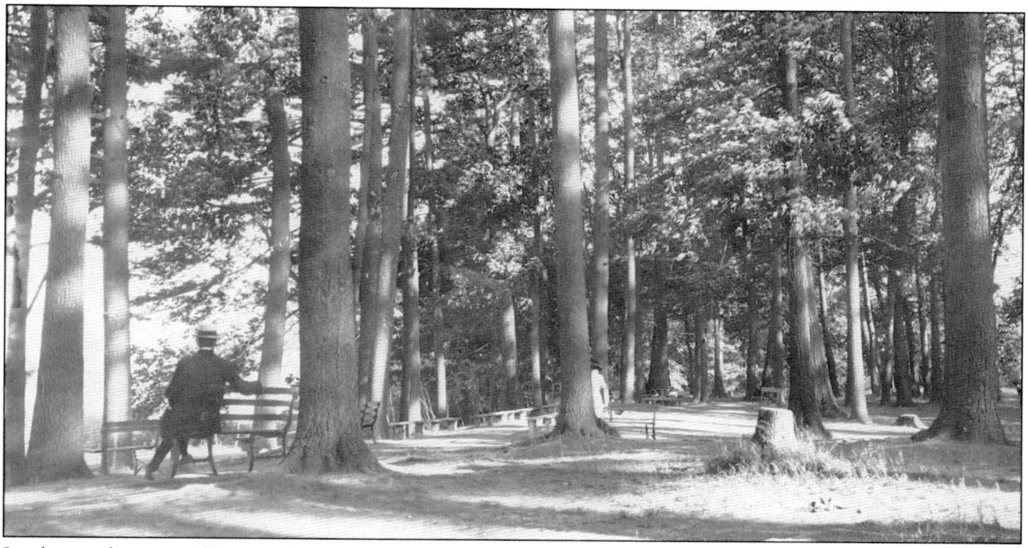

In this early view of Riverside Grove, its attraction is clear: the tall stand of pine trees offered a cool and relaxing respite during the hot summer months in the years before central air-conditioning. The Smiths operated the grove on "strictly temperance principles" and worked to attract "the custom of first-class picnic parties."

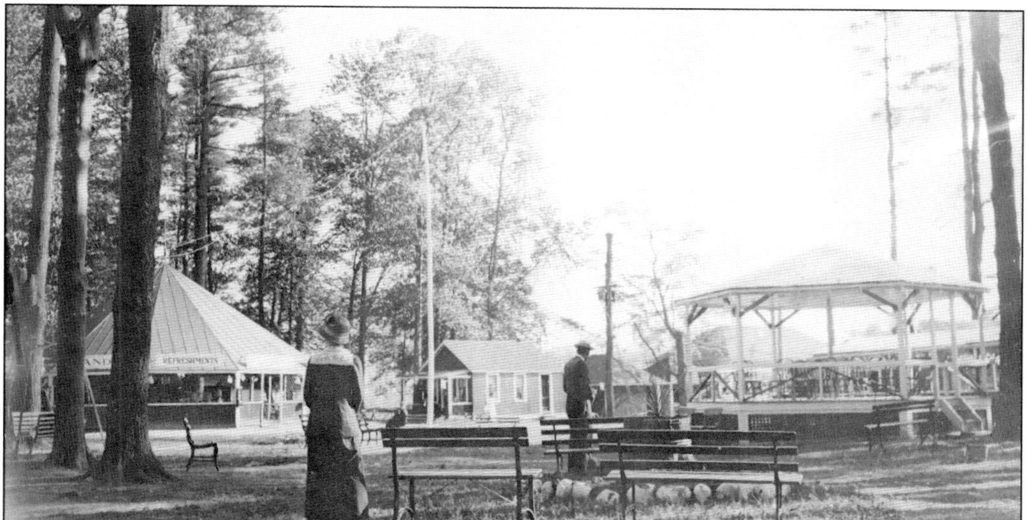


This early view of Riverside Grove includes the refreshment stand (left) and the bandstand (right). Afternoon and evening concerts were very popular events. A 1905 concert by Coate's Orchestra consisted of the following program: the march "Yankee Girl," overture "Tambour de Garde," serenade "Moonlight," caprice "Corncracker Dance," operatic selections "The Defender," "Apple Blossoms," and "Yankeeiana," the "Loveland Waltz," "Timely Tunes" medley, and the finale, "Phonograph."

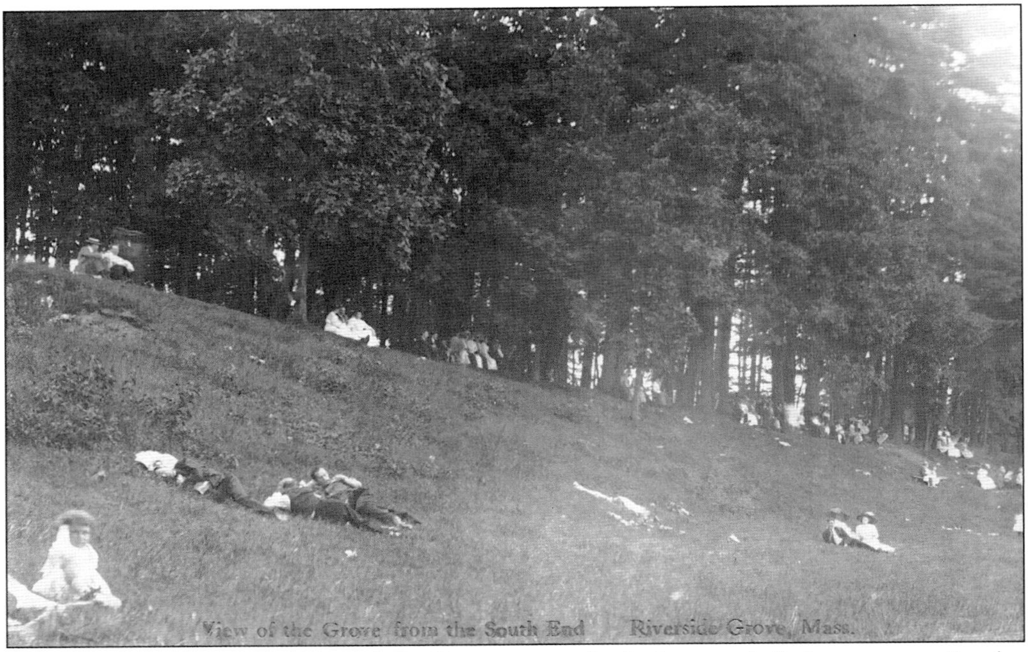


"View of the Grove from the South End" captures perfectly the mood of a lazy summer Sunday afternoon 100 years ago. Couples sit in the meadow enjoying the cool breeze as they watch boats on the river pass them by. The three men on the left are relaxing on what may be their only day off by lying in the grass, and one appears to be fast asleep.

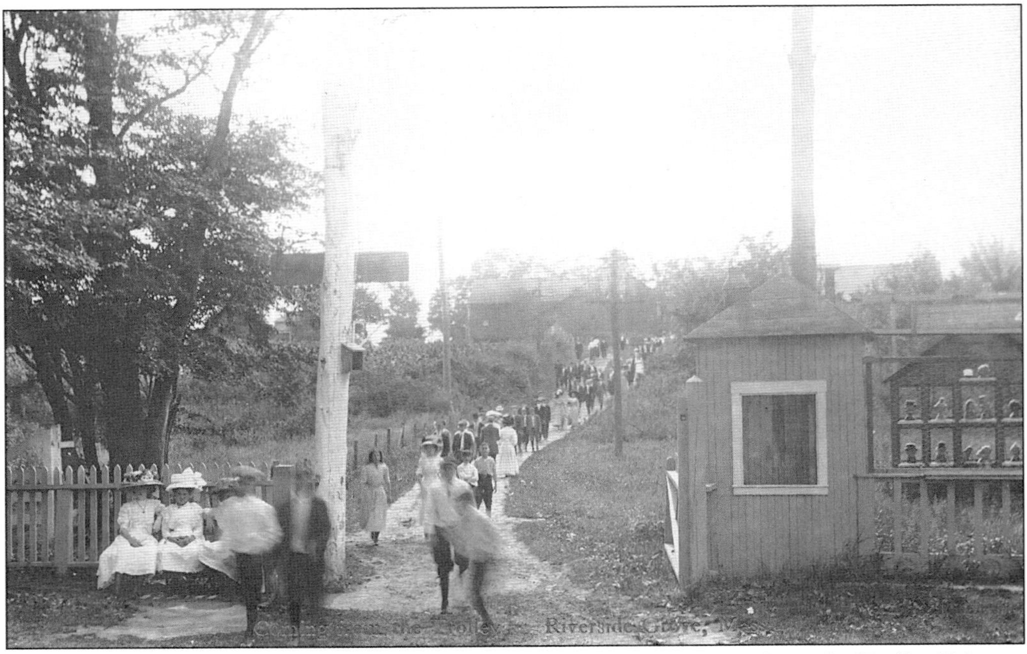

Grove patrons follow the path from Main Street in this view, "Coming from the Trolley." Notice of an 1896 proposal by the West Springfield, Agawam, and Suffield Street Railroad Company to build an "electric road" on Main Street stated that "Agawam people are of course anxious for the road . . . running as it does by Riverside Grove and within a quarter mile of Calla Shasta."

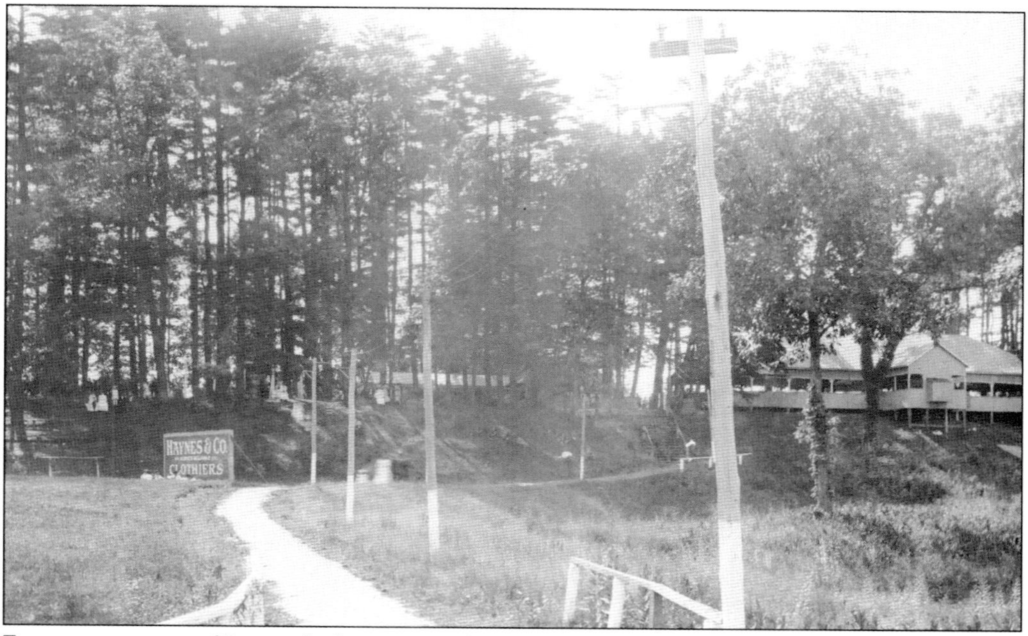


For years, patrons of Riverside Grove came by way of the river. The path across the meadow just past the steamboat landing is pictured, with the dance hall at right. The sign advertises Haynes & Company, a well-known clothing store on Main Street in nearby Springfield. Around the time this photograph was taken, Stanford Haynes was attempting to sell his Peerless Town Car Limousine because, as an ad in the *Springfield Daily Republican* noted, he had "bought a new car, same model, with body design a little more fitted to [his] personal needs."

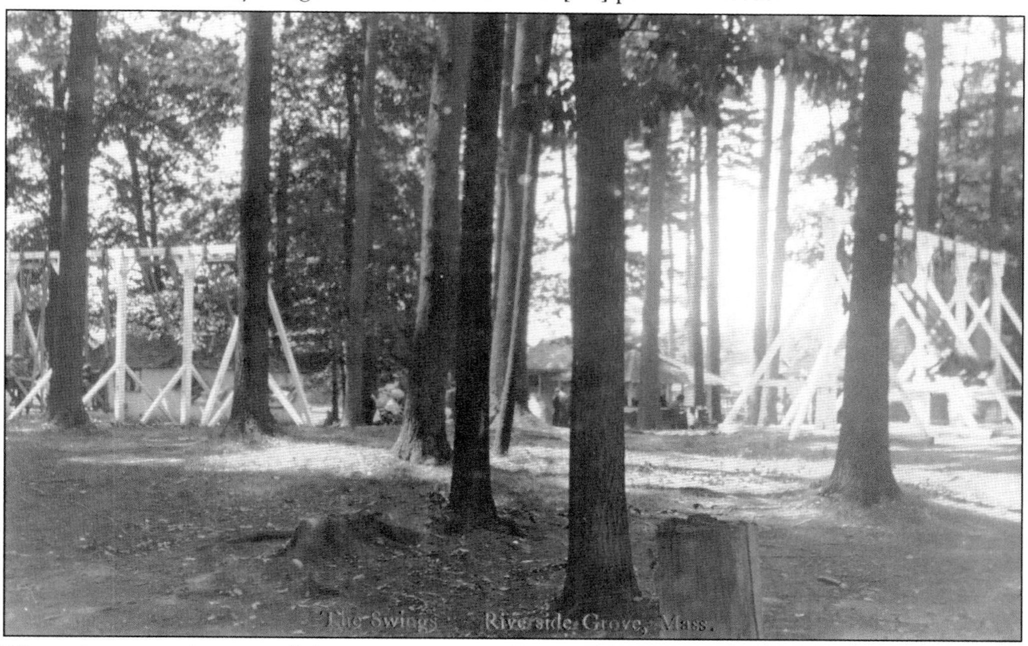


The swings were just one of the amusements at Riverside Grove available for early visitors. New attractions for 1892 included bowling alleys and a Razzle Dazzle. Riverside Grove was a very popular picnic destination for Sunday schools, fraternal organizations, clubs, trade groups, and businesses from around the area. The addition of amusements and attractions only added to its appeal.

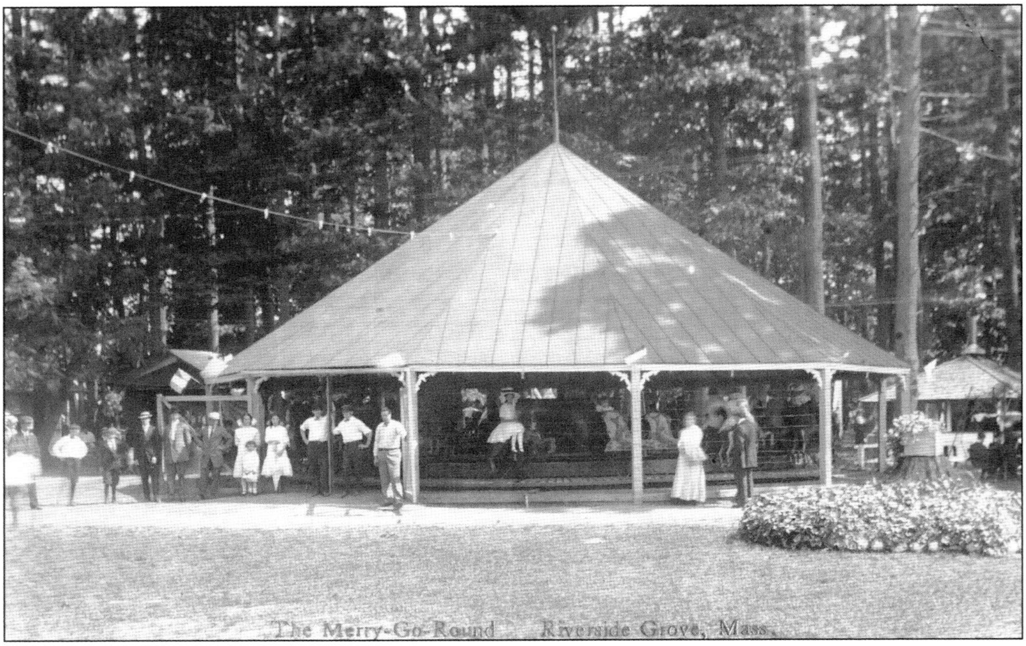


There was a merry-go-round at Riverside Grove as early as 1906. In 1908, it proved a favorite of the more than 1,000 children who attended the Playground Association picnic that year. Although it dates from roughly the same era, this modest ride contrasts greatly with the ornate 1909 M.C. Illions Coney Island–style carousel that was brought to Riverside Park by Ed Carroll Sr. in 1940.

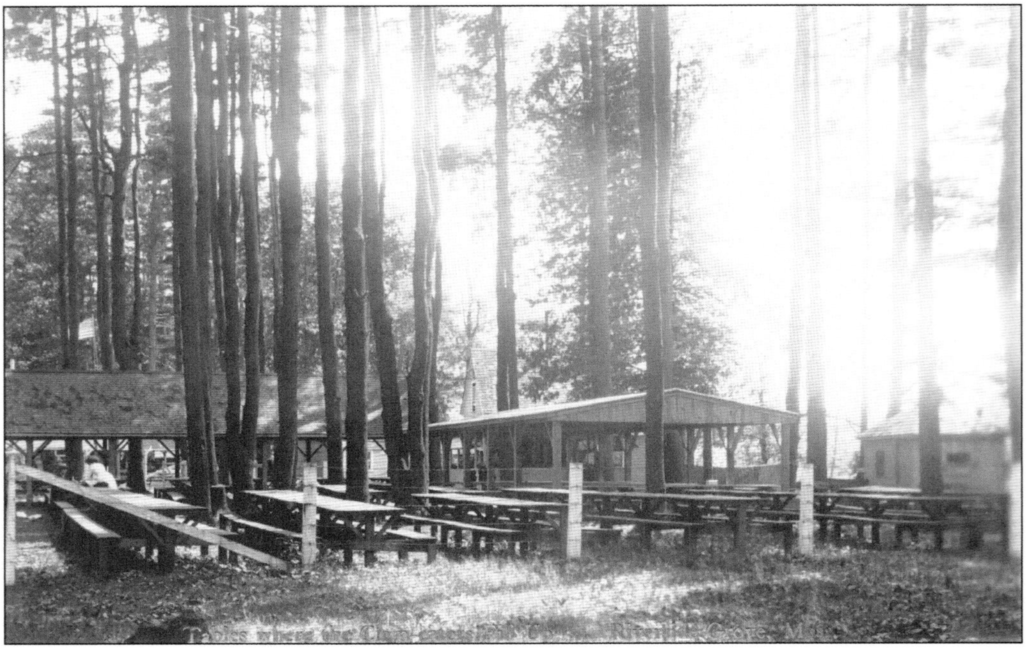

This photograph, entitled "Tables Where the Clam-Eaters Fill Up," illustrates the prominence of the legendary Riverside Grove clambake. Once the cooking began, a newspaper account reads, any really hungry people would have to walk "clear to the other side of the woods" to escape the "savory fumes which presently began to arise from that wagon load of steaming clams."

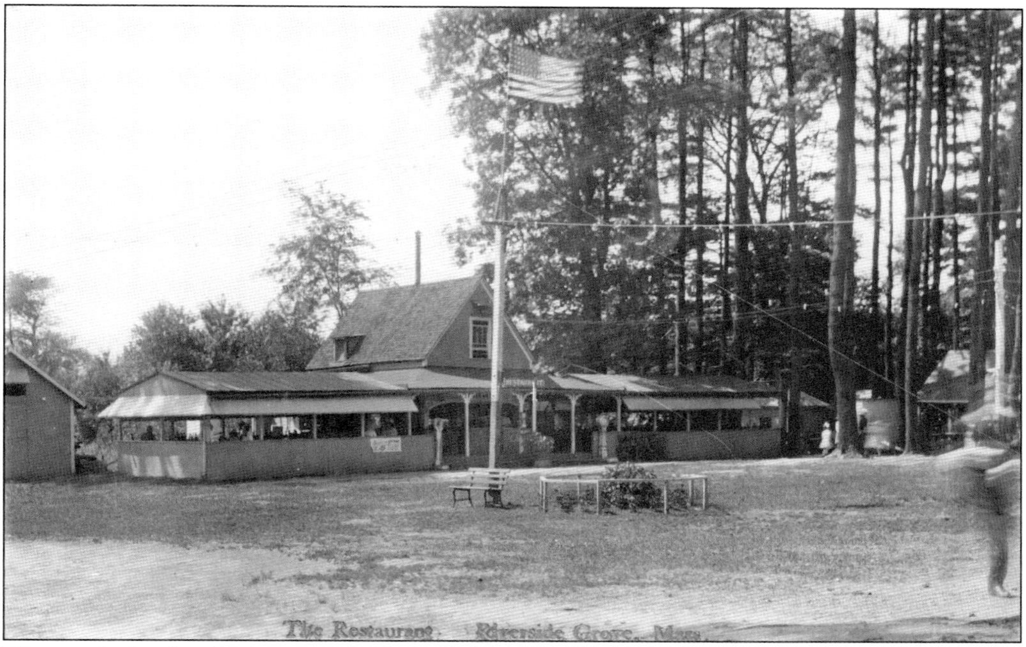


This might be the 300-seat restaurant Smith planned to build when he bought the property in 1887. It seems small, however. The history of Riverside is filled with announcements and plans that never materialized. In January 1906, it was announced that Riverside Grove had been sold to Lloyd, Walsh & Company, a Pennsylvania firm that intended to spend $100,000 developing the property into a large amusement park. The same month, it was reported that, despite such news, the Springfield Street Railway had not given up on the idea of building an amusement resort on Tubbs Hill in West Springfield. By March, the deal with Lloyd, Walsh & Company had fallen through. Smith included "no change in management" in his advertising for most of the 1906 summer season.

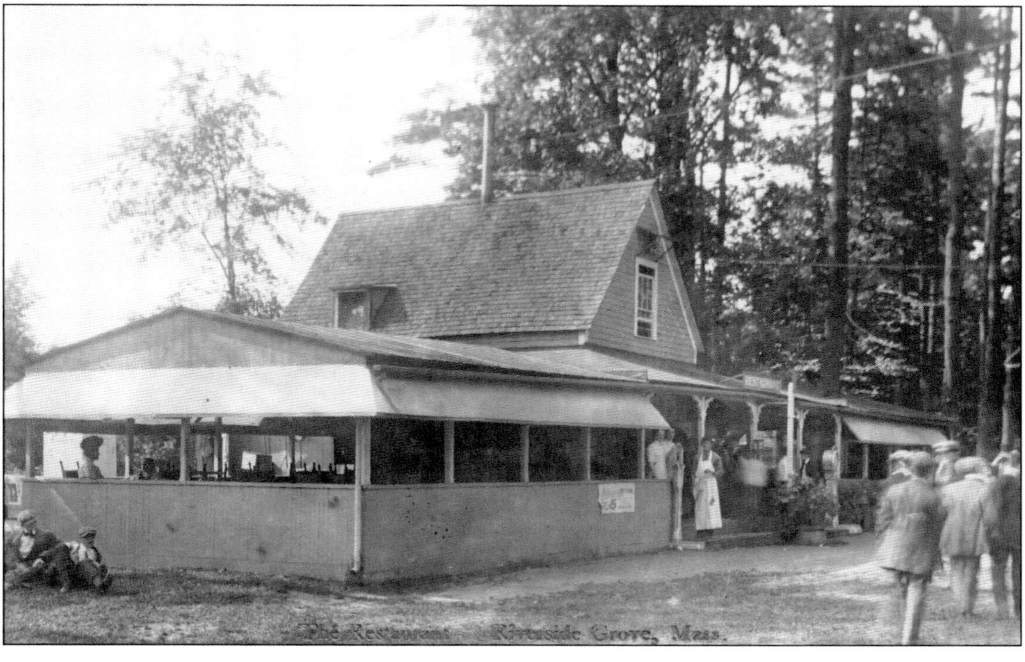

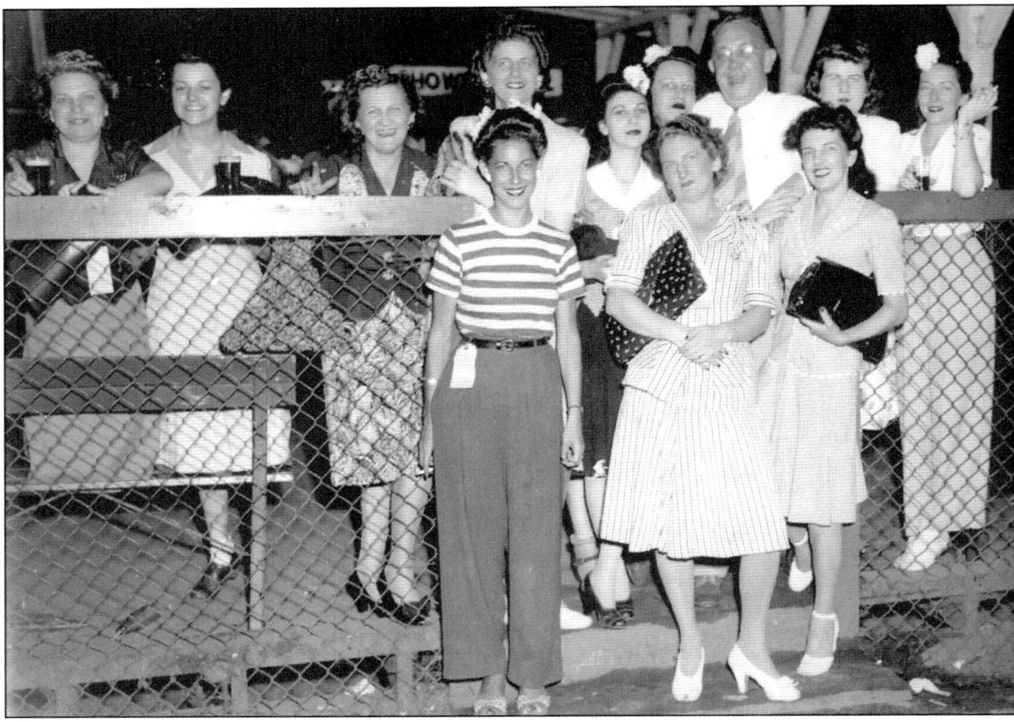

As the years went by and the amusement park aspect of the property began to overshadow the picnic grounds, Riverside Grove held its own, eventually becoming as well known for its chicken dinners as it was for its clambakes. The list of companies booking picnics at the grove continued to grow and by the 1940s included American Bosch, Milton Bradley, Stanley Tool, Coca-Cola, Bemis & Call, and department stores Forbes & Wallace, Steiger's, and Haynes & Company. Steiger's annual trip to Riverside was a summertime tradition from the 1920s until the chain ceased operations in the 1990s. Stores closed early for an afternoon of athletic games, comedic sketches, and dinner. Steiger's employees pose in the grove pavilion on July 27, 1944 (above), and enjoy their dinners at the 1947 gathering (below). Bill Morgan is the gentleman in the photograph above. (Both, courtesy of Mary Jane Murat.)

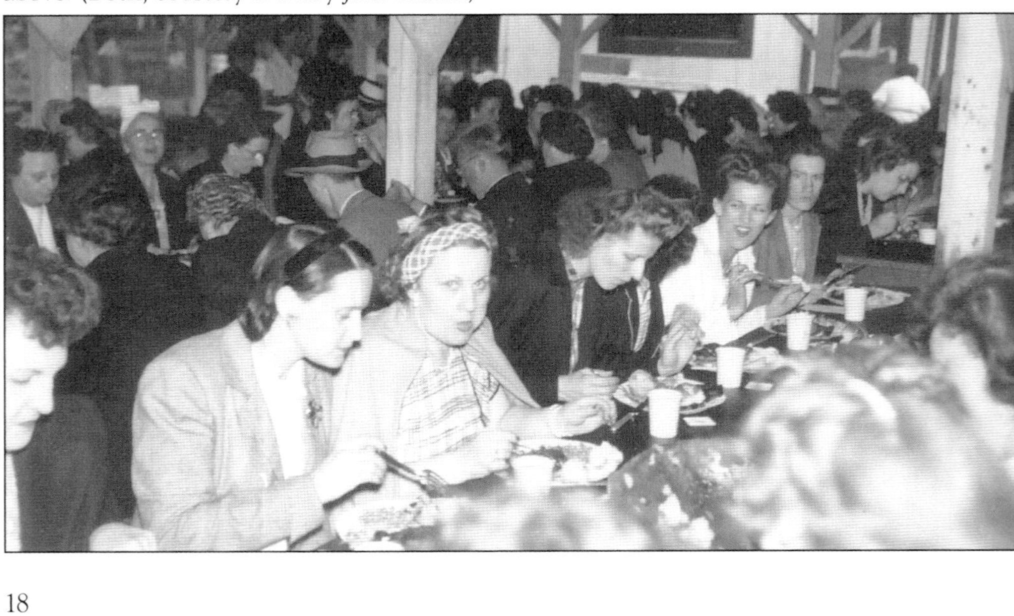

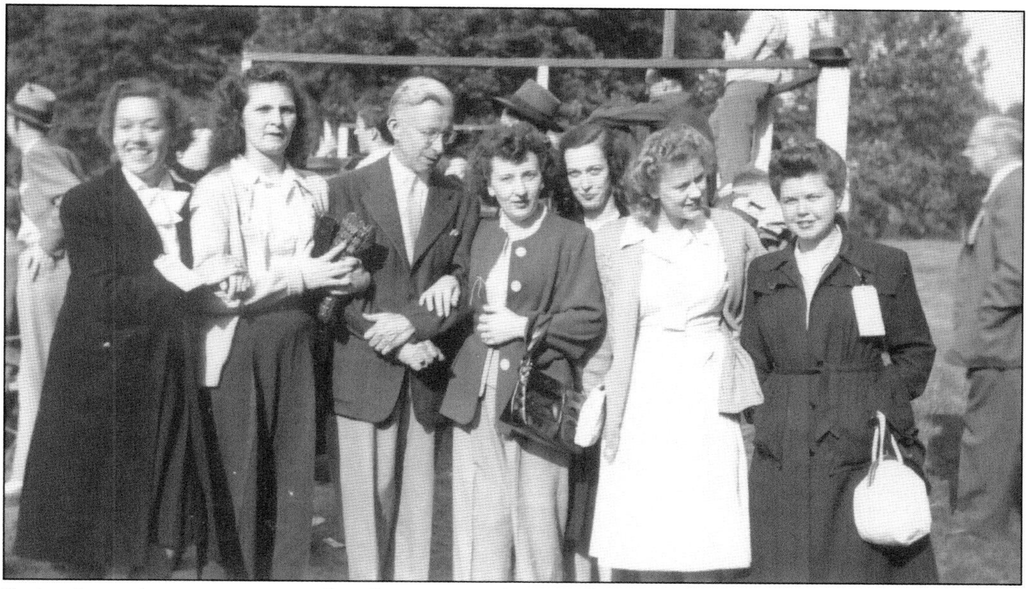

Steiger's employees are pictured at the company's annual summer picnic at Riverside Park in 1947. With two separate picnic groves in operation, Riverside could now hold outings for two parties simultaneously, as was the case on July 22, 1944, when Cogswell Manufacturing Company and Belmont Laundry held their summer gatherings. (Courtesy of Mary Jane Murat.)

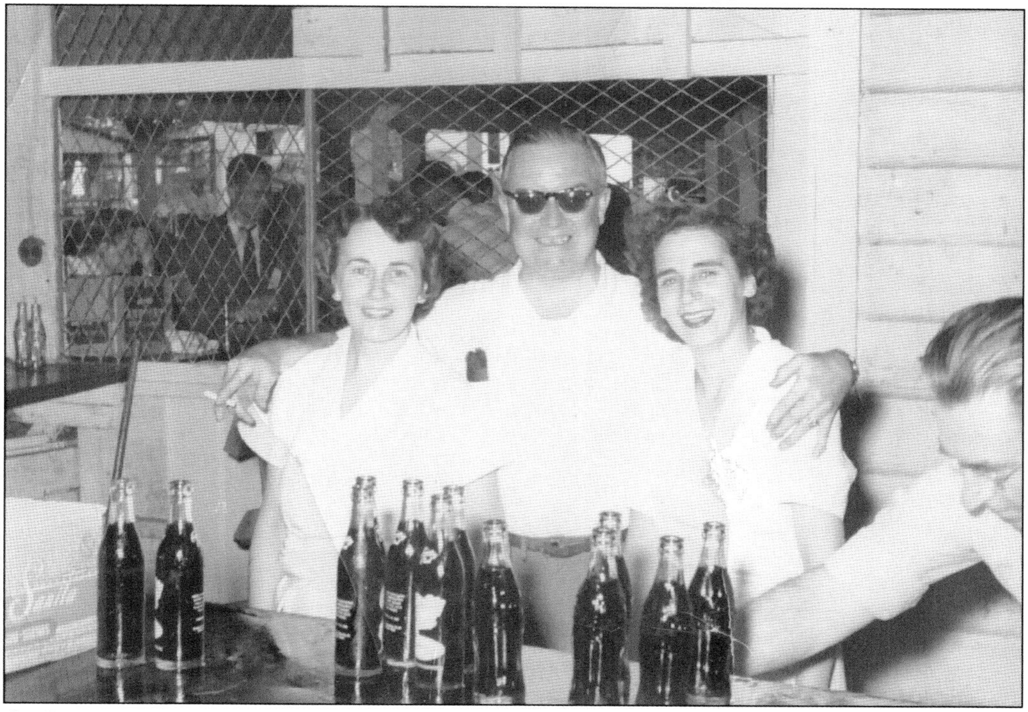

On June 24, 1943, Colonial Beacon Oil Company held its employee clambake, the first of six functions in six days at the grove. According to Harry Storin, Riverside Park's public relations director (center), this was the first time in park history so many events had been booked in one week. Visitors were transported to the park in the Transmobile (see page 73), which was credited with attracting all six bookings. (Courtesy of Florence Frasco.)

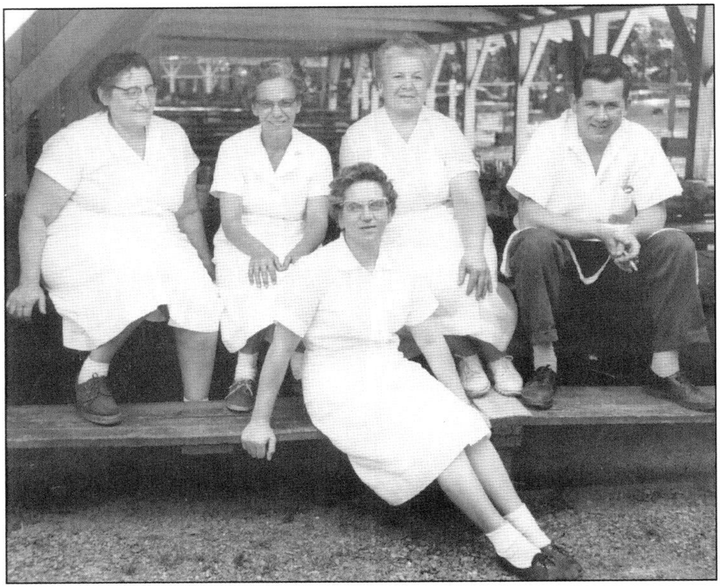

Grove employees take a break in this c. 1950 photograph. On the tabletop are, from left to right, Mary Ghedi, Rose Hall, Stella Doy, and Bob Stefanik. Florence "Flo" Frasco is seated in front of the others. Flo started at the grove in 1947, cleaning chickens for 60¢ an hour. To mark her 50th anniversary at the park, Ed Carroll Jr. presented Flo and her husband with a trip to Las Vegas. Flo still works when needed. (Courtesy of Florence Frasco.)

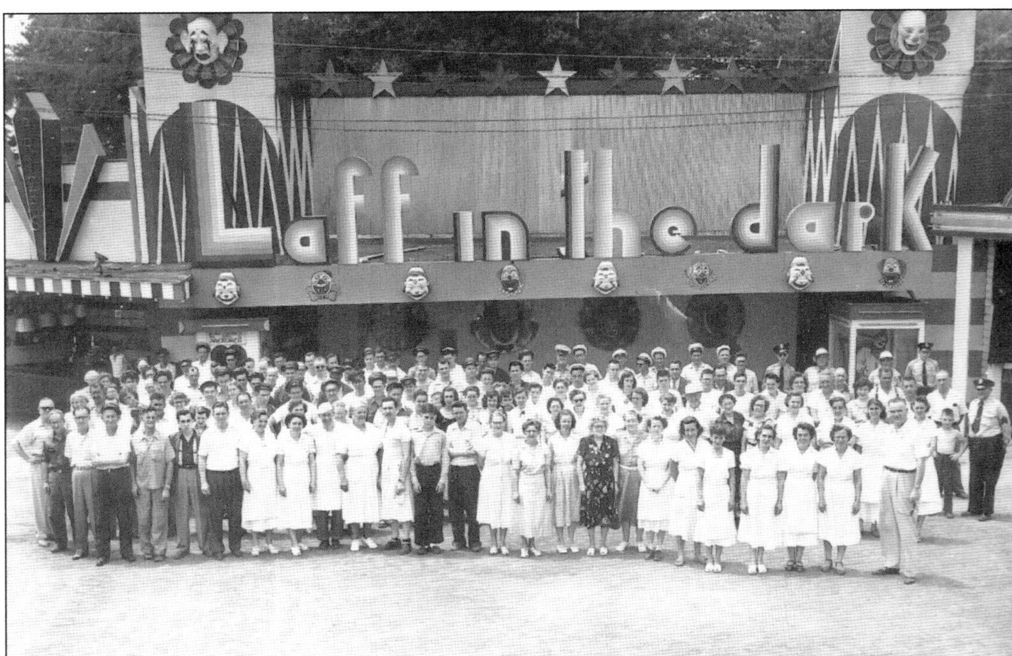


One of Riverside's most popular "dark rides," Laff in the Dark, opened in 1941. That same year, improvements to the grove included new equipment, athletic fields, open roasting ovens, and a new private entrance at the north end of the property. The Riverside Park grove staff is pictured around 1950.

# *Two*

# LET'S GO!

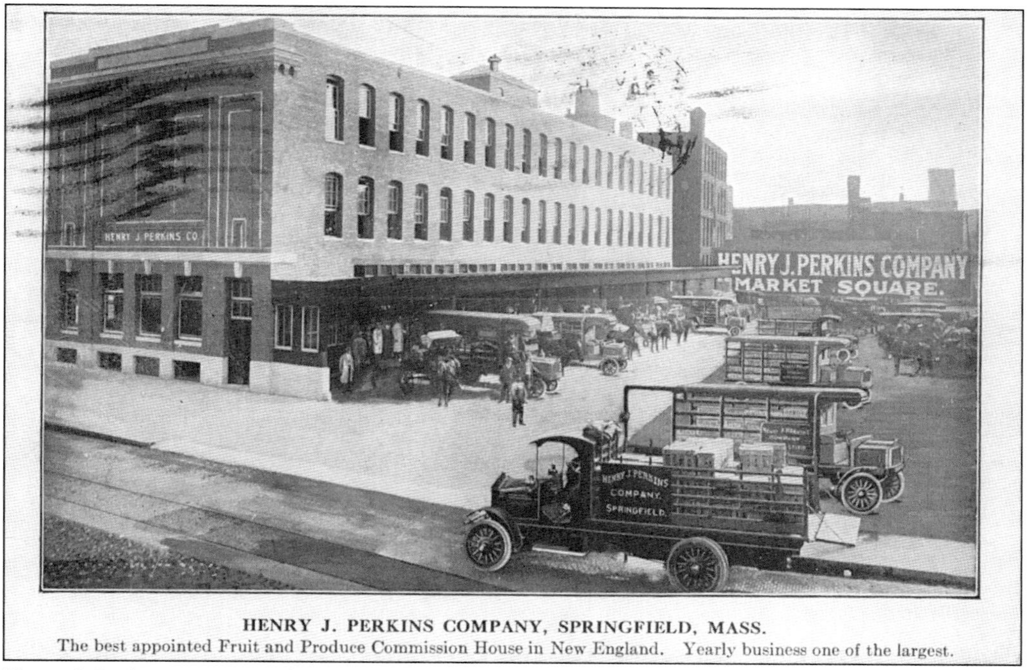


Henry J. Perkins is responsible for the transformation of Riverside from picnic grove to amusement park. Perkins, who purchased the park in 1911, was president and treasurer of the wholesale fruit and produce concern Henry J. Perkins Company and very active in local fraternal and trade groups. His 1927 obituary described him as "one of the outstanding figures in the business and civic life of this city and widely known throughout the Connecticut Valley."

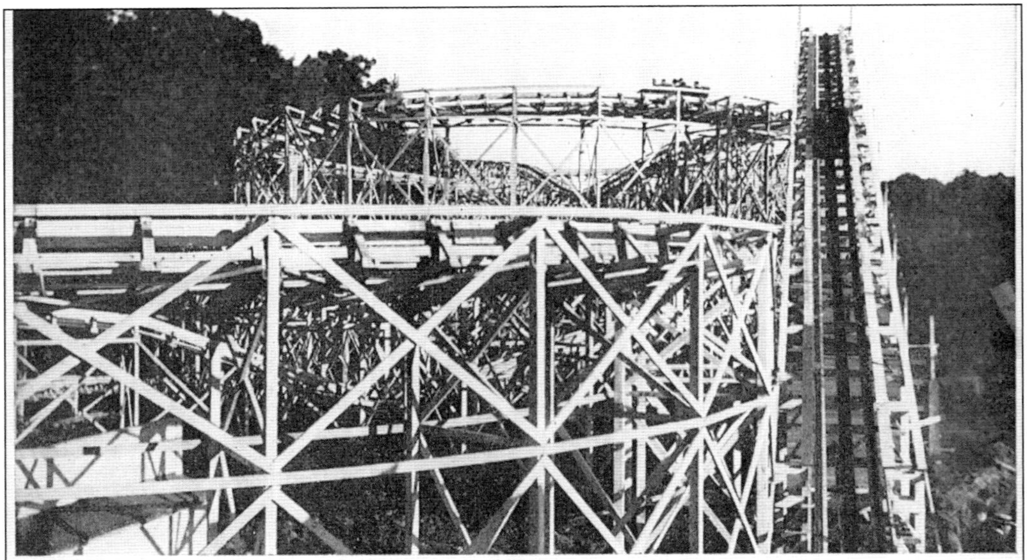

Riverside Park (Springfield, Mass.). Giant Dip Coaster. Thousands ride on this every day.

The Giant Dip Coaster was the main attraction when Riverside Park opened for the 1912 season. Billed as one of the largest roller coasters in the country, it was the first in a storied line of bigger, longer, and more spectacular roller coasters at the park. These two early postcards detail the ride's popularity. Advertisements for opening day proclaimed, "A half a mile in a minute and a half! That's the speed you travel. Going some, eh? And it's as safe as a baby carriage!" Newspaper accounts demystified the romantic appeal: "The young man who has been trying vainly to win a smile from his particular fair one takes her on the trip and the delightful little screams of semiterror that she gives and her frantic clutchings at his arm make him press his way forward for another ticket when the ride is over."

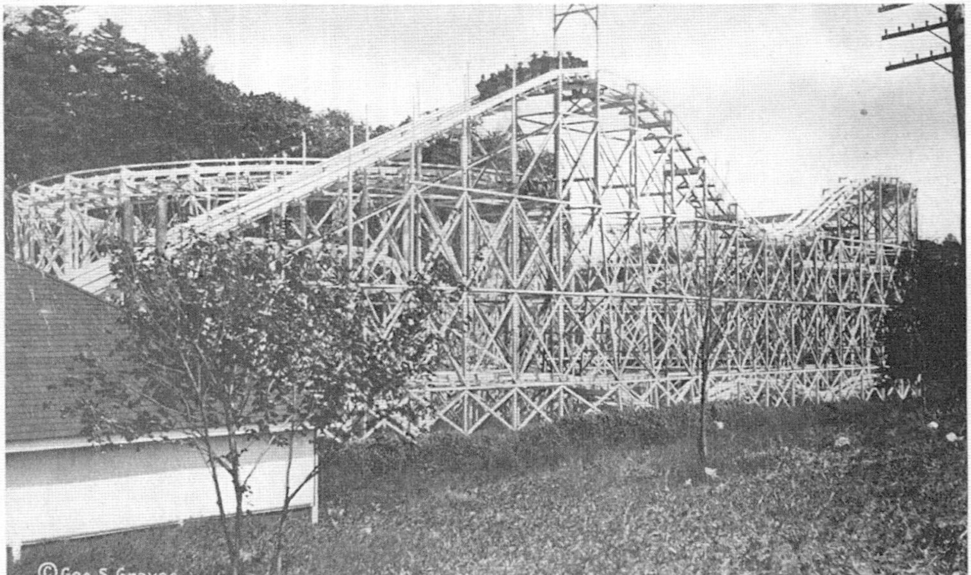


RIVERSIDE PARK, SPRINGFIELD, MASSACHUSETTS. THE GIANT COASTER, the greatest thriller in this region. Always a crowd waiting for a ride. A 678

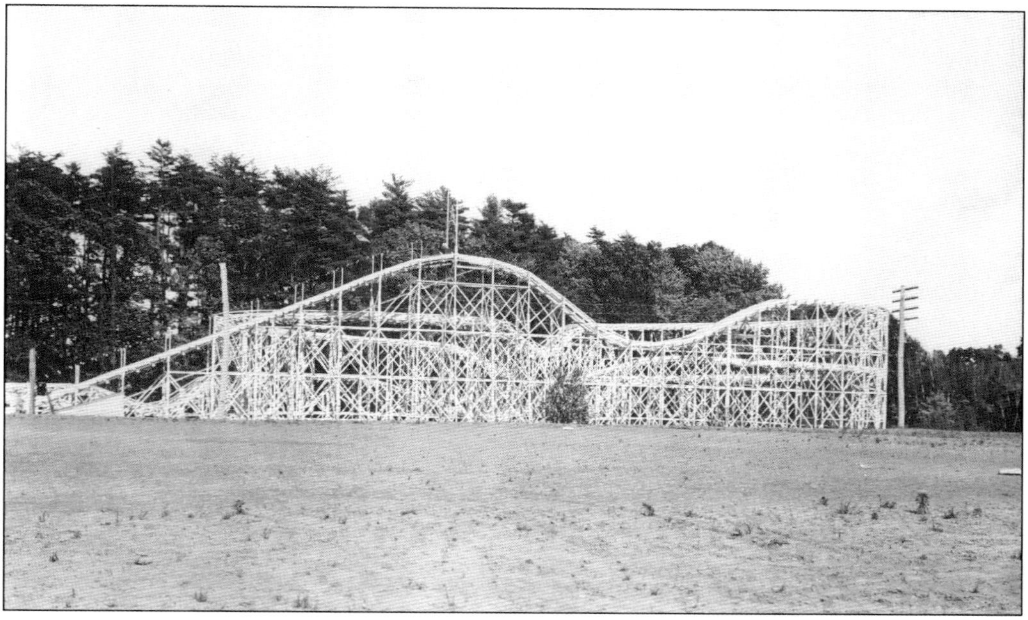

The development of Riverside Park into a full-fledged amusement park can be dated to the construction of its first roller coaster. The dip coaster was located toward the river, away from the Main Street entrance. In the early years of the park, most patrons arrived by steamboat via the river route; others came by trolley and jitney. As the automobile grew in popularity in the coming years, the empty field pictured would soon enough be filled with Model Ts and other flivvers. Riverside's original dip coaster was replaced by a larger roller coaster in 1920.

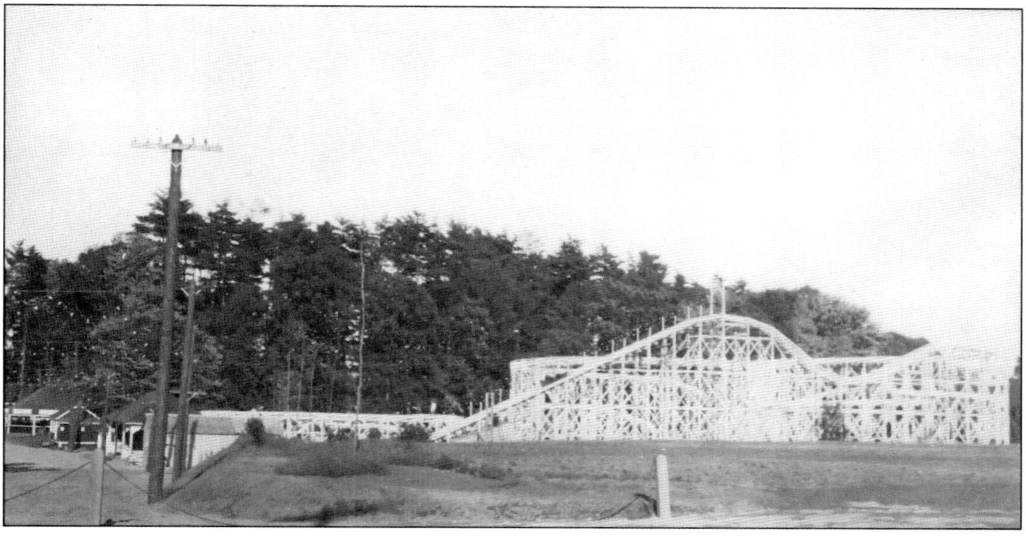

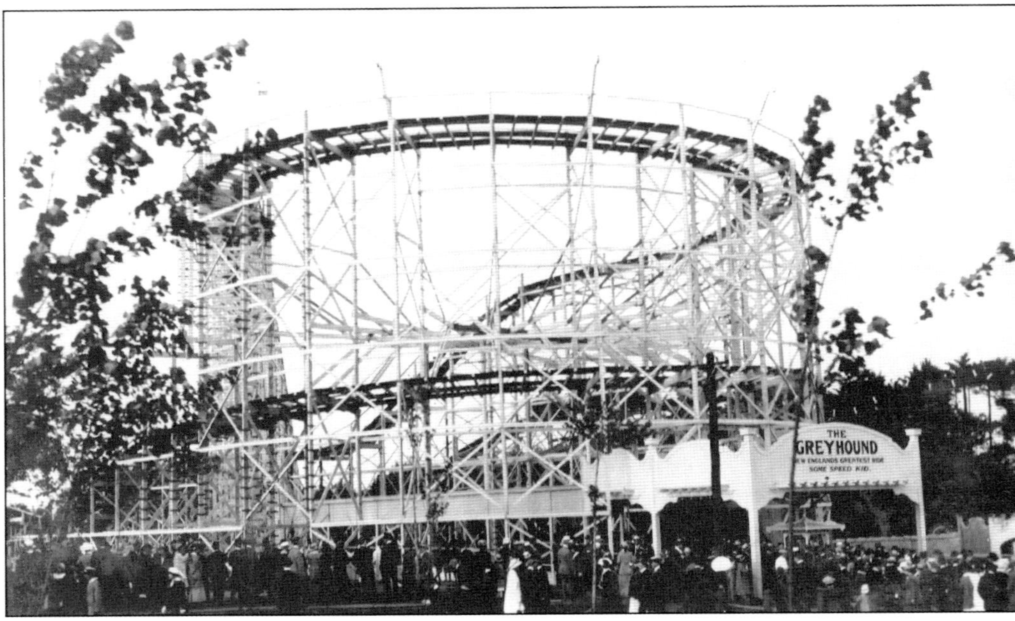


Thrill-seekers are a demanding lot, and the dip coaster was soon joined by the Greyhound. The Greyhound was built in 1915 at a cost of $60,000 by Josiah Pearce & Sons of New Orleans. It was 80 feet high, covered 60,000 square feet, and was touted as the largest, fastest, and finest roller coaster in New England. The layout included dips, glides, tunnels, and other novelties. Shown shortly after its opening in May 1915 (above), the unfinished marquee over the entrance of the Greyhound proclaims it "New England's Greatest Ride. Some Speed Kid." A postcard view (below) dating from 1917 refers to the ride as "one of the favorite forms of amusements."

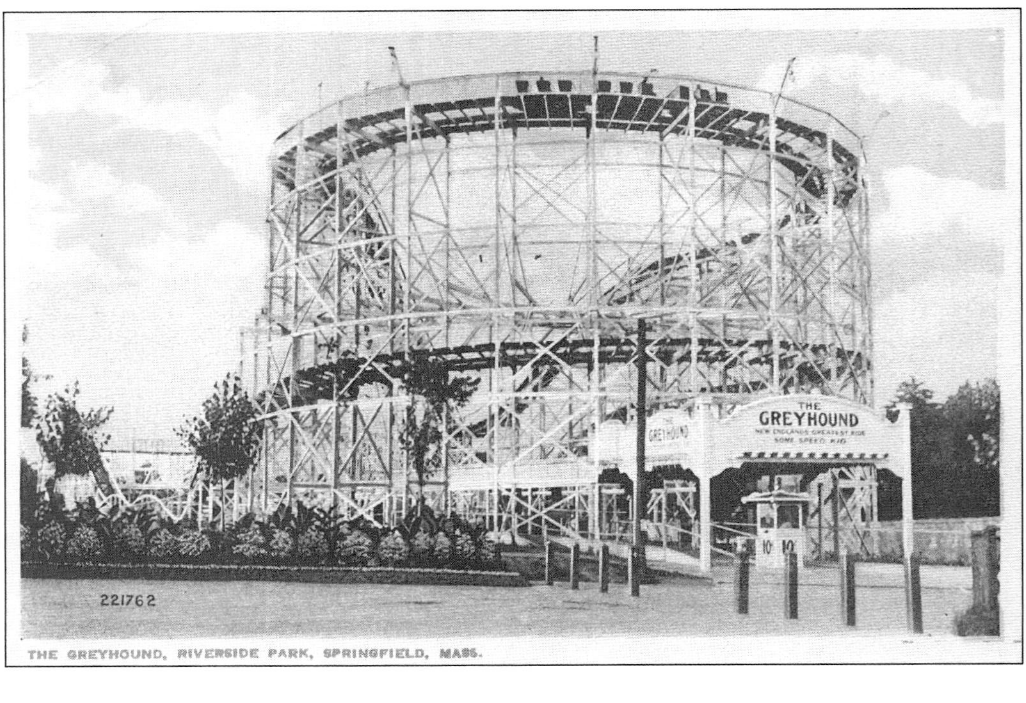

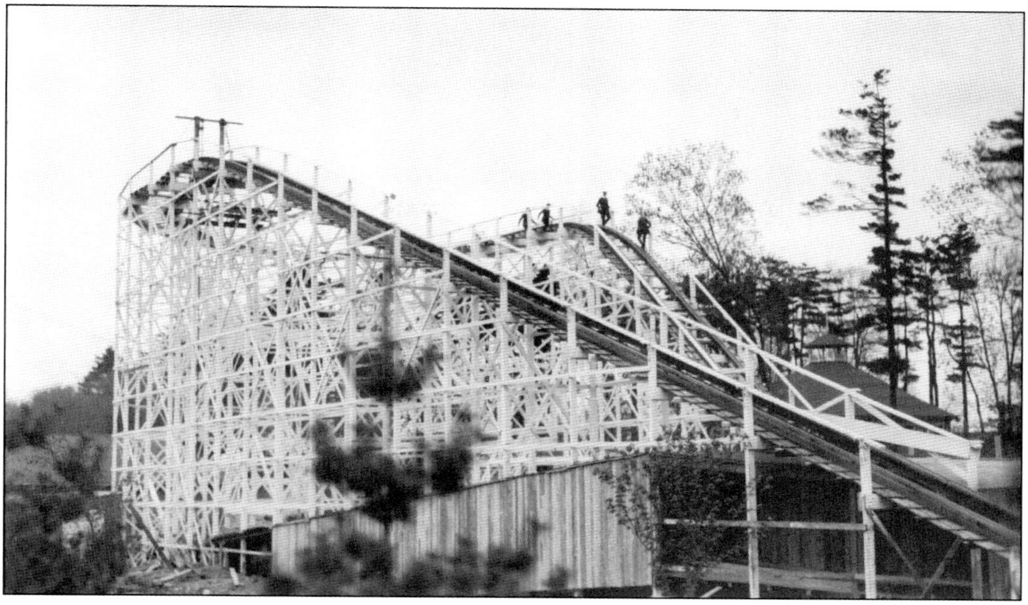

Less than a decade after it was built, the dip coaster was replaced by a roller coaster double its size. The new ride, built on the site of the dip coaster, debuted when the park opened for the season on May 22, 1920. At one mile long, the $70,000 coaster, later known as the Lightning, was the largest in the country. Anthony Ventrice and his father were among those on the construction crew. Riverside had grown to become one of the largest amusement parks in the United States. Other new midway attractions that joined the Lightning in 1920 were the Whip, the Funny House, and Airplane Swings. Two seaplanes were also stationed on the Connecticut River at Riverside for passenger and commercial flights. Henry J. Perkins was among the first aloft.

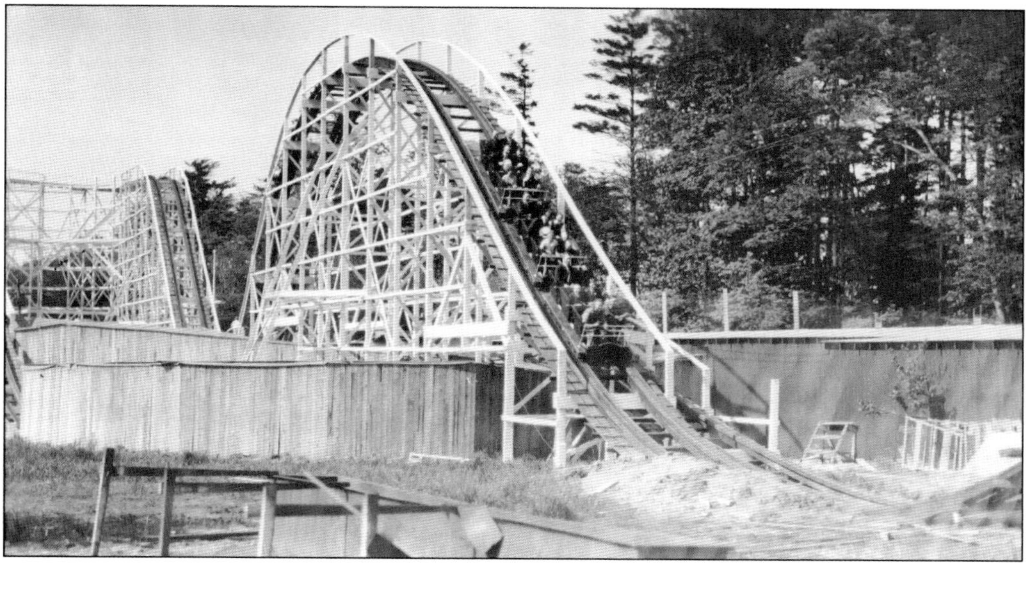

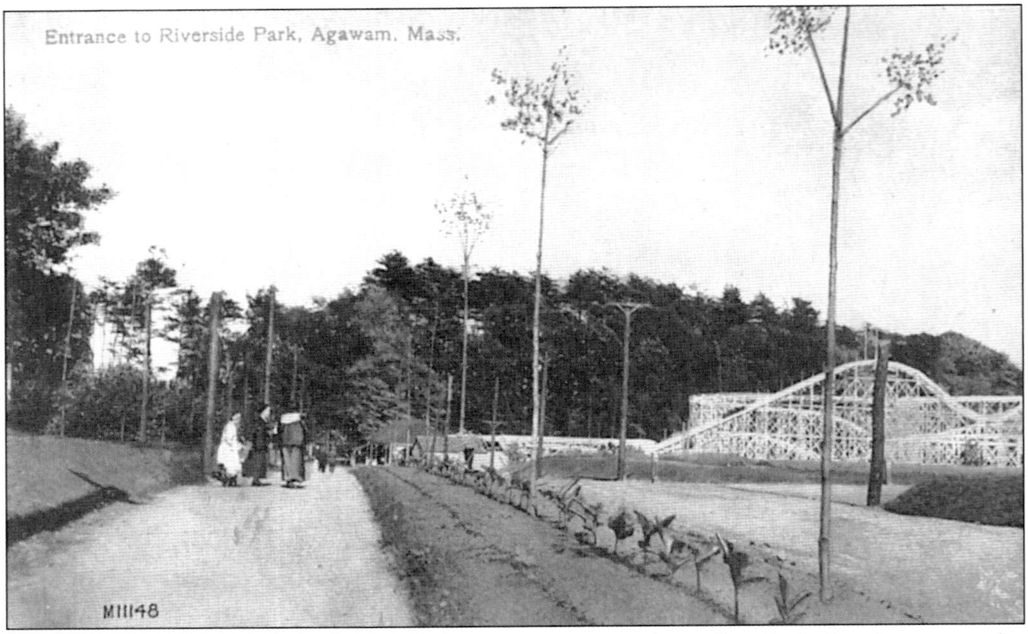


The entrance to Riverside Park, as seen by visitors arriving by trolley, is depicted on a popular postcard of the day. By 1915, Riverside was Agawam's largest taxpayer and employer, a distinction is has held off and on (mostly on) ever since. As Henry J. Perkins poured money and improvements into the park during the 1910s and 1920s, the crowds continued to grow.

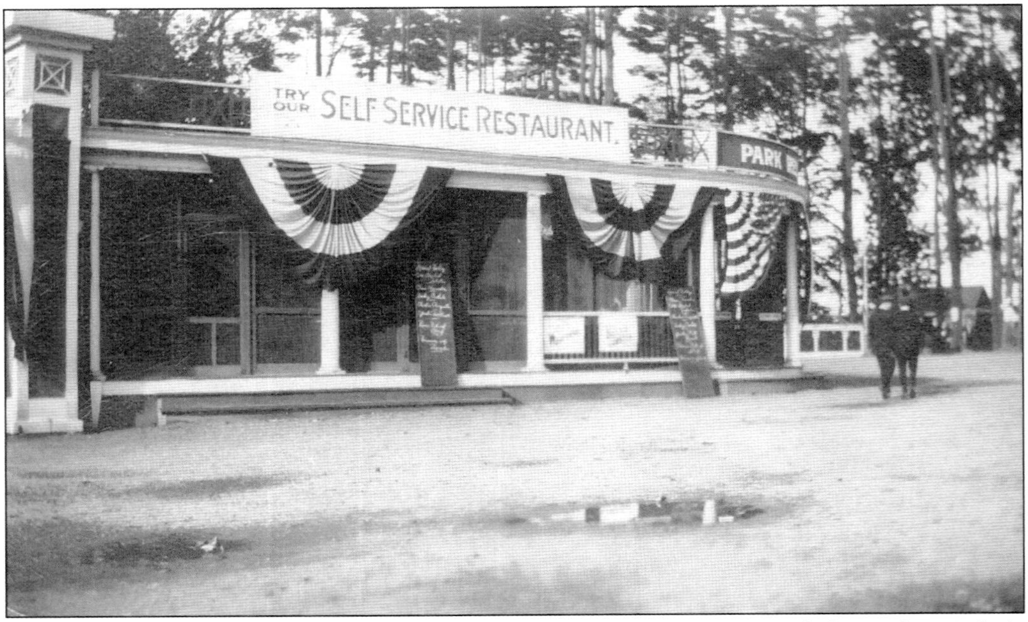


When the new Riverside Park Restaurant opened in 1915, it was presided over by Michele Canavosio, one of the best-known chefs in New England. Canavosio was formerly associated with the exclusive Holyoke Club and the Hotel Hueblein in Hartford. Price for a special Sunday and holiday luncheon of one whole chicken, lobster, bread, butter, and coffee was 75¢ in 1920. (Courtesy of June Cook.)

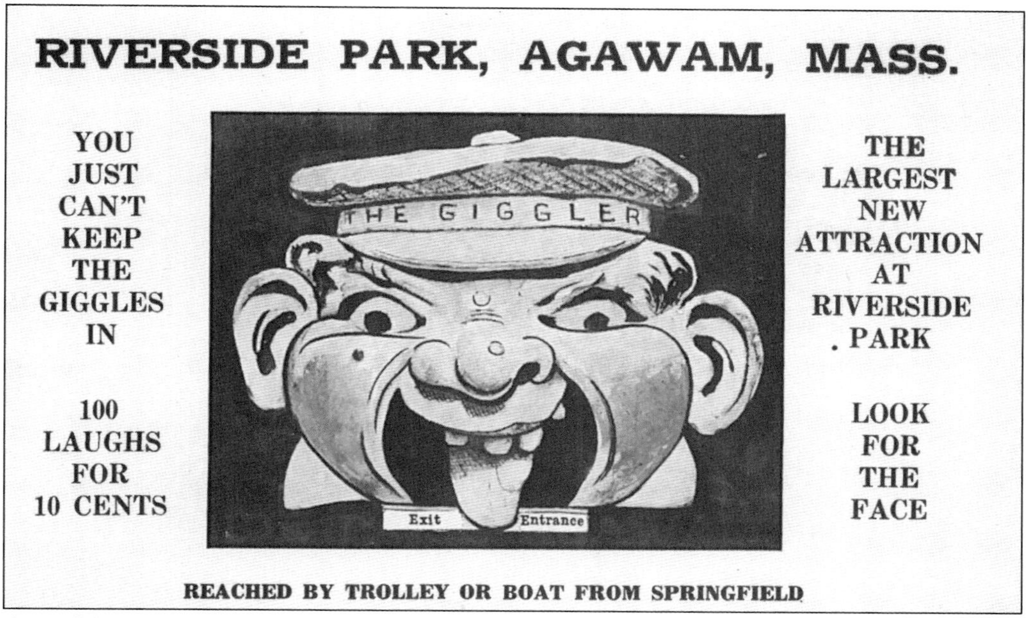


One of the most anticipated new attractions for the 1914 season was the Giggler. It is described in the May 3, 1914, *Springfield Sunday Republican* as "a real innovation in this part of the country. Its exterior is a great face, broadened into a happy smile. Electrical apparatus will make the eyes move and gleam, and there will be other effects that will be startling and amusing. Within the building will be many laughable surprises for patrons."

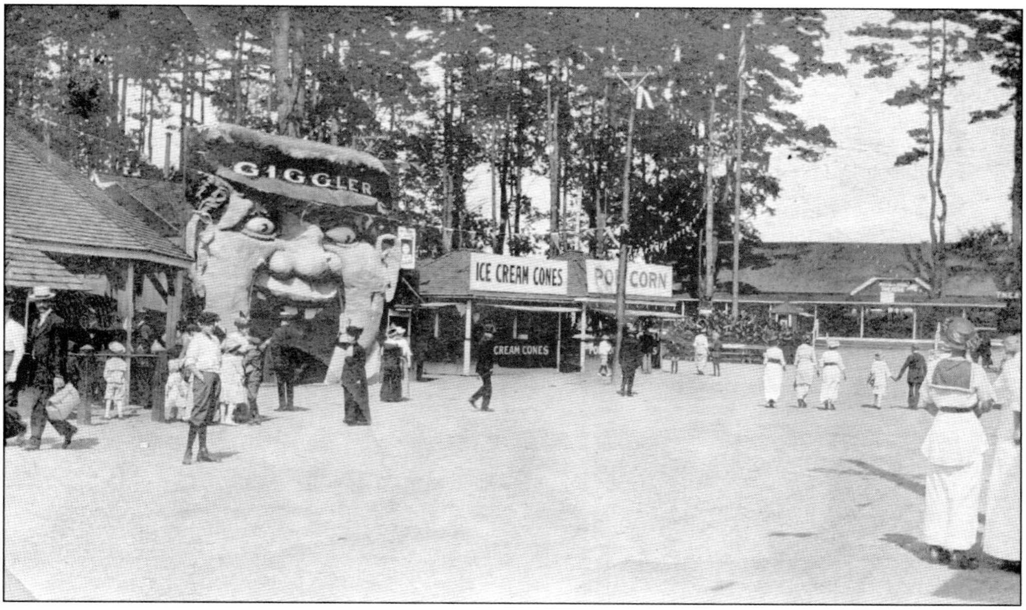


The *Springfield Sunday Republican* further describes the Giggler: "There will be rocking bridges, movable doors, sliding stairways, "joy rooms" where one does not recognize one's own reflection, and dozens of entertaining features. Compressed air devices will add to the gayety of the place, and the management declares that if one can go through this attraction and come out with a solemn face it will be because that person is deaf, dumb, blind, and insensate." (Courtesy of June Cook.)

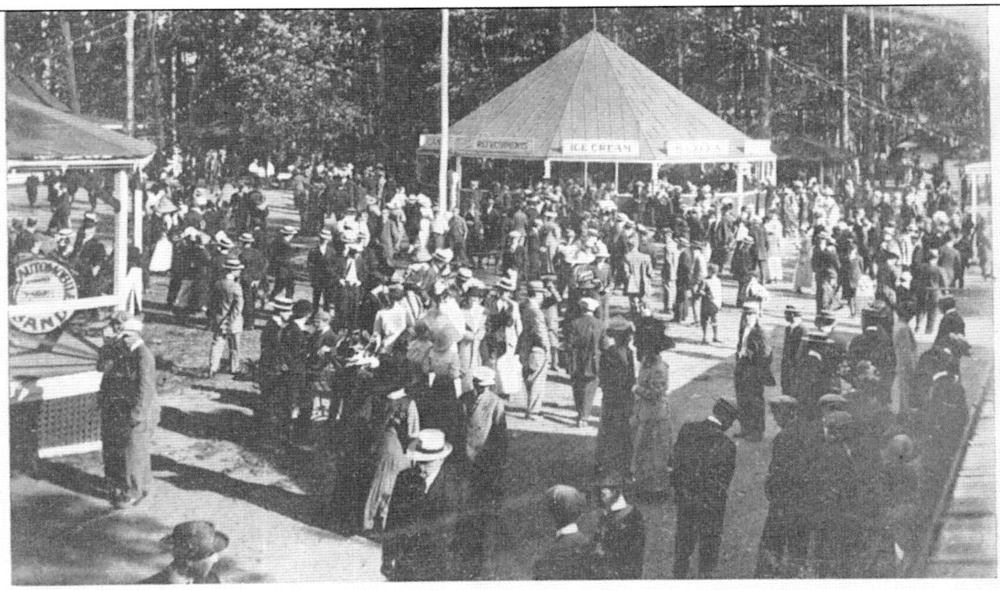


Riverside Park (Springfield, Mass.). The equipment of refreshments and music is the best.

The Knox Automobile Band (on the bandstand at left), directed by Albert E. Short, plays for the midway crowd on a Sunday afternoon. Throngs of people swarmed Riverside on Sundays, much to the consternation of Agawam residents, who at one time sought to close amusements such as the merry-go-round and roller coaster on Sundays. In August 1916, Agawam selectmen banned Sunday baseball games at the park, citing the general Lord's Day Law of Massachusetts.

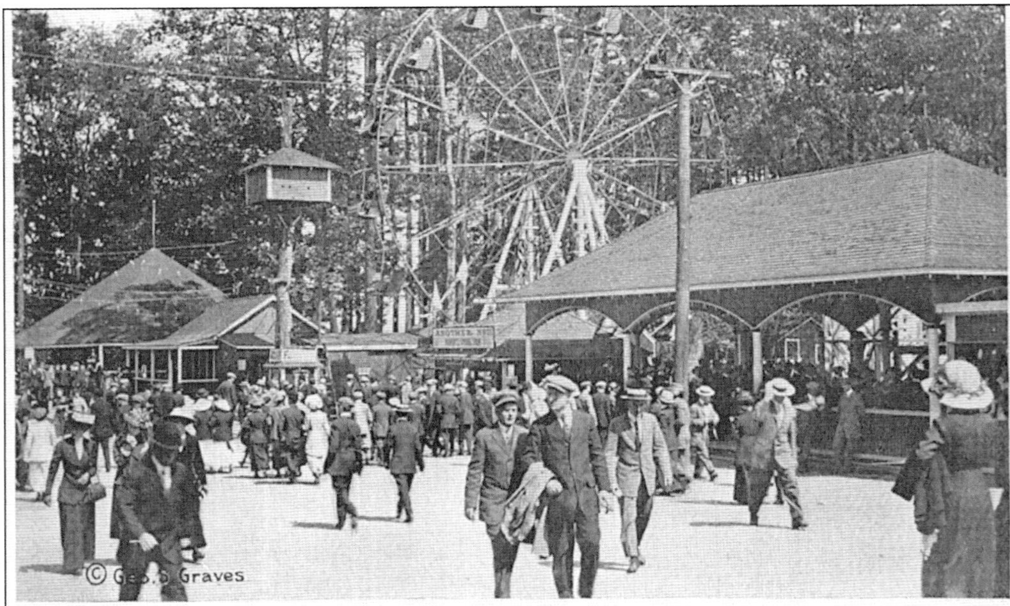


RIVERSIDE PARK, SPRINGFIELD, MASS. On the crowded "Midway." The Ferris Wheel, a ride on which gives you a gentle thrill. A-680

Riverside opened for the 1913 season with several new attractions. A 60-foot Ferris wheel was added, as was the Panama Canal ride, with 3,000 feet of waterways surrounded by scenery and "electrical effects and illusions galore" inspired by the isthmus-spanning marvel that had captured the nation's attention and would open to ship traffic the following year.

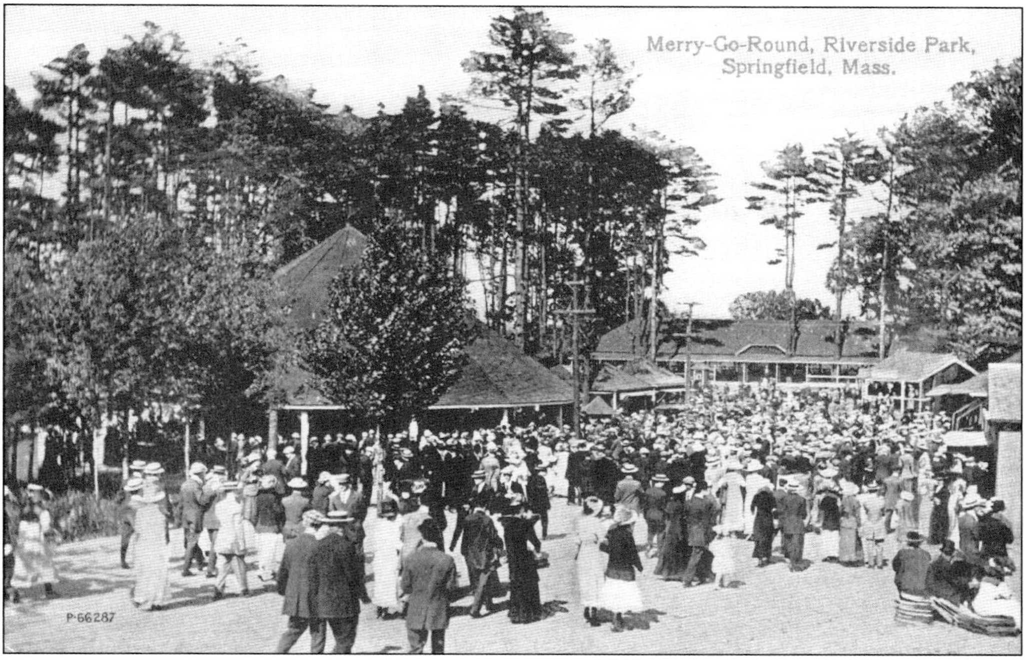


Advertisements crowed, "Some call it a merry-go-round, but the name doesn't fit." Riverside Grove's early carousel was replaced with a new $10,000 model in 1912, "the most luxurious, delightful, magnificent, elaborate pleasure vehicle between New York and Boston." It was one of the largest of its kind in use, and run by electricity, which eliminated the "annoying steam engine" that had run the previous attraction.

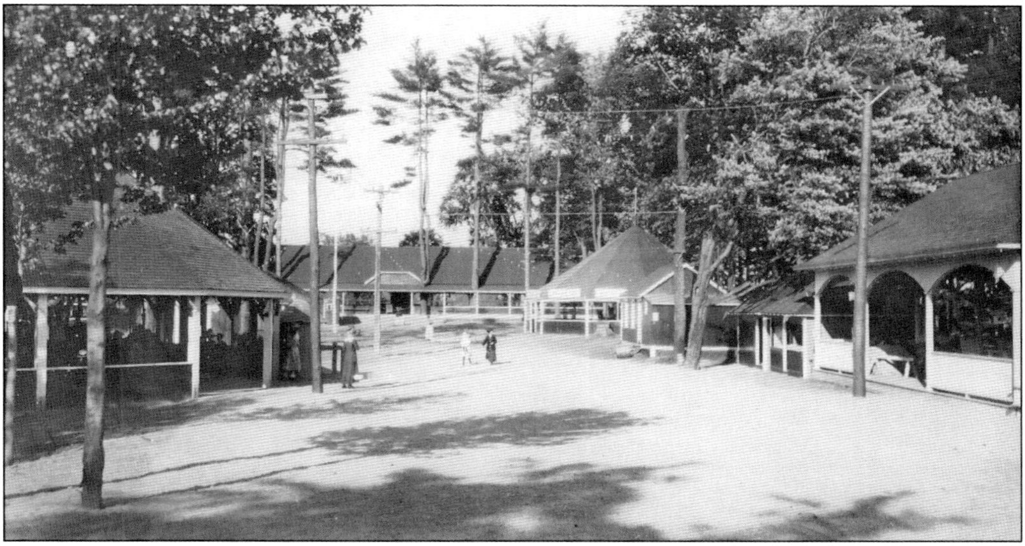

Compare this view of the midway with the one above. Within a few years of this photograph being taken, the 1912 carousel would be joined by a new $20,000 carousel, and the dance hall, seen in the center of the photograph, would be replaced with a larger pavilion measuring 220 feet long by 110 feet wide. In 1917, the Riverside Park Natatorium, a 300-foot-diameter swimming pool, would also join the list of attractions.

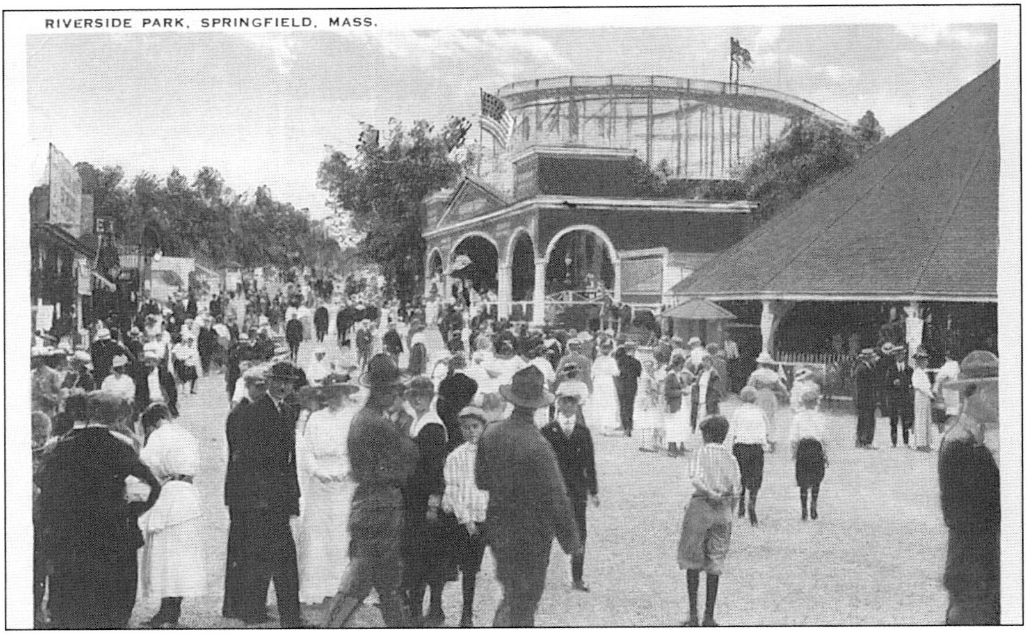


The Riverside midway is captured in these c. 1917 photographs. The back of the postcard below reads, "Springfield's Wonderland—Where every Summer Diversion is at its Best. Where the crowds go. Riverside Park among the pines has a natural situation unsurpassed. Lying close to the edge of the Connecticut River and well shaded by pine and other trees affords one of the coolest, most popular, and up-to-date amusement parks in New England. It was long ago chosen as an ideal picnic and outing place by local trade and social organizations and the Riverside Grove clambakes of years gone by are fragrant in memory. Fond traditions have not been disturbed, for while the natural advantages of the site have been greatly improved, a large section is set aside where clambakes and picnics are still held as of yore."

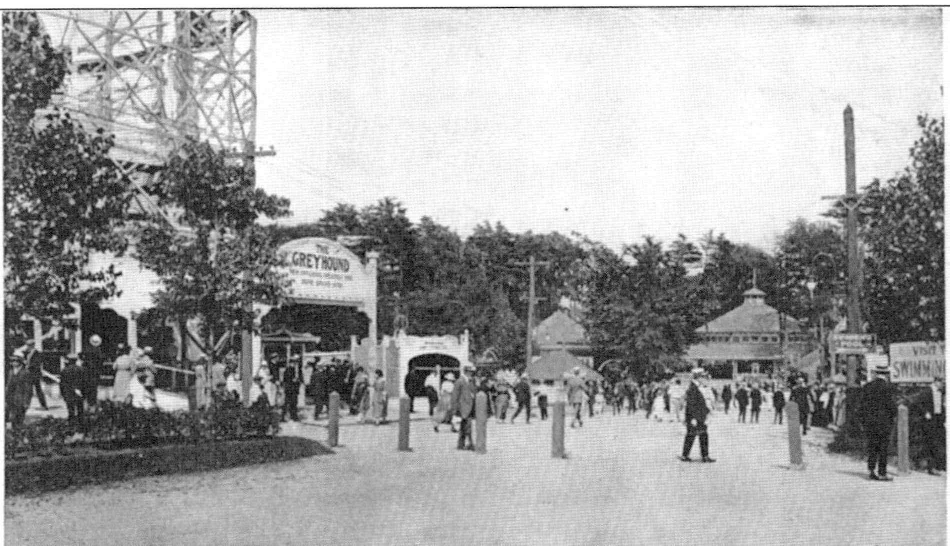


"THE MIDWAY," RIVERSIDE PARK, SPRINGFIELD, MASS.
Incidental fun-making features are all along up and down "THE MIDWAY." At the left "The Greyhound" roller coaster is crowded every minute. The new $20,000 carousal or "Merry-go-round" at the rear is always busy.
(See other side) A-750

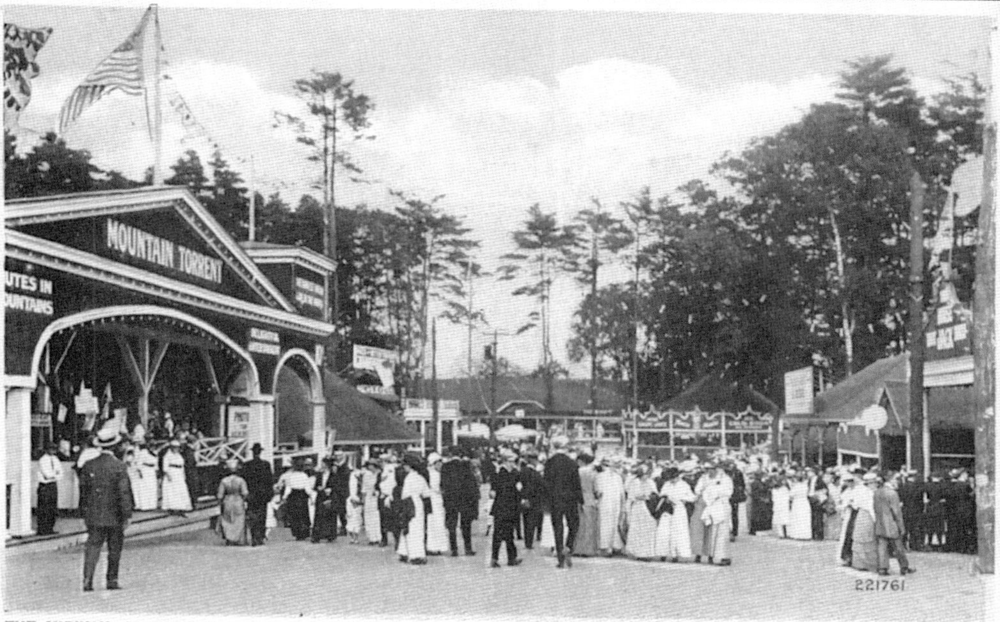


THE MIDWAY, RIVERSIDE PARK, SPRINGFIELD, MASS.

The Riverside midway never looked the same for long. The real Panama Canal opened in 1914, and the public soon lost interest; the Mountain Torrent (above) replaced the Panama Canal ride in 1915 after just two seasons. The 1912 carousel building can be seen just to the right of the Mountain Torrent, with the Giggler barely visible beyond that. Another new attraction for 1915, the Whip, had only been installed at Coney Island and at the Panama Pacific Exposition in San Francisco. By 1920, the midway had changed again. The Mountain Torrent was replaced with the Coal Mine ride (below), in which guests rode through the dark in coal cars pulled by donkeys.

A SCENE AT RIVERSIDE PARK, SPRINGFIELD, MASS.

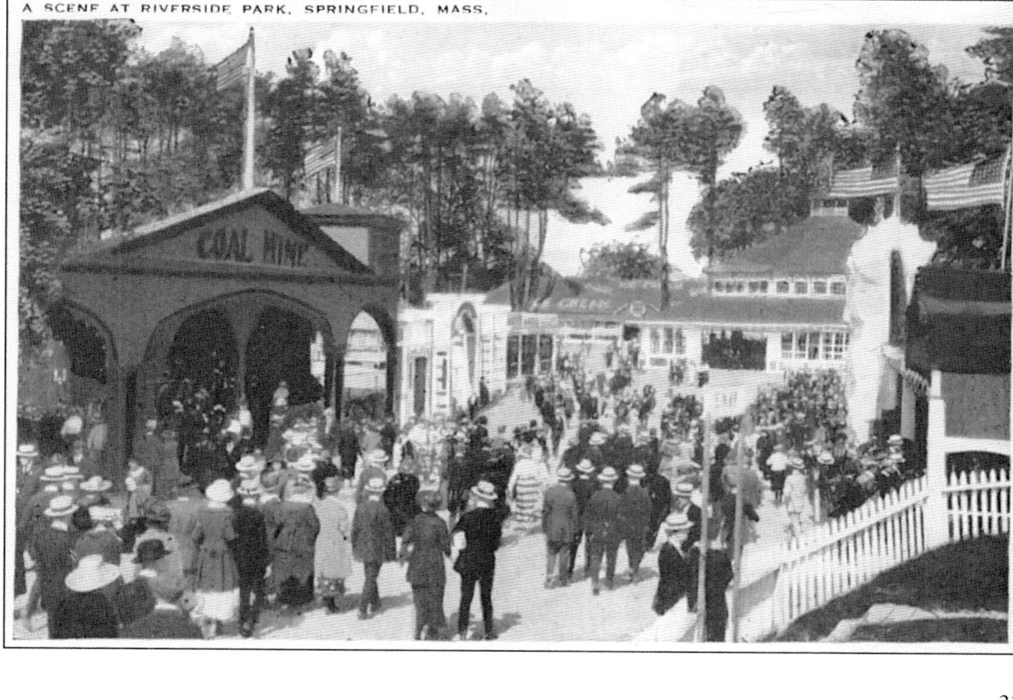

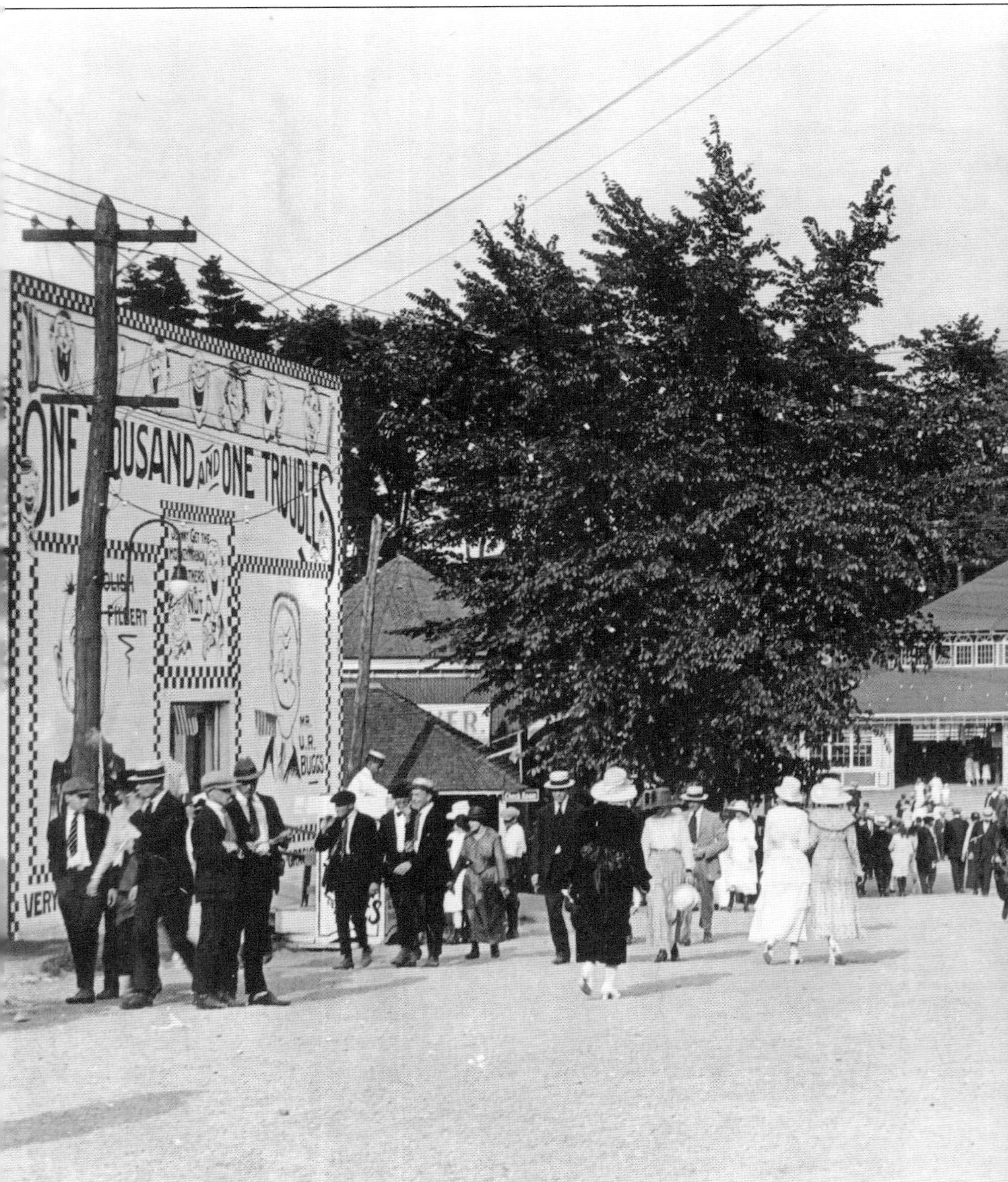


World War I had ended the previous fall, but the public's interest had yet to wane. One of the new attractions when Riverside Park opened in 1919 was a display of ruined French and Belgian cathedrals and towns. Another new attraction was One Thousand and One Troubles (at left), an

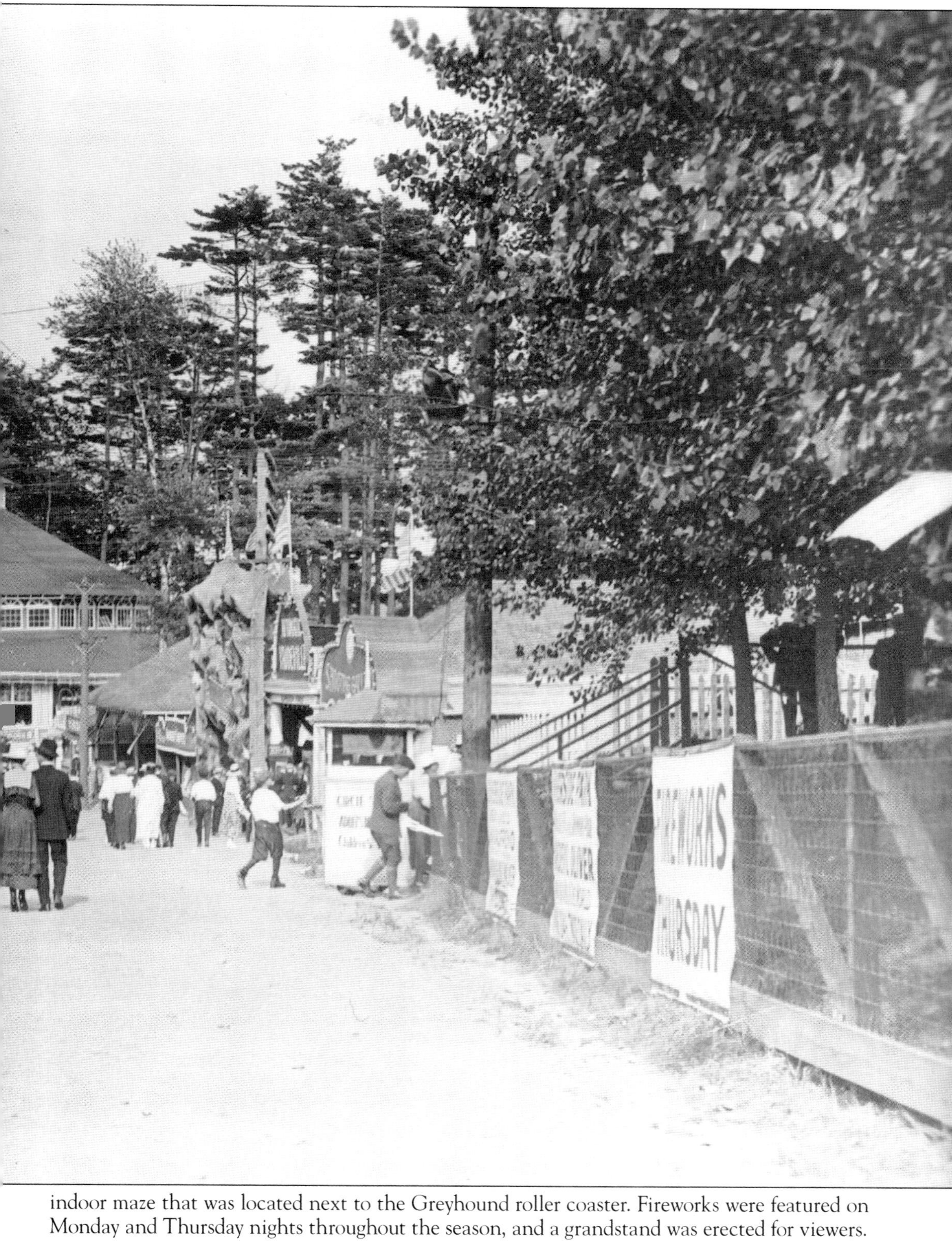


indoor maze that was located next to the Greyhound roller coaster. Fireworks were featured on Monday and Thursday nights throughout the season, and a grandstand was erected for viewers.

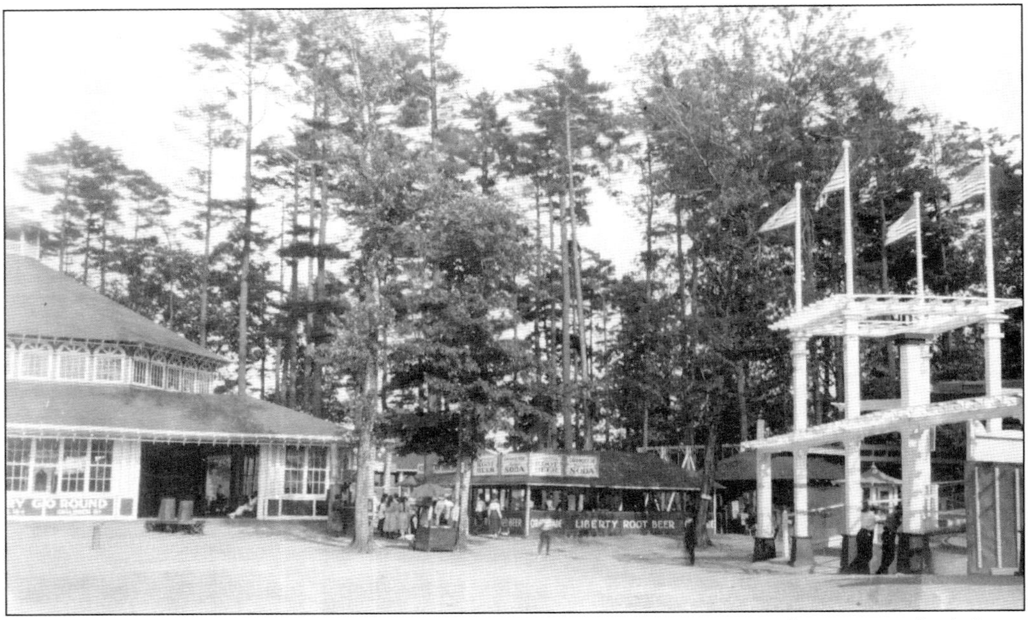


The 1917 carousel building (left) and the entrance to the Lightning roller coaster (right) are pictured before the crowds arrived on Memorial Day, May 31, 1921. The elaborate carousel, housed in an 80-square-foot building, had a capacity of 500 people, according to newspaper accounts. The swings (see page 15) are visible just beyond the refreshment stand (center). Sadly, the peacefulness of this scene was not universal; on that same day, a race riot in Tulsa, Oklahoma, left 39 people dead.

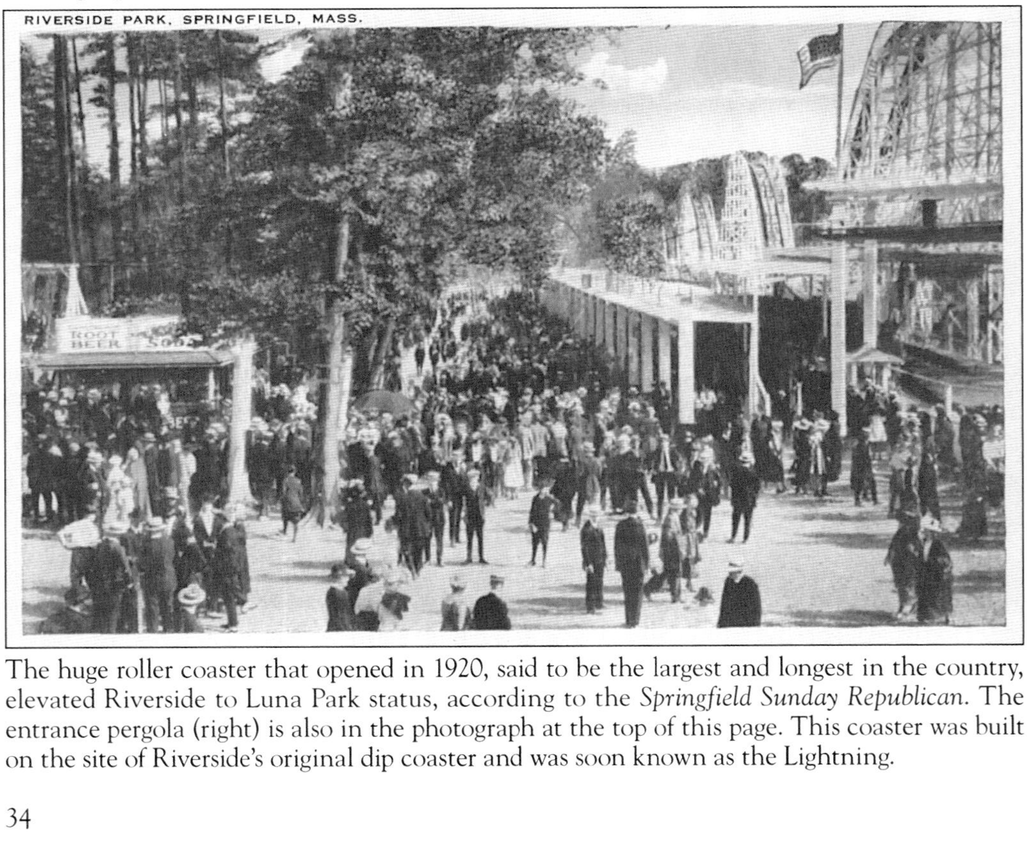


The huge roller coaster that opened in 1920, said to be the largest and longest in the country, elevated Riverside to Luna Park status, according to the *Springfield Sunday Republican*. The entrance pergola (right) is also in the photograph at the top of this page. This coaster was built on the site of Riverside's original dip coaster and was soon known as the Lightning.

MISS AMERICA SEEKING PRETTIEST RIVERSIDE GIRL

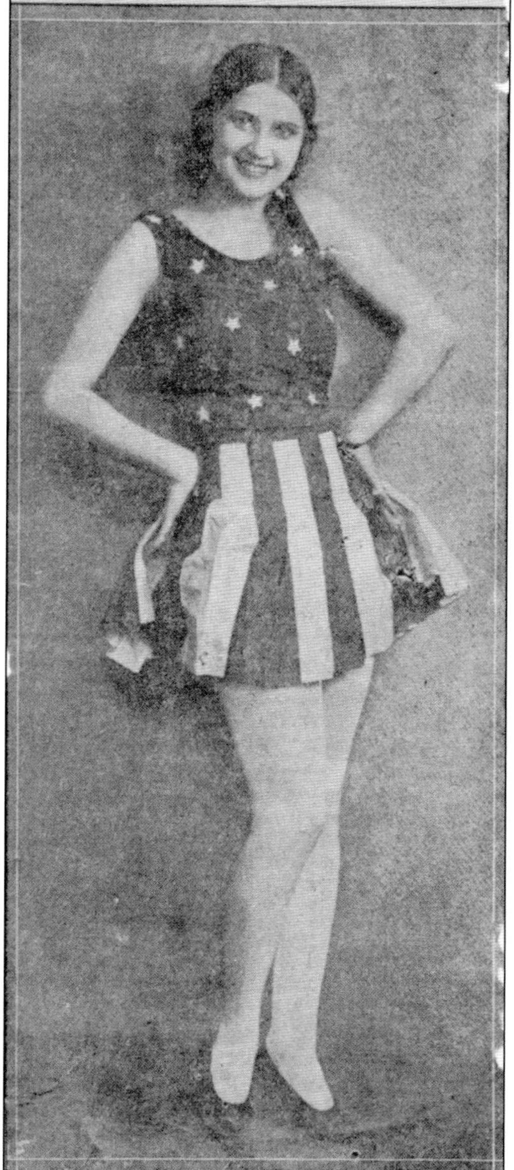

FAMOUS American beauty, winner of 1926 national beauty pageant in Atlantic City, will be at the Crystal Ballroom at Riverside Park tomorrow night. She will personally select the prettiest girl on the floor and present her a beautiful silver loving cup as a memento. Miss America is Miss Norma Smallwood of Tulsa, Ok., and she will appear at the ballroom in several changes of costume, including the bathing suit in which she won her title.

On July 27, 1927, Norma Smallwood, the reigning Miss America, was at Riverside's Crystal Ballroom to select the most beautiful girl on the floor. Helen Fitzgerald was chosen from the hundreds in attendance, and in addition to receiving a silver loving cup, she was crowned Miss Riverside. Smallwood returned to Riverside later in the week to swim in Lake Takadip. The selection of a Miss Riverside was revived by Ed Carroll Sr. in the 1940s. (Courtesy of Ann LaPalme.)

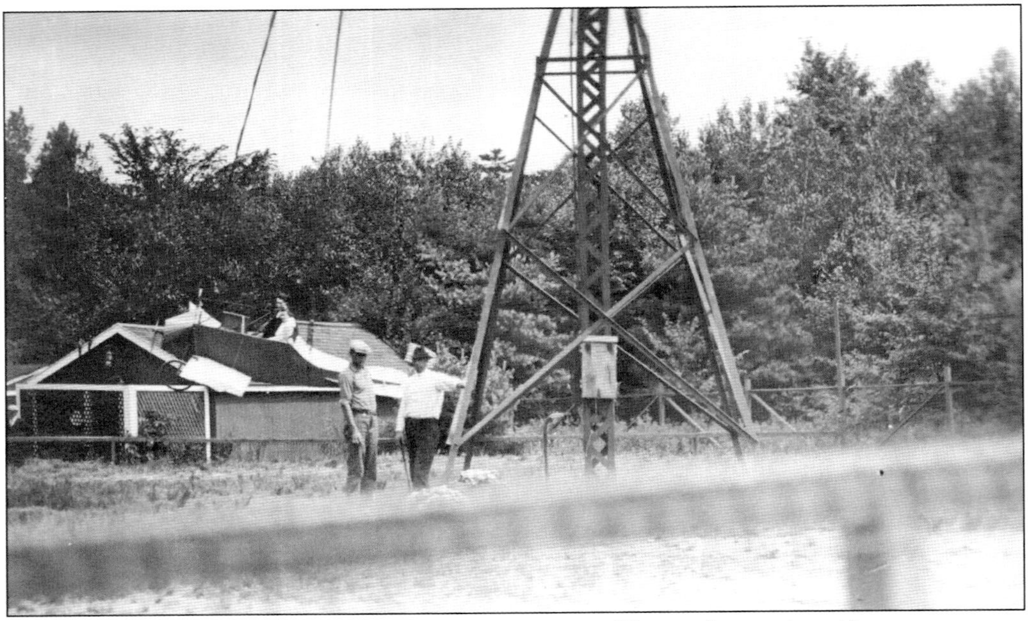

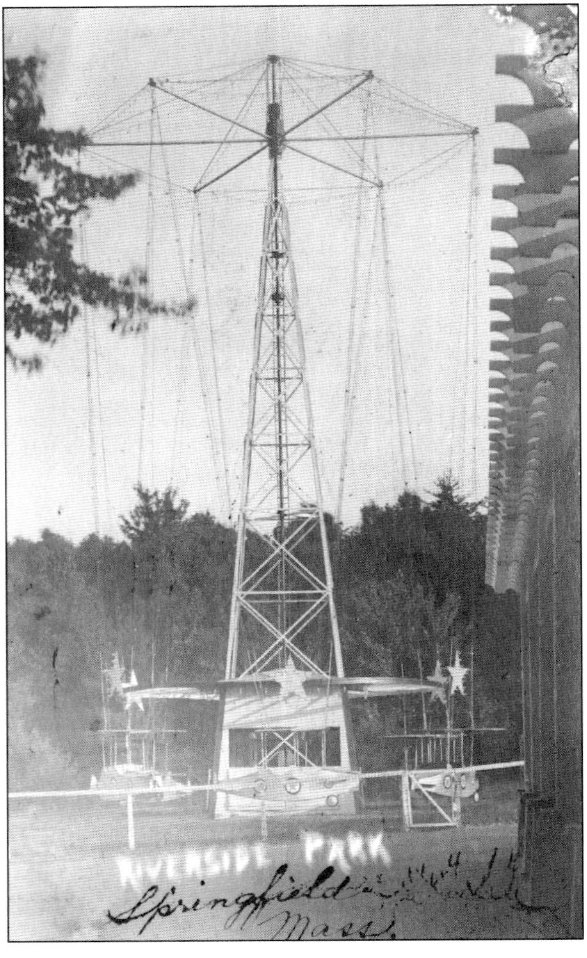


The airplane swing ride was very popular due to America's fascination with aeronautics in the early decades of the 20th century. The ride is shown shortly after it opened in the late 1910s (above) and then after it was moved and modernized in the 1920s (left). In 1913, Riverside hosted Nels J. Nelson, "the Swedish Aviator," who gave flying demonstrations over the area in his Dionne hydroaeroplane; it was the first such demonstration in the Connecticut Valley. The craft's top speed was 60 miles per hour. The year 1913 also saw a visit by aeronaut George E. Dion, who made two balloon ascensions and parachute drops in September of that year.

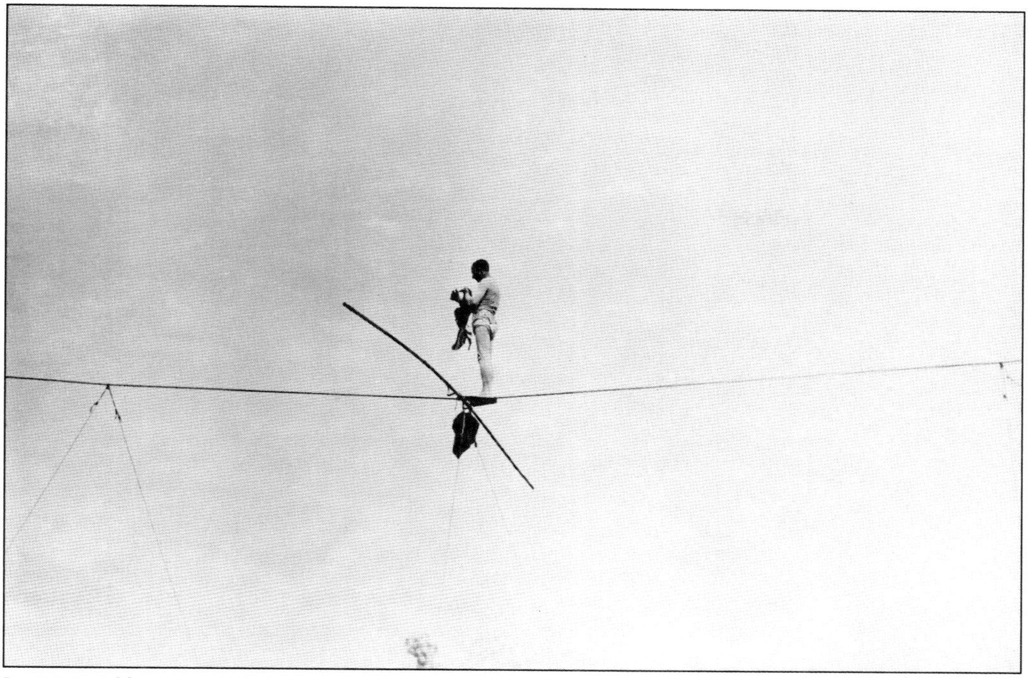

In 1919, Alfreno and his high-wire act appeared at Riverside during the month of July. He gave performances daily at 4:00 p.m. and 9:00 p.m. The highlight of the evening show came when he appeared in women's attire, disrobed, and went to bed on the wire.

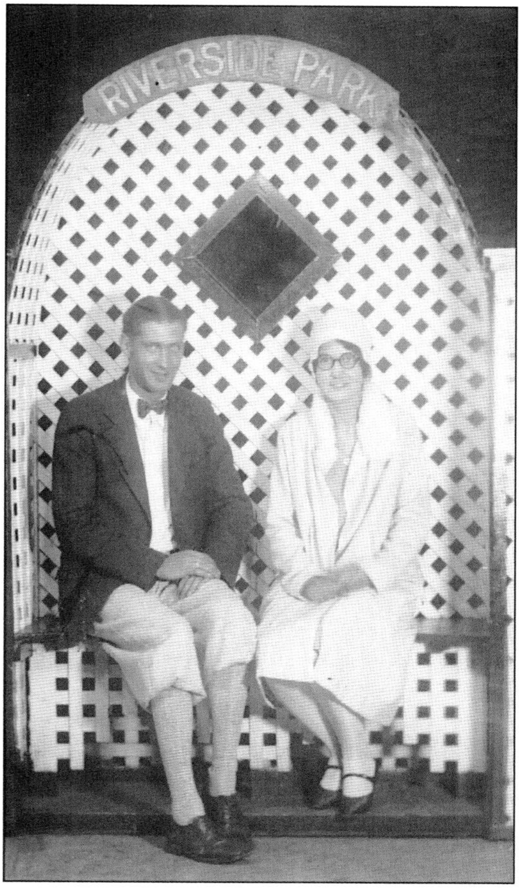


Agawam natives Bea Daly and Leonard Johnson are pictured at Riverside Park in the early 1920s. Both the Daly and Johnson families lived on Elm Street. The couple was later married and made their home on Elm Street as well. (Courtesy of Jack Hess.)

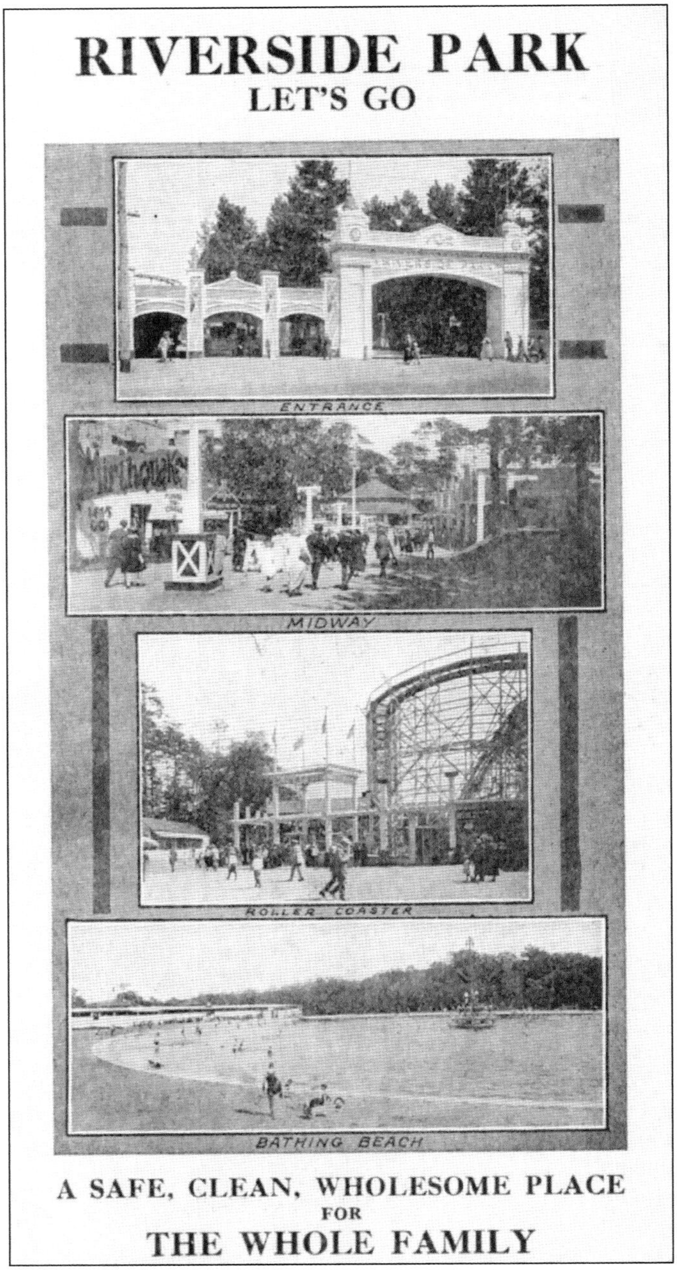


This promotional card from the 1920s declares Riverside Park a "safe, clean, wholesome place for the whole family." Riverside worked hard to "cater only to the best part of the population" and "attract everybody that is a gentleman or lady." With 30,000 or more visitors on Sundays (more than 10 times the population of Agawam at that time), it was inevitable that some bad eggs slipped in. As early as 1914, reports of "young foreigners" whose idea of a good time when intoxicated "do not correspond with the best interests of the community" appeared in the local press. Offseason visits to Riverside were also of concern. "Another place of improper conduct on the part of the young foreigners is at Riverside Park. The people who go out there at this time of the year [February], when the park is not in operation, have a free hand. What goes on is not of a proper character for publication." (Courtesy of June Cook.)

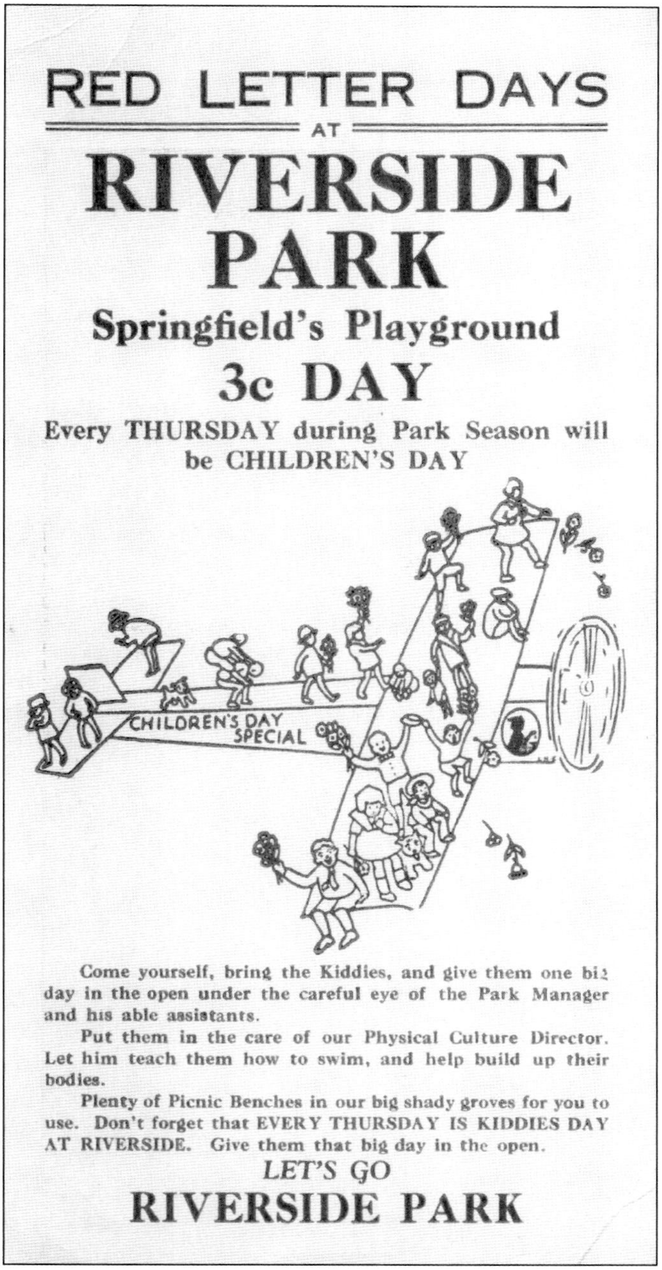


Riverside Park has always been a favorite of area children. Thursdays were designated Children's Day for several years in the late 1920s, with special rates for youngsters on all rides. In 1928, the Springfield Day Nursery (now Square One) held its annual outing at Riverside for 70 mothers and their children. The following year, 15,000 children attended the Hathaway Baking Company's annual Hathaway Bread Day at the park. Alton B. Hathaway, president of the company, gave away $100 in gold to winners of the day's athletic events, and 200 winners of the Lucky Name contest each went home with a loaf of bread. Between 1929 and 1932, Country Club Soda Day attracted crowds of between 20,000 and 35,000, mostly children. More than 2,300 newsboys, who consumed more than 150 gallons of orangeade, were the guests of the Springfield Newspapers at the park on August 10, 1932. (Courtesy of June Cook.)

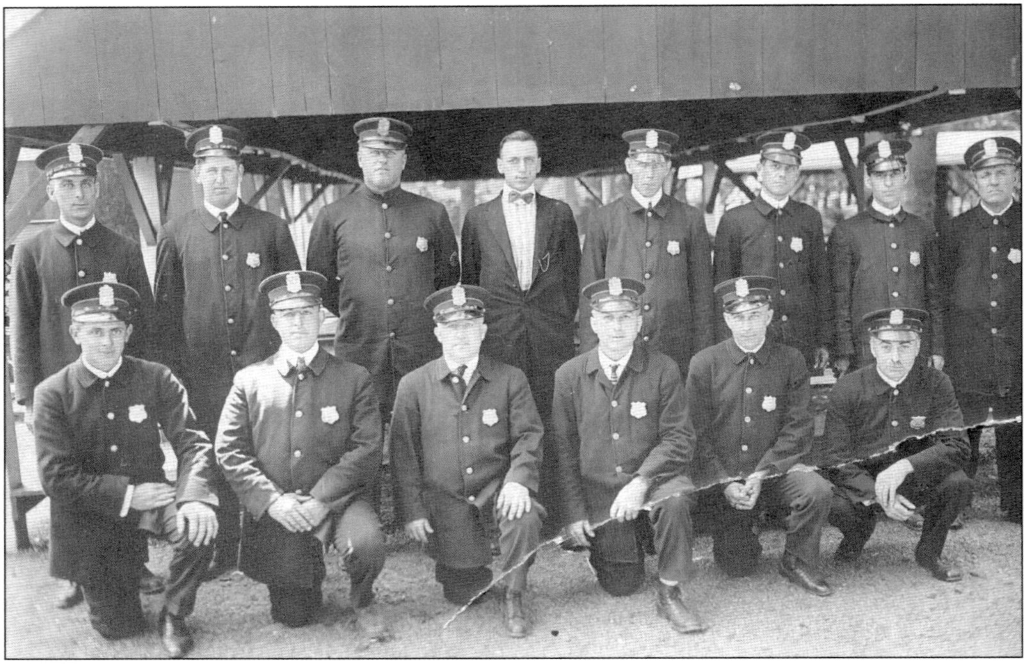

The Agawam Police Department, seen here at the Riverside Park picnic grove in the 1920s, has seen its share of action at the park. In 1921, a Buick touring car stolen in Springfield was found two hours later at Riverside by police officers. In 1932, Agawam police chief Perley J. Hewey and motorcycle officer Roland C. Reed arrested the Cedarville brothers for stealing gasoline from a car in the Riverside Park lot.

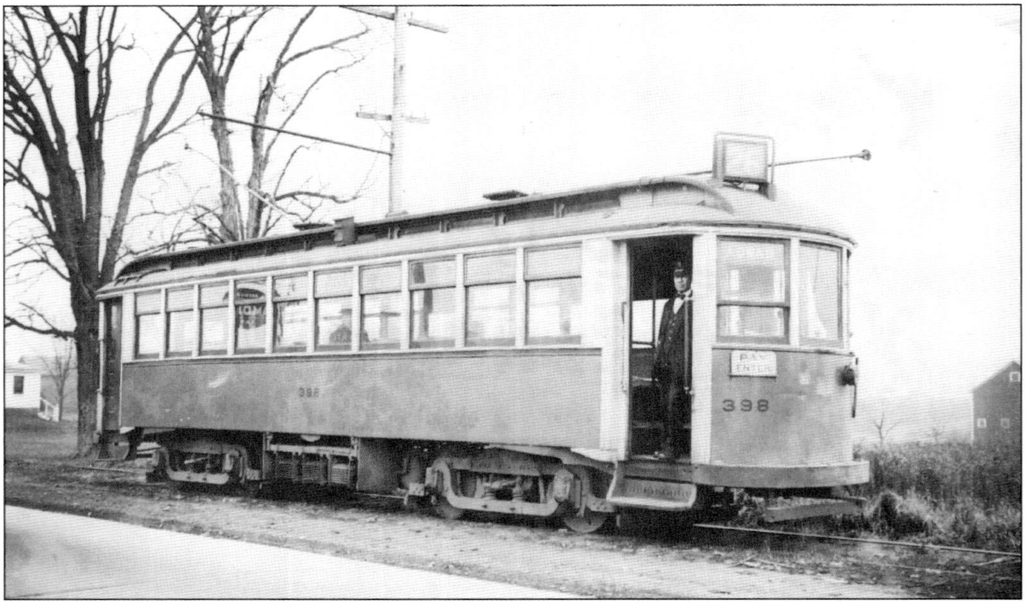


When Springfield Street Railway car no. 398 was photographed at the end of the line near Riverside Park on November 18, 1934, no one knew the trolleys would be gone in just two years. During their last run on November 14, 1936, retired motorman Ezra F. Paddock told the *Springfield Sunday Union and Republican*, "I've seen 15 packed cars in a line going to the park on a Sunday afternoon. Everyone was dressed in their best and carried picnic lunches. Sunday was our busiest day."

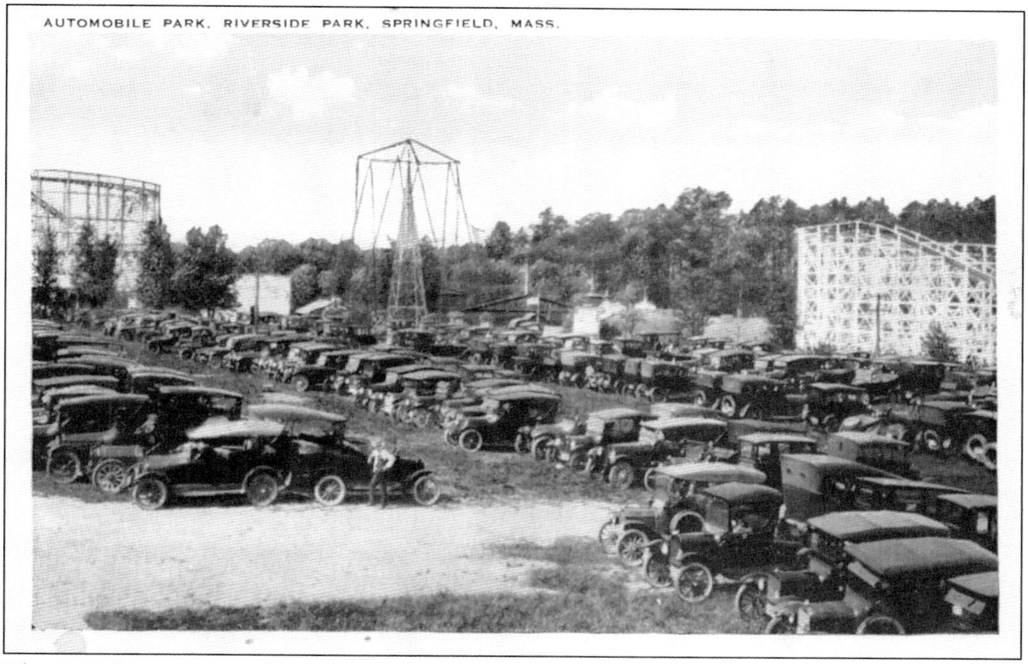


The steamboats to Riverside Park ended their run in the mid-1920s, and the trolleys ended theirs in the mid-1930s; both were victims of the rising popularity of the automobile. The parking lot at Riverside is shown around 1915. The park has continued to grow, and by the first decade of the 21st century, the parking situation had become a somewhat controversial issue.

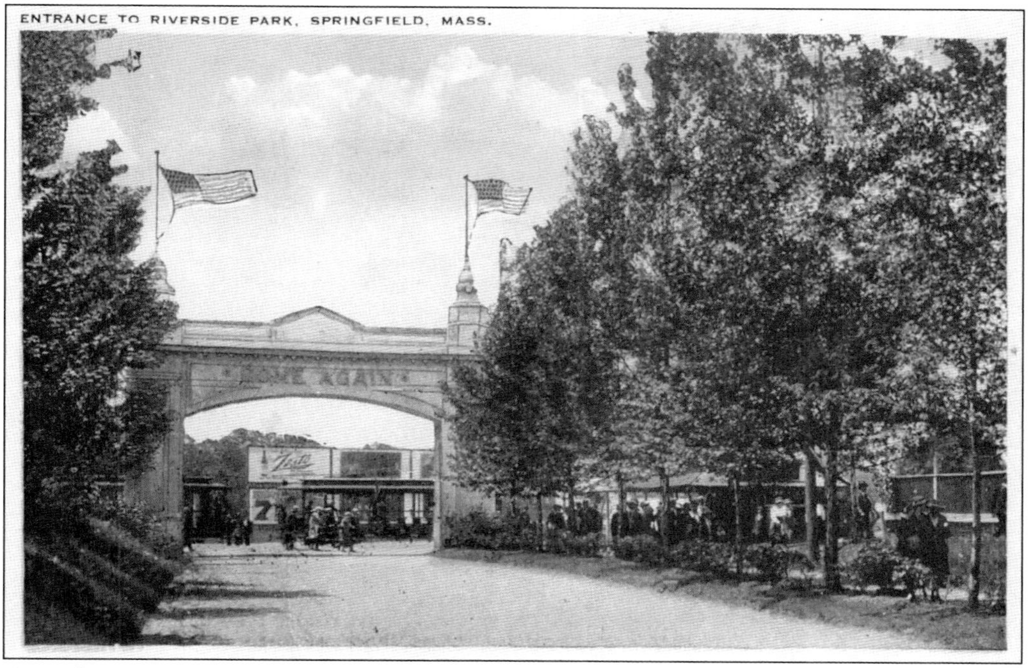


An early open-air trolley car is seen through the entrance arch at Riverside Park. A 1932 real estate assessment describes the arch as an "ornamented structure" with a fair valuation of "not less than $500." The lower section was stucco on metal lath over frame, and the upper part was wood. The side columns measured about six feet square, with the opening between columns about 33 feet wide.

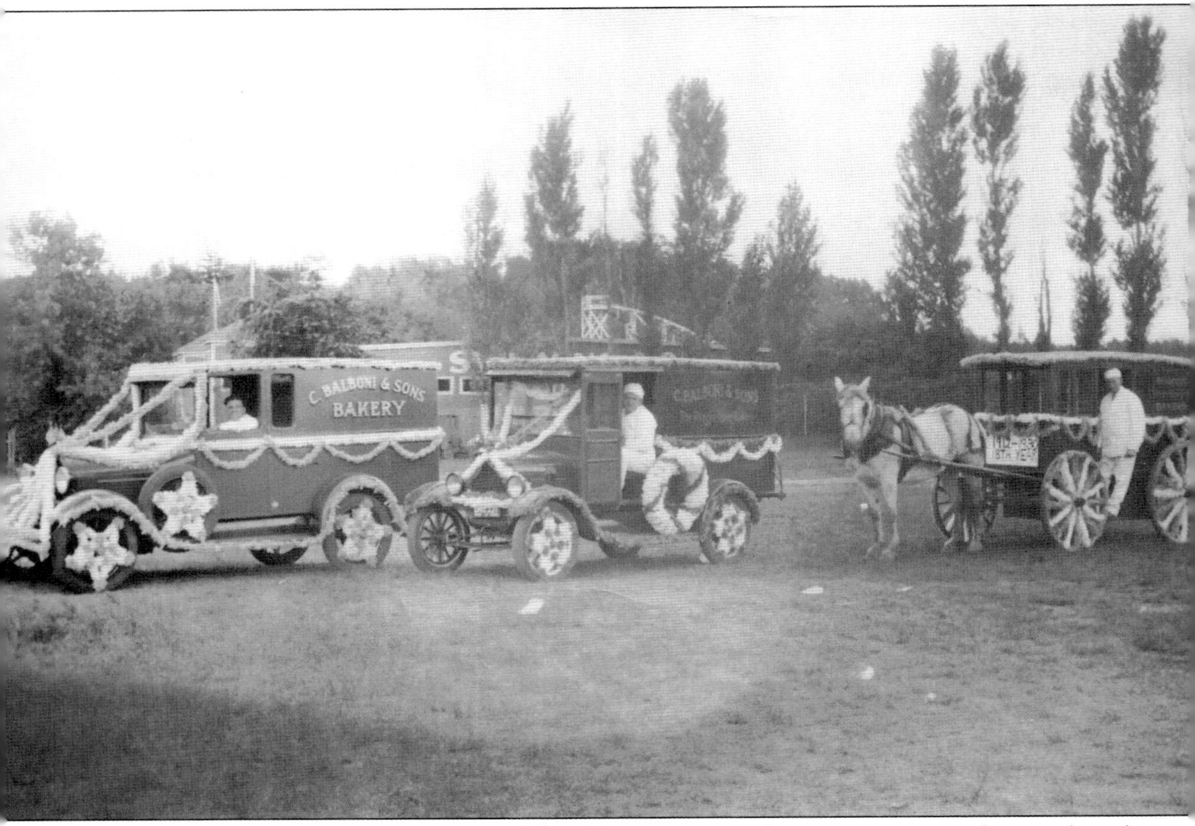


On August 12, 1930, Agawam celebrated the 75th anniversary of its incorporation with a parade and pageant. The parade traveled from Feeding Hills Center down Springfield Street to Maple, Bridge, River, Walnut, and Main Streets to Riverside Park, arriving in time for a noon picnic lunch. The Balboni Bakery parade contingent is pictured at Riverside with the roller coaster visible between the trees. At 1:00 p.m., Rev. C.B. Jackson of the Feeding Hills Congregational Church gave an address that included the following remarks: "The town of Agawam is a normal community. It is doubtful if we shall ever see a rapid influx of citizens attracted from other communities. It is likewise doubtful that the town will ever attract any great enterprise to locate within its borders unless some radical changes are made in transportation facilities in the future." A program of athletic events followed the address, and later that evening, the Pageant of Agawam was presented before more than 3,000 spectators at the Riverside Park amphitheater. Performing in the pageant, which was written by George Pelletier, were 300 citizens. (Courtesy of Mae Balboni.)

# *Three*

# LET'S DANCE!

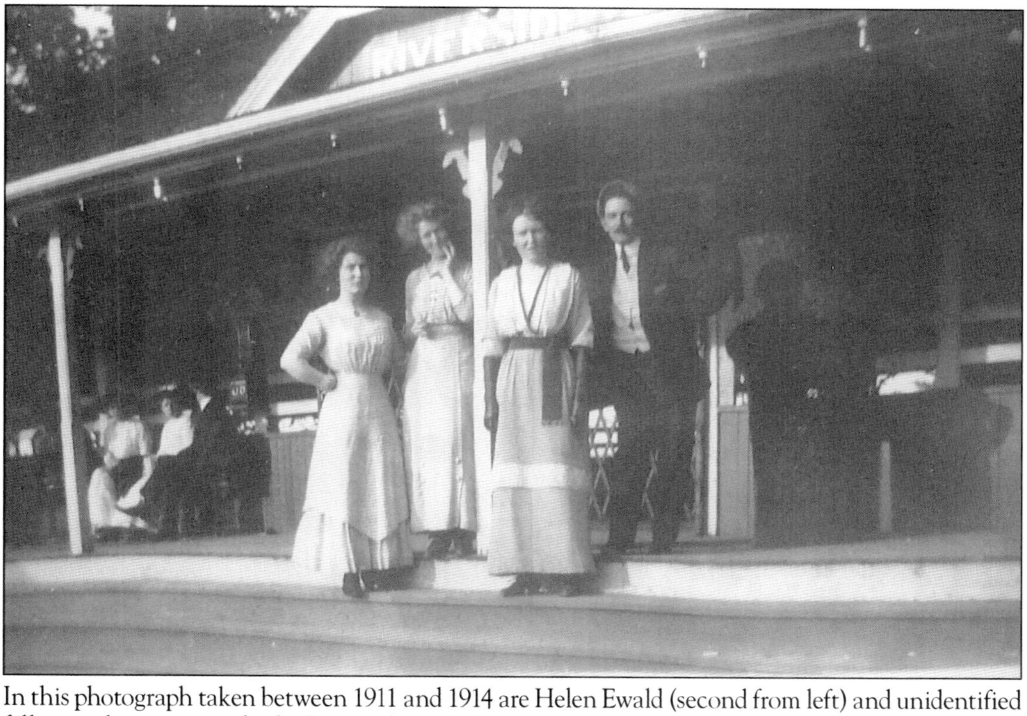

In this photograph taken between 1911 and 1914 are Helen Ewald (second from left) and unidentified fellow park goers outside the Riverside Park dance hall. Helen later married Robert Schilling. He played piano for and managed the popular Hollywood Orchestra, which played at Riverside often during the 1920s and 1930s. (Courtesy of Geraldine Schilling-Nordal.)

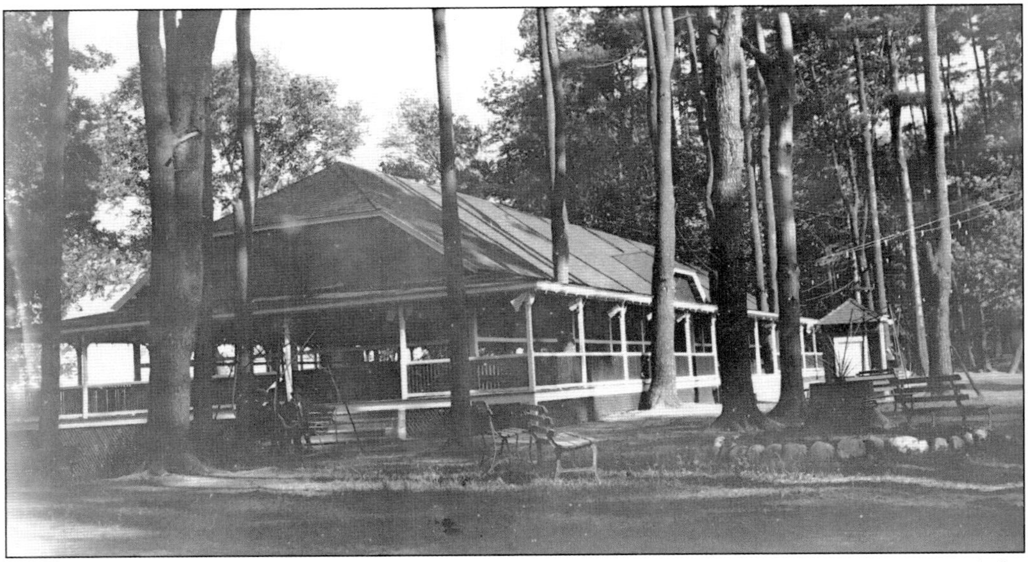

In 1900, W.J. Cook leased the pavilion at Riverside Park for dancing purposes. He managed the hall for years, even through the 1930s, when the park itself was inactive. During the off-season, Cook also operated the Butterfly Ballroom in Springfield. His proudest achievement was bringing John Philip Sousa to Riverside in 1920 and 1925. Sousa's 70-piece band attracted over 9,000 listeners. Cook died in 1941 at the age of 76.

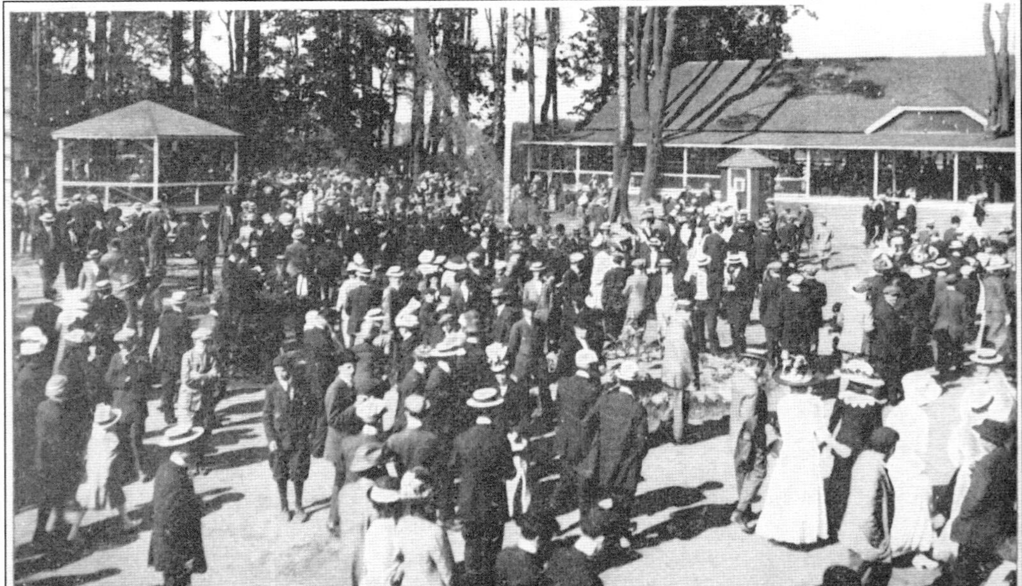

Riverside Park (Springfield, Mass.). Many feet keep time to the best of music.

Great concern was expressed in the local papers about what Henry J. Perkins had in mind for the dance hall when he purchased the park, but those concerns were soon put to rest. Springfield's *Republican* newspaper declared, "Public dance halls are generally associated with some form of vulgarity, but such is not the case at Riverside." The "excellent manner in which the dance hall is conducted and the entire elimination of all objectionable features" was commended.

"The Riverside Waltz Song," music by Howard I. Smith, was published by Riverside Music Company in 1913 and is called "the only authorized Riverside song." The lyrics, by Ella M. Smith, included the following chorus: "Riverside! That's the place to go / You will have a good time tonight / If your spirit is only right / If you're out for fun when the day is done / Take the boat or trolley, Oh won't that be jolly, to Riverside!"

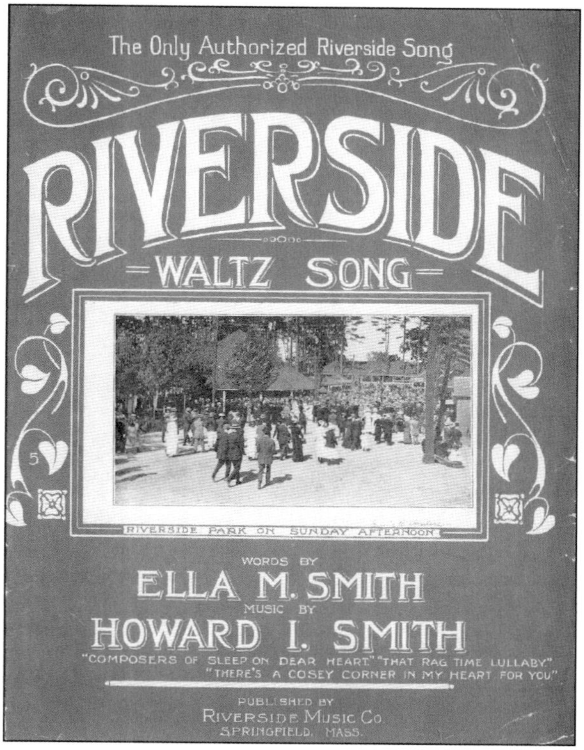


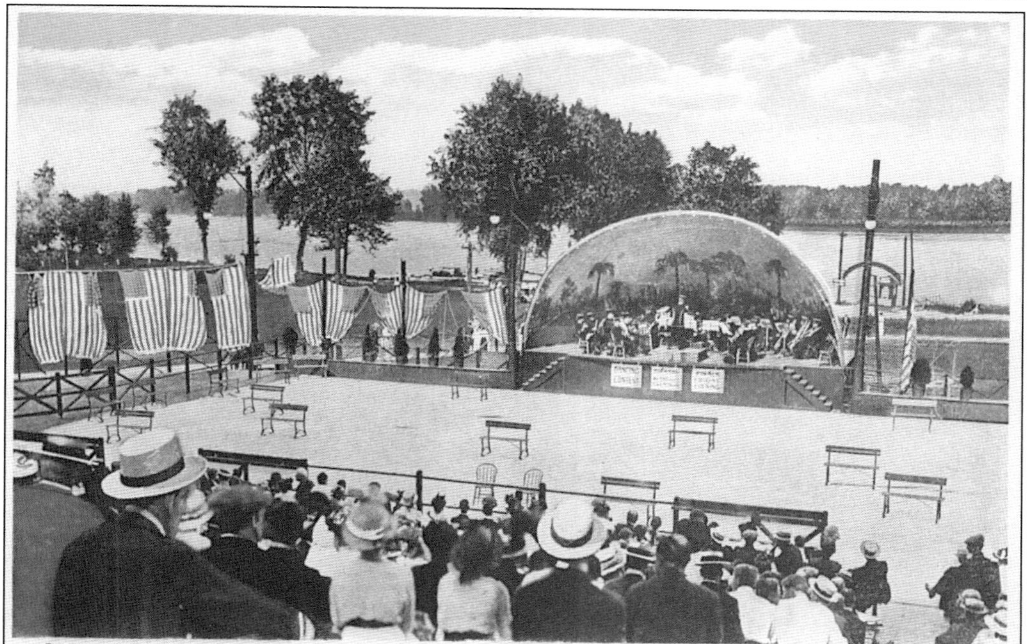
OPEN AIR DANSANT PAVILION, RIVERSIDE PARK, SPRINGFIELD, MASS.

Dancing had become so popular that by 1914 the old dance hall proved inadequate for the crowds. A new grandstand was built facing the river, and a platform measuring 165 feet by 50 feet was constructed to handle the overflow. This open-air dance floor was used for the modern dances and was considered a temporary solution until a new dance hall could be built. Traditional dances, such as the waltz or two-step, would continue to be offered in the covered dance hall.

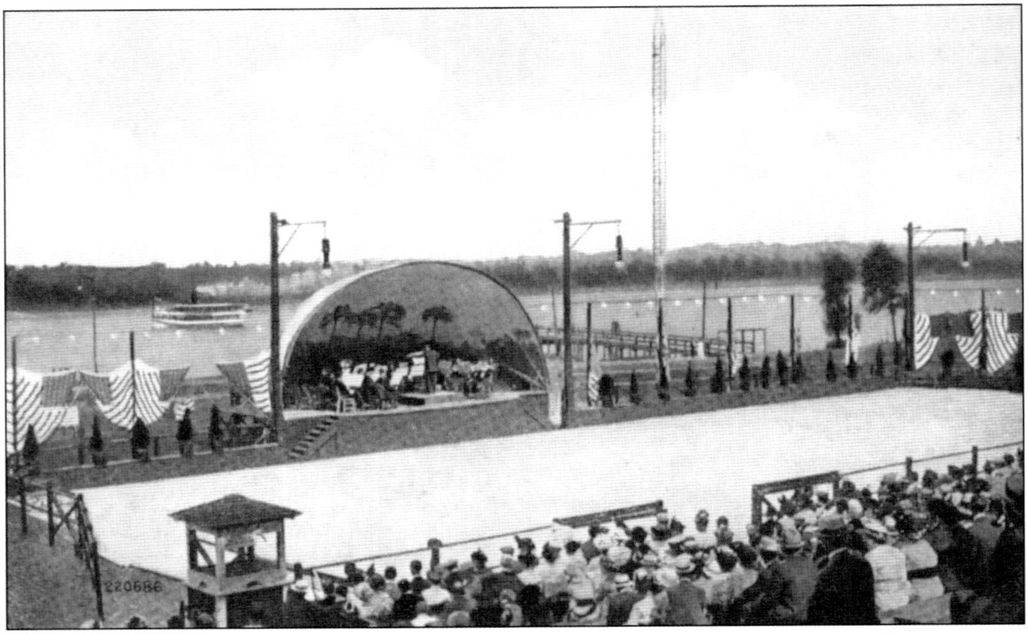


The May 21, 1915, *Springfield Daily Republican* announced that in preparation for the upcoming season, the dance floor of the open-air dance pavilion had been planed and "made as nearly perfect as it is possible for a dancing surface to be." The Riverside Singing Orchestra debuted that same year to rave reviews. Daniel J. Harrington was dance floor director, a position he had held since 1912. William F. O'Brien, chief dancing instructor, and 10 assistants offered dancing lessons to all "very cheaply and delightfully."

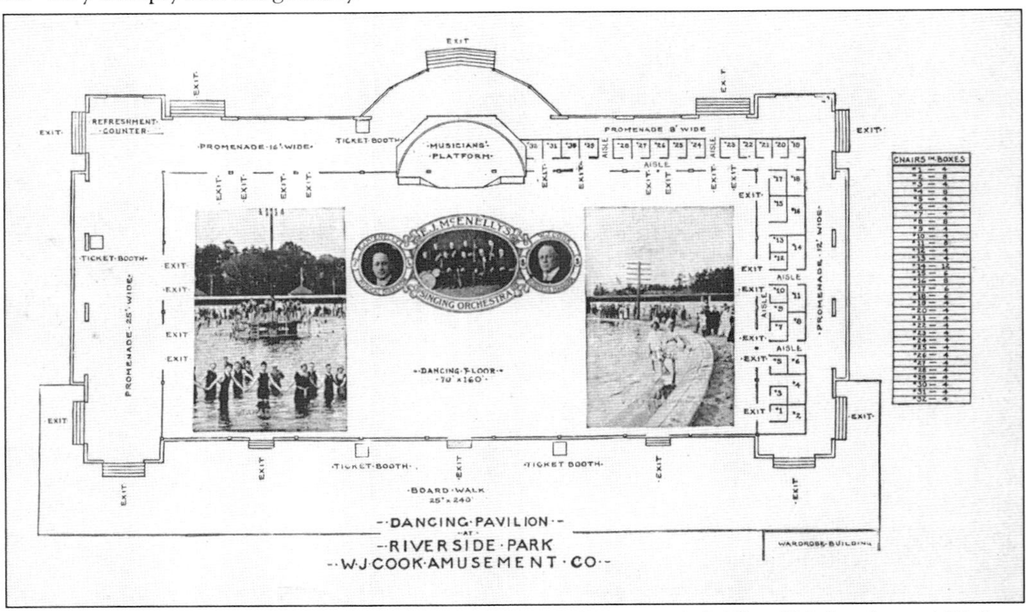


Cook's Dancing Pavilion opened in time for Memorial Day in 1917. The 220-foot-long, 100-foot-wide building with 22-foot ceilings was built around the former open-air dance floor. The new pavilion served as the summer home of McEnelly's Singing Orchestra, which was led by Edwin "the Waltz King" McEnelly. He rose to national renown as a recording artist for Victor Records with songs such as "I Like Pie, I Like Cake (but I Like You Best of All)."

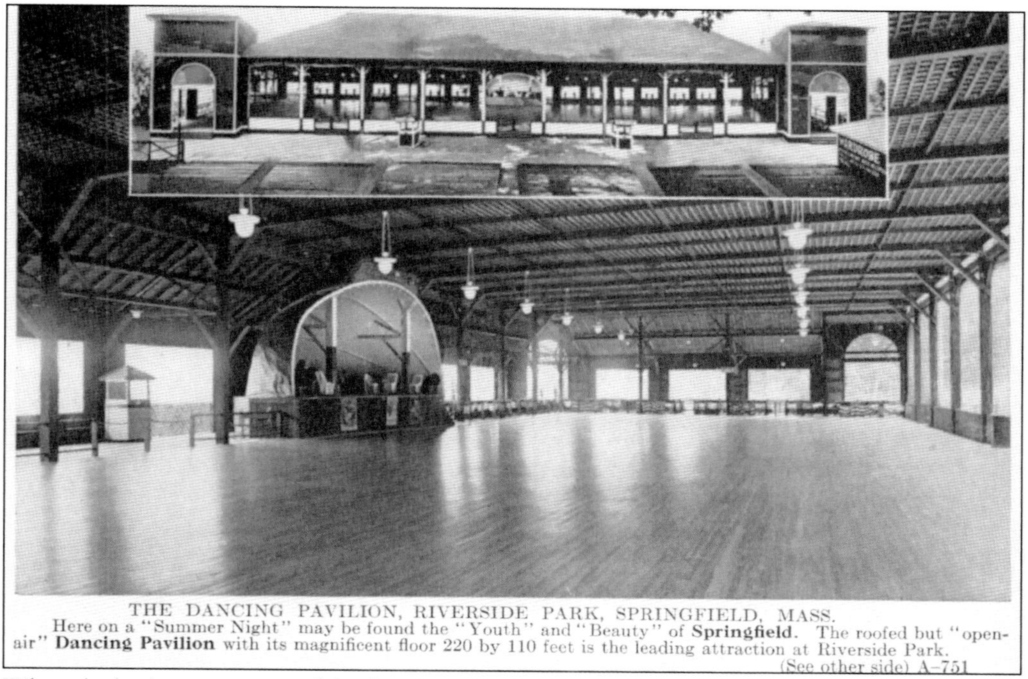


When the leading musicians of the day were not on the bandstand, the "giant orthophonic Victrola" was put into use, beginning in 1927. Sound could be projected as far as a half mile through the instrument, the likes of which could not be found within 100 miles of Riverside. The May 15, 1927, *Springfield Sunday Union and Republican* says of the device: "Benito Mussolini's greeting to the American people [his April 1927 "Message of Friendship"] can be heard as if Italy's famous statesman were speaking in person."

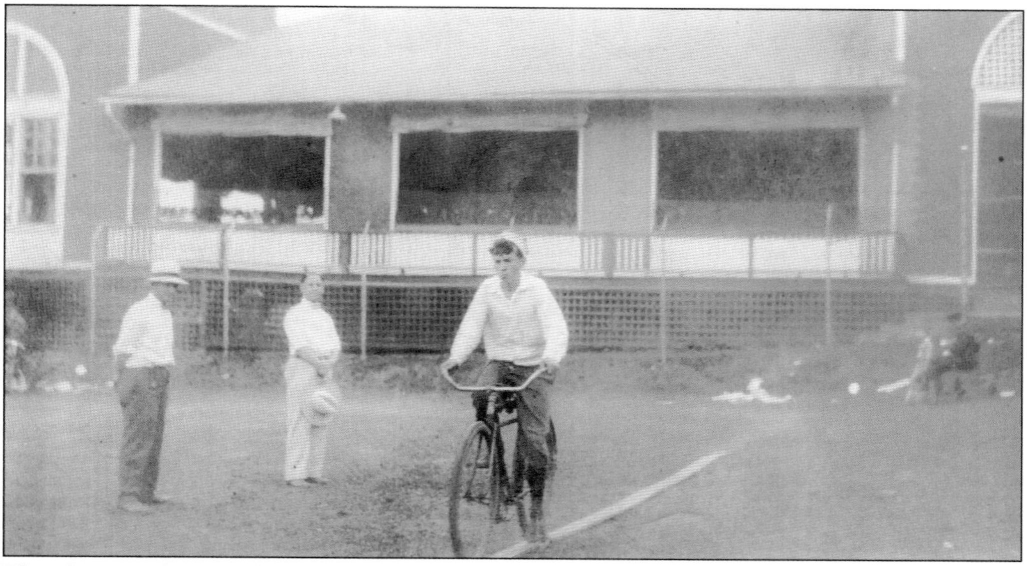

This photograph was perhaps taken on August 25, 1933, before Fred Waring and his Pennsylvanians were stopped in Connecticut for a motor vehicle violation en route to their engagement at Riverside. Later that day, Waring was detained by Springfield police after running a red light and becoming belligerent when he could not produce a license or registration. More than 2,000 people waited almost an hour for the tardy bandleader to arrive for his show. (Courtesy of June Cook.)

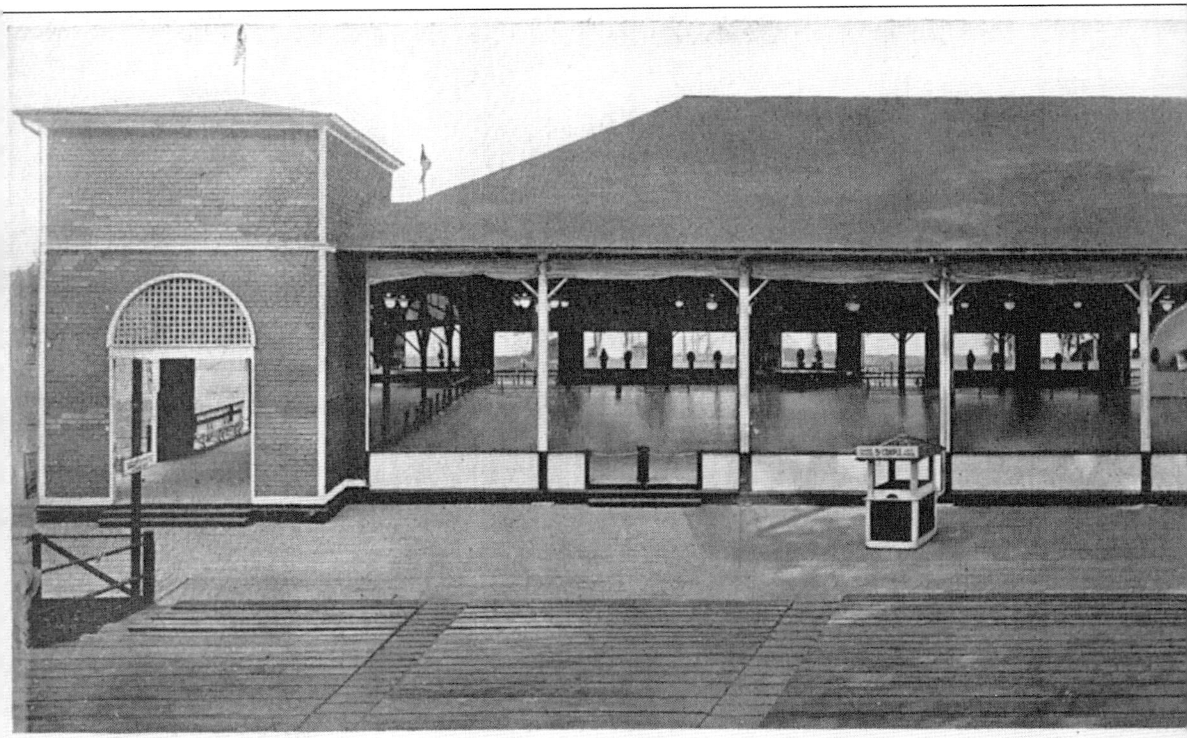

COOK'S DANCING PAVILION, RIVERSIDE PARK, SPRINGFIELD, MASS.
"Where the crowds go." Situated on a broad plateau close to the edge of the West Side to Hartford, **"Cook's Dancing Pavilion"** affords one of the

On Wednesday, August 29, 1928, nearly 6,000 people attended a concert by Paul Whiteman and his orchestra at Riverside Park. Whiteman, "the King of Jazz," was the most popular bandleader of the 1920s, and in 1928, he would score No. 1 hits with "Ol' Man River," "Among My Souvenirs," "Ramona," "Together," and "My Angel." He was just one in a long list of top performers to appear

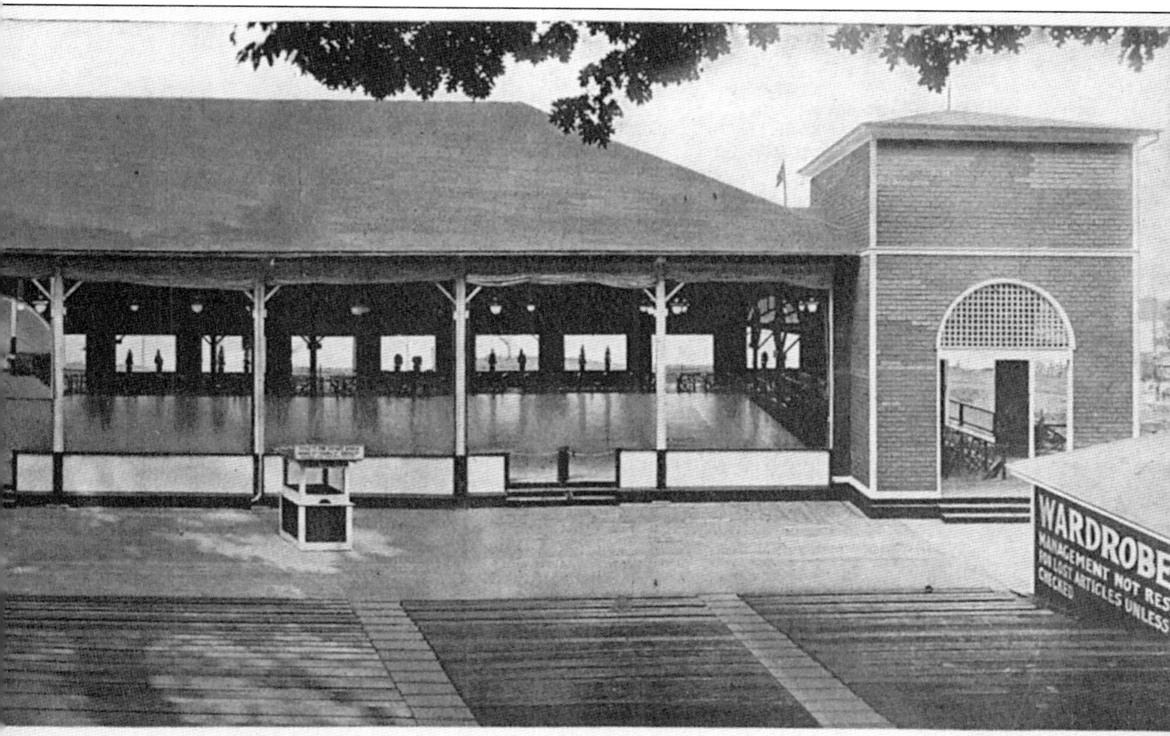


SUMMER HOME OF McENELLY'S SINGING ORCHESTRA
ticut River and "among the pines," a few minutes' ride from Springfield on
coolest places for **Summer Dancing in New England. "Let's Dance."**

at Riverside Park. Later years would see Rudy Vallee, Cab Calloway, Benny Goodman, Guy Lombardo, Harry James, and Tommy Dorsey at the popular venue. On May 14, 1945, Springfield Armory employees and their guests enjoyed a huge Victory Ball featuring Vincent Lopez and his Orchestra. In 1948, the storied ballroom was replaced with a racetrack by Ed Carroll Sr.

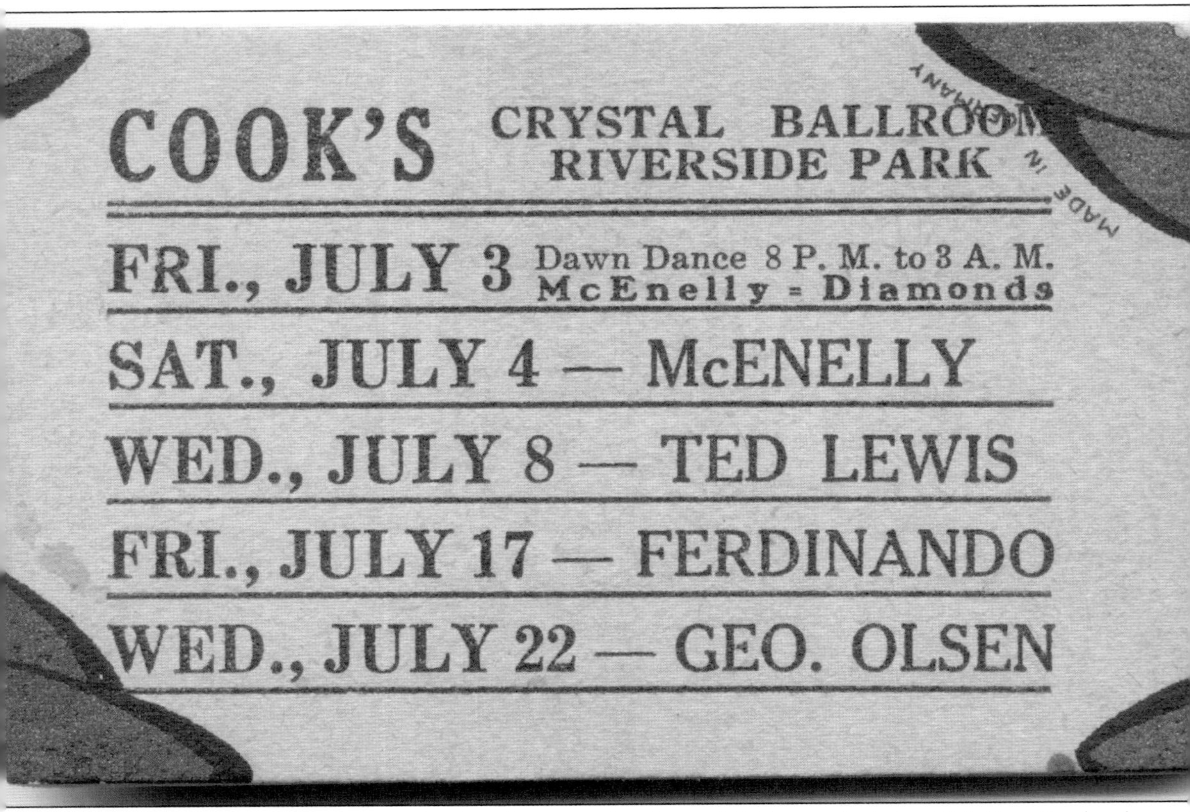


This dance card documents the headliners at the Crystal Ballroom for July 1925. New England favorite McEnelly's Singing Orchestra, led by violinist Edwin McEnelly, played regularly at Riverside and Cook's Butterfly Ballroom. The band also recorded 21 sides for Victor Records between 1925 and 1929. Jazz pioneer Ted Lewis and his band were one of the best-selling jazz groups of the 1920s and the top-selling artist for Columbia Records at the time. Benny Goodman, Fats Waller, Jack Teagarden, and Jimmy Dorsey were all Ted Lewis alumni. Felix Ferdinando and His Havana Orchestra was a popular group from Connecticut. George Olsen and His Music, as another band was known, signed with Victor Records in 1924 and was one of the label's most prolific recording artists.

*Four*

# Come on in, the Water's Fine!

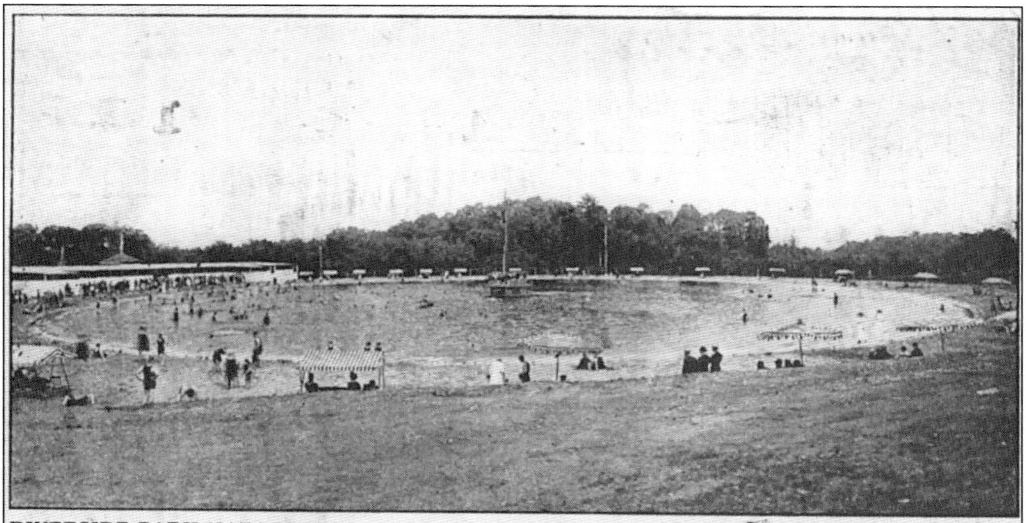

RIVERSIDE PARK NATATORIUM. The most sanitary bathing pool in the world, 300 feet in diameter, filtered water, 98% pure, 3000 gallons per minute flowing in and out of the pool. Riverside Park, Agawam, Mass. Post Office Address, Box 956, Springfield, Mass.

The Riverside Park Natatorium Company was formed in February 1916 and soon unveiled plans to build a giant swimming pool at Riverside. Originally planned for the area between the river and the open-air dance pavilion, the 300-foot-diameter pool as built by C.P. Kibbe Construction differed also in size from the 400-foot-by-200-foot structure initially designed by Springfield architects Bliss & Lavelle.

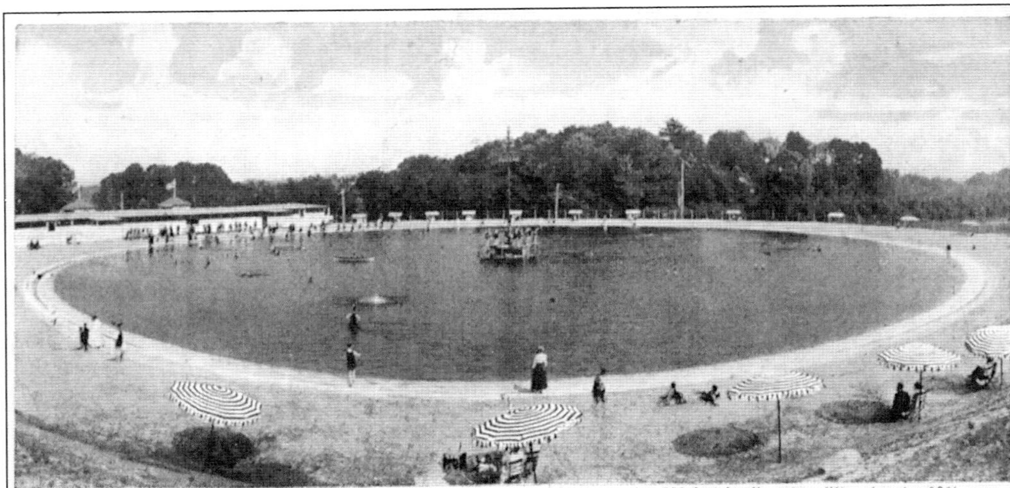


The great pool was something "all Springfield has been waiting for," according to a quarter-page advertisement that appeared in the *Springfield Sunday Republican* on April 1, 1917. The advertisement further states, "It is common knowledge that there is not even one satisfactory and accessible bathing place in Springfield. The facilities at Watershops Pond never have been and never can be satisfactory, and Loon Pond is far from the trolley and from the city. The river is not safe."

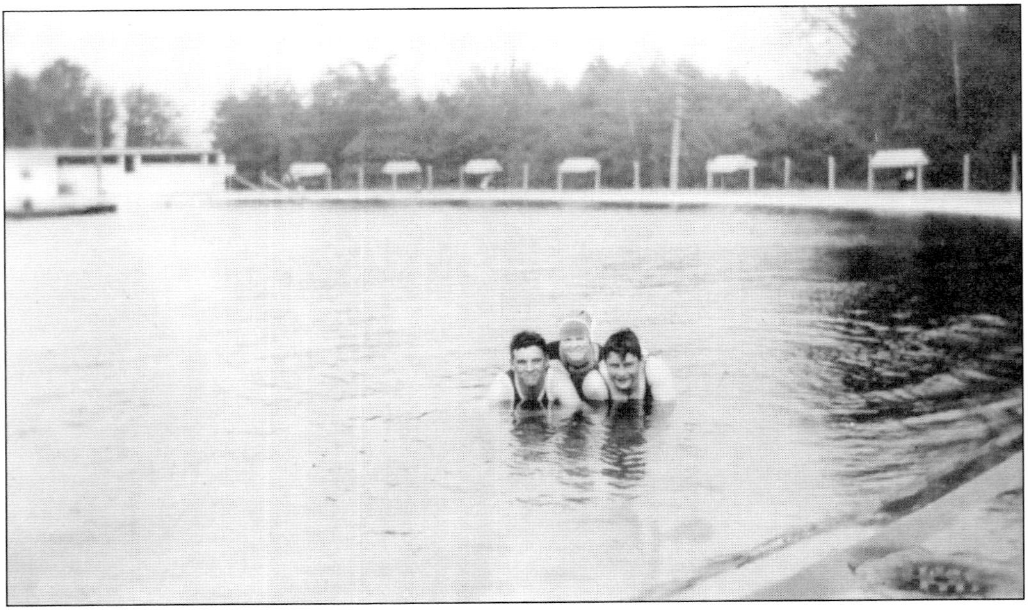

The huge pool boasted more shallow water than deep water, due to the fact that, according to the ad, the "majority of people want to wade and splash about—they are not anxious to swim." The water started at one inch deep and ran to five feet deep when 125 feet from the shore. The center of the pool was 11 feet deep and featured a diving platform that survived long after the pool was filled in and forgotten (see page 94). (Courtesy of Jane D. O'Donoghue.)

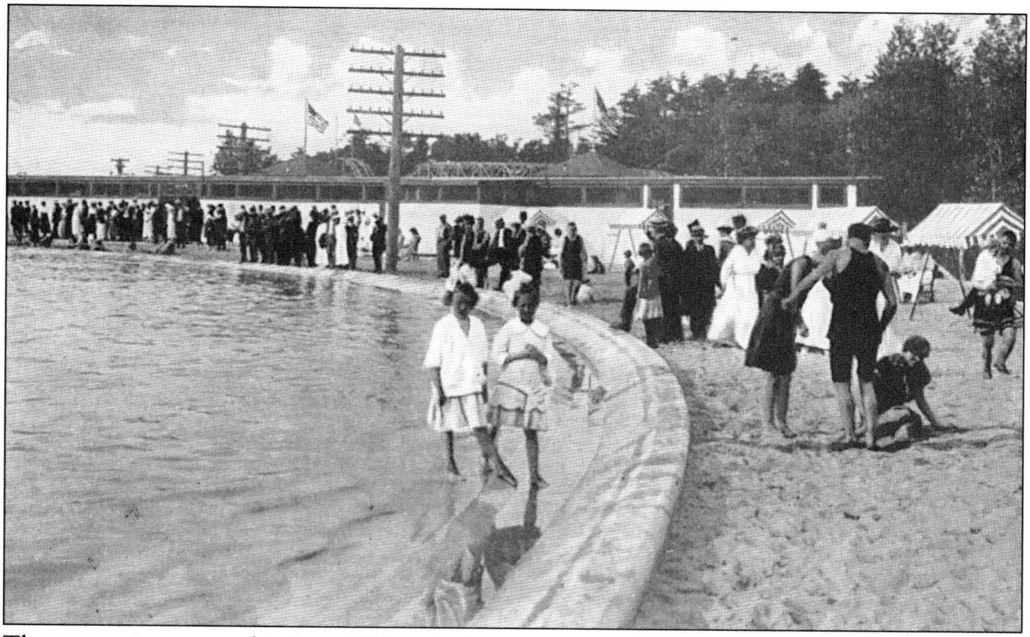

The natatorium opened in June 1917 with the invitation, "Come on in, the water's fine!" At the time, few people owned their own bathing attire, and 25¢ was charged for a "clean, sterilized bathing suit" and towel, with special rates for mothers with large families. That August, the price of admission was doubled, a move that proved unpopular with the 2,000 to 3,000 people a day who used the facility.

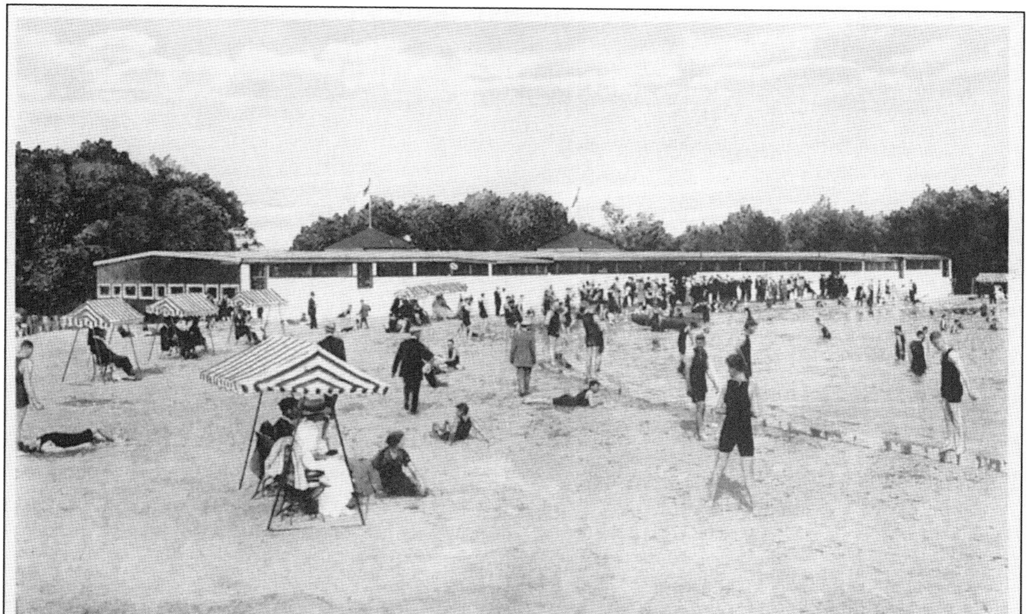

BATH HOUSES AND BEACH, LAKE TAKADIP, RIVERSIDE PARK, SPRINGFIELD, MASS.

Ads placed in the *Republican* newspapers touted the purity of the pool's water: "It will be filtered and re-filtered and will flow continuously through the tank; there will be a complete change of water every few hours. All the water entering the pool is guaranteed to be 98 per cent pure—thousands of dollars have been spent to insure the purity of the water."

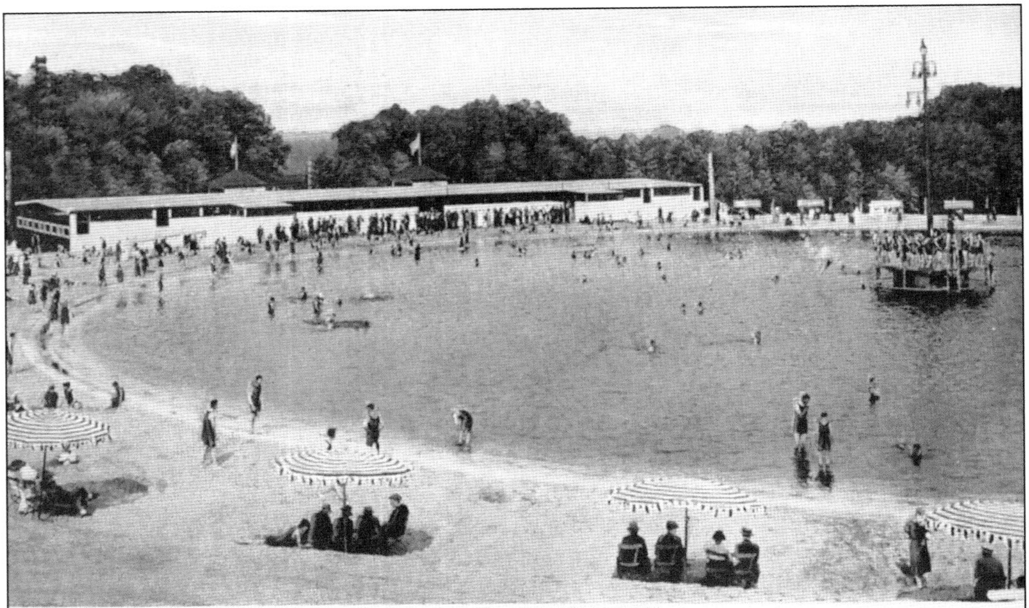

BATH HOUSES, LAKE TAKADIP, RIVERSIDE PARK, SPRINGFIELD, MASS.

Advertisements urged swimmers to "take a dip" in the pool, and within a month, the pool was forever known as Lake Takadip. Advertisement copy from July 26, 1917, read, "Come down and take a dip in Lake Takadip. That is the name of the big artificial lake—thousands like it, it's so clean. Pure filtered water—clean sand beach, clean lockers, clean people. A quarter covers all expenses."

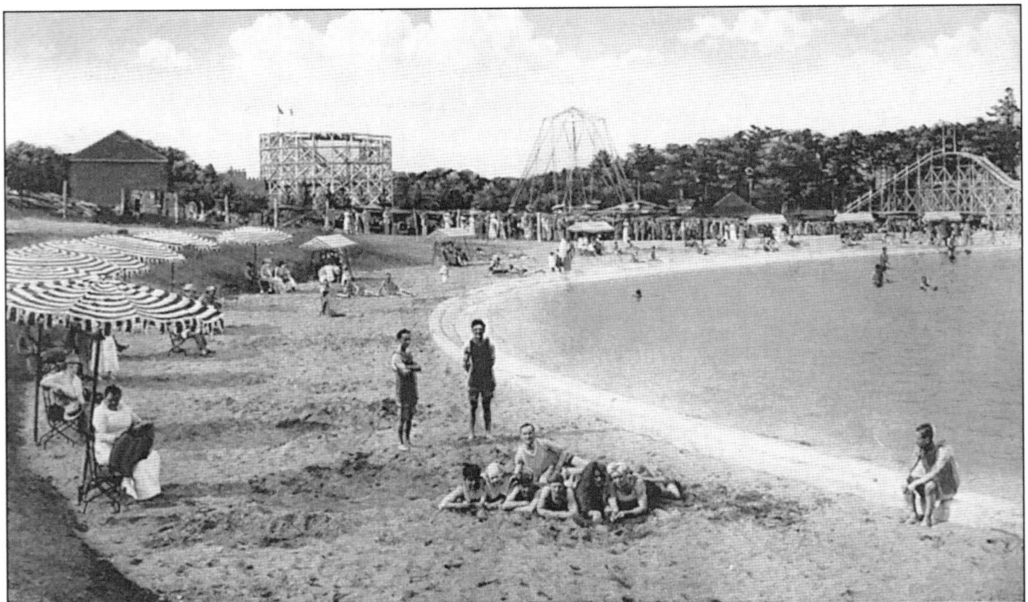

THE BEACH, LAKE TAKADIP, RIVERSIDE PARK, SPRINGFIELD, MASS.

In an attempt to prove conclusively just how clean the water was, the pool was emptied on August 13, 1917, so that thousands of curious onlookers could verify the operator's claims. It took three hours to drain, and the *Springfield Daily Republican* confirmed that there "was practically no objectionable sediment on the bottom." Ads further stated that the only thing found in the pool was "the sand carried in on bathers' feet—no sediment, no dirt, nothing at all." It took seven hours to refill the pool.

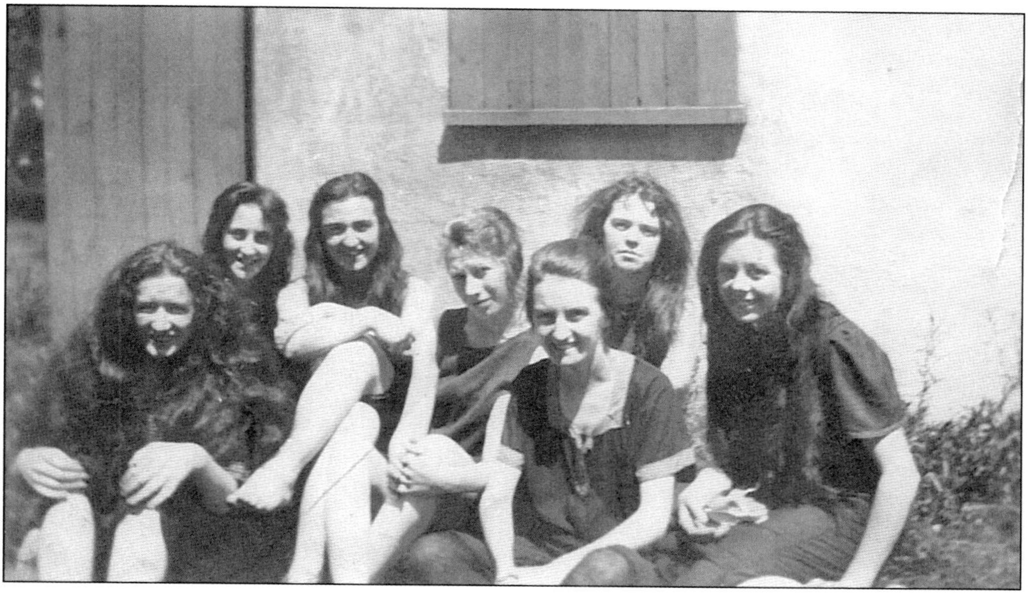

With the increasing independence of women in the early 20th century (and the right to vote to be achieved just a year after these 1919 photographs were taken), they were a growing part of the pool's visiting public. Advertisements promoting the pool stated that management watched the water "as a mother does her handsomest daughter" and proclaimed the facility safe for the fairer sex: "Competent lifeguards and instructors . . . [are] always on duty; special policemen . . . [are] on guard at the beach to protect . . . against annoyance. Women and children are absolutely safe at the Riverside Natatorium. Keep that in mind—safe against accident and safe against annoyance." Among those seen here outside the bathhouse (above) and in the pool (below) are Catherine Morrison (above, left; below, fourth from right) and Catherine Garvey of Chicopee (above, far right; below, third from left). Legendary longtime Agawam High School teacher and coach Harmon A. Smith was one of the pool's lifeguards. (Both, courtesy of Jane D. O'Donoghue.)

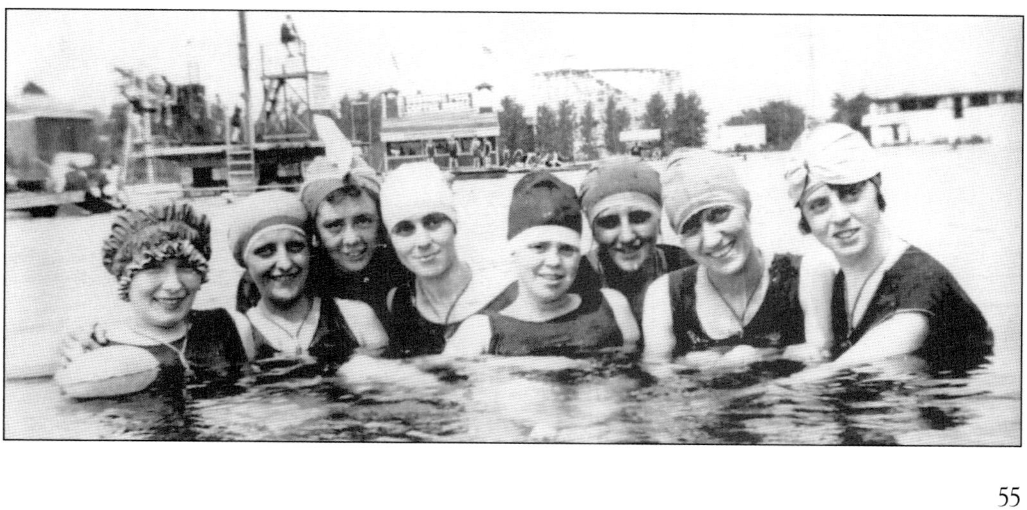

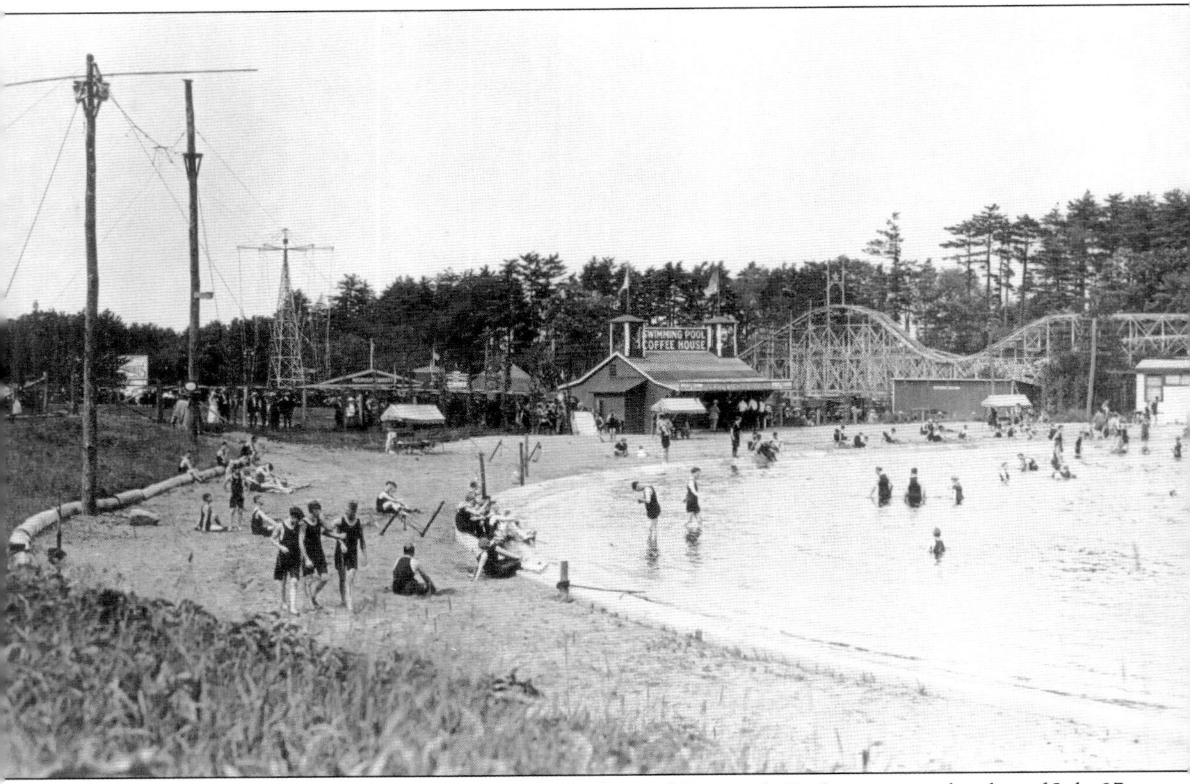


This incredible panoramic shot of Lake Takadip and Riverside Park captures the day of July 27, 1919. The advertisement that appeared in that day's *Springfield Daily Republican* reads, "At the swimming pool—life-saving demonstration with lung motor this afternoon at 3:30. Also, Alfreno walks the high wire at 4 and 9 o'clock. Concerts by 104th Regt. Band afternoon and evening. Today, *Sylvia* leaves foot of Elm St. at 2, 4, 6, and 8:15 p.m. Fare ten cents. Dare-Devil Oliver all

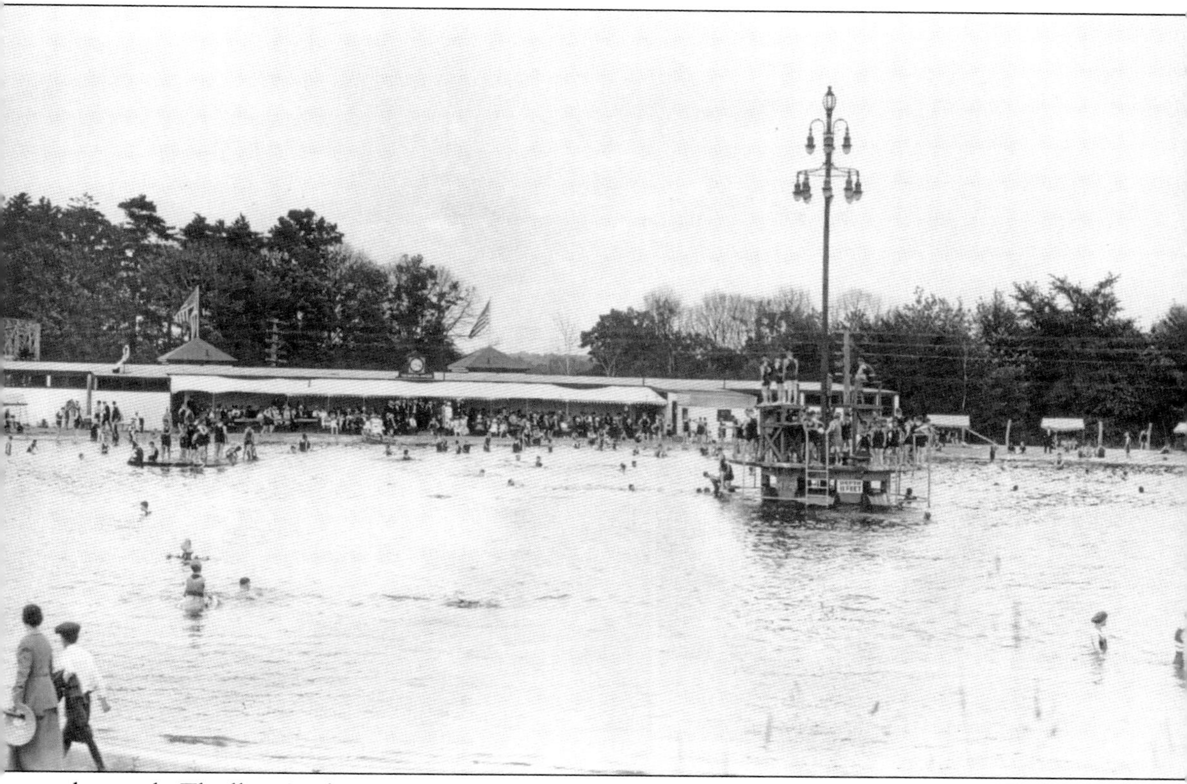

this week. Thrilling High Dive Act. Let's Go!" Daredevil Oliver was accompanied by a diving dog named Uno. The pool was open from 10:30 a.m. until 10:30 p.m. And, in addition to these attractions, Riverside also hoped to attract the public to its Park Restaurant, where manager Charles Young would provide "American or Chinese dishes at a cost that will not be greater than if you stayed at home."

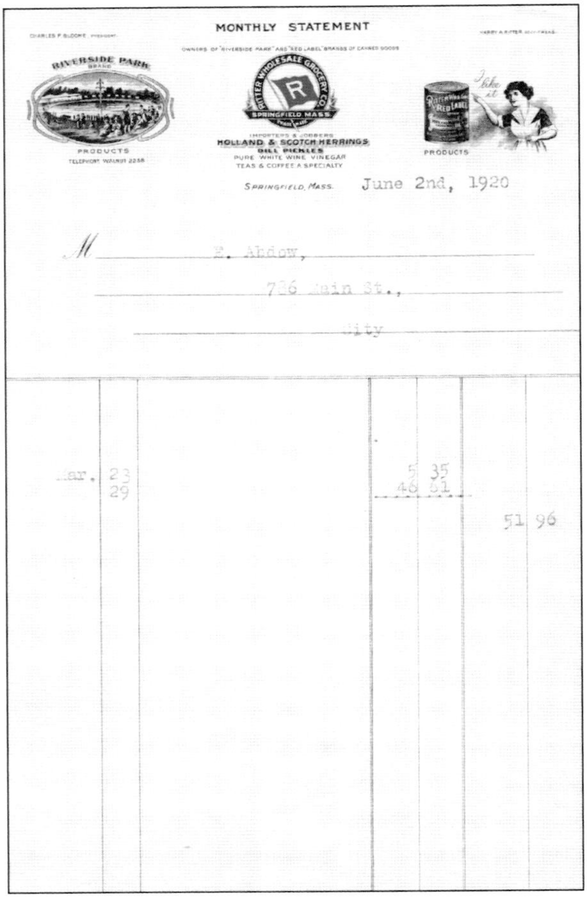

MONTHLY STATEMENT

OWNERS OF "RIVERSIDE PARK" AND "RED LABEL" BRANDS OF CANNED GOODS

RIVERSIDE PARK BRAND PRODUCTS

TELEPHONE WALNUT 2258

RITTER WHOLESALE GROCERY CO. SPRINGFIELD MASS.

IMPORTERS & JOBBERS
HOLLAND & SCOTCH HERRINGS
DILL PICKLES
PURE WHITE WINE VINEGAR
TEAS & COFFEE A SPECIALTY

RED LABEL PRODUCTS

I like it

SPRINGFIELD, MASS. June 2nd, 1920

M E. Abdow,
7[illegible]6 [illegible]ain St.,
[illegible]ity

| | | | | |
|---|---|---|---|---|
| [illegible]ar. | 23 | | 5 35 | |
| | 29 | | 46 61 | |
| | | | | 51 96 |

Riverside Park and its pool proved so popular with the public that the Ritter Wholesale Grocery Company of Springfield, Massachusetts, created a line of Riverside Park Brand products and featured Lake Takadip on its label and letterhead. The pool was used for more than just swimming, too; in 1928, it was the site for a fly-casting competition during the state convention of the Izaak Walton League.

Like the dance hall and Riverside Park itself, the pool attracted the celebrities of the day. In 1918, professional swimmer, vaudevillian, and early film star Annette Kellerman and her company of divers and swimmers spent a week at the pool to raise money for the Springfield Rotary Club's war-work fund. Kellerman is often credited with the invention of synchronized swimming, and she was well known for her controversial one-piece bathing suits.

SWIMMING POOL, RIVERSIDE PARK, SPRINGFIELD, MASS.

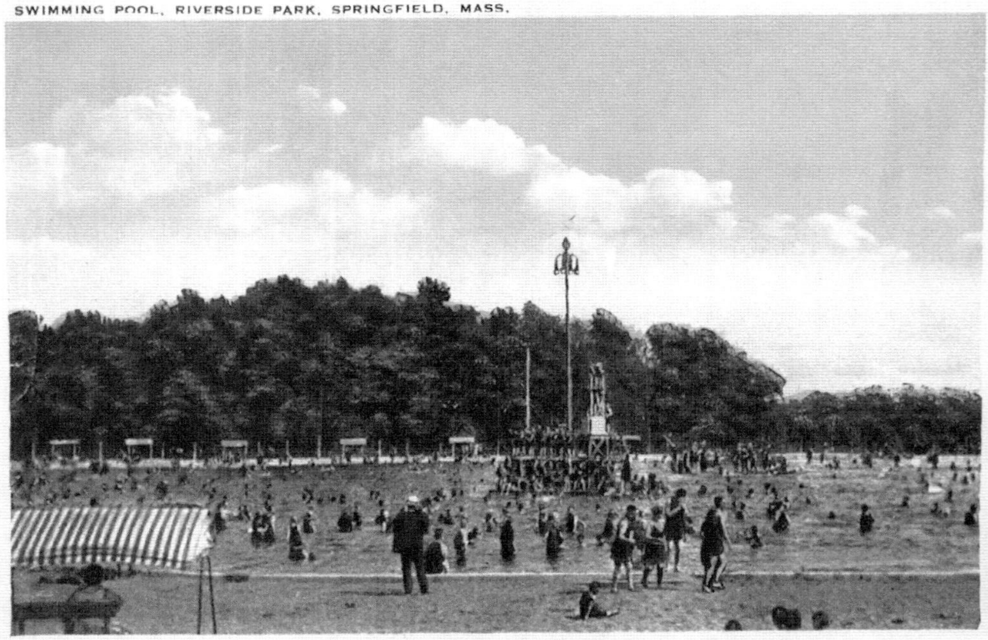

# *Five*

# ON THE RIVER SIDE

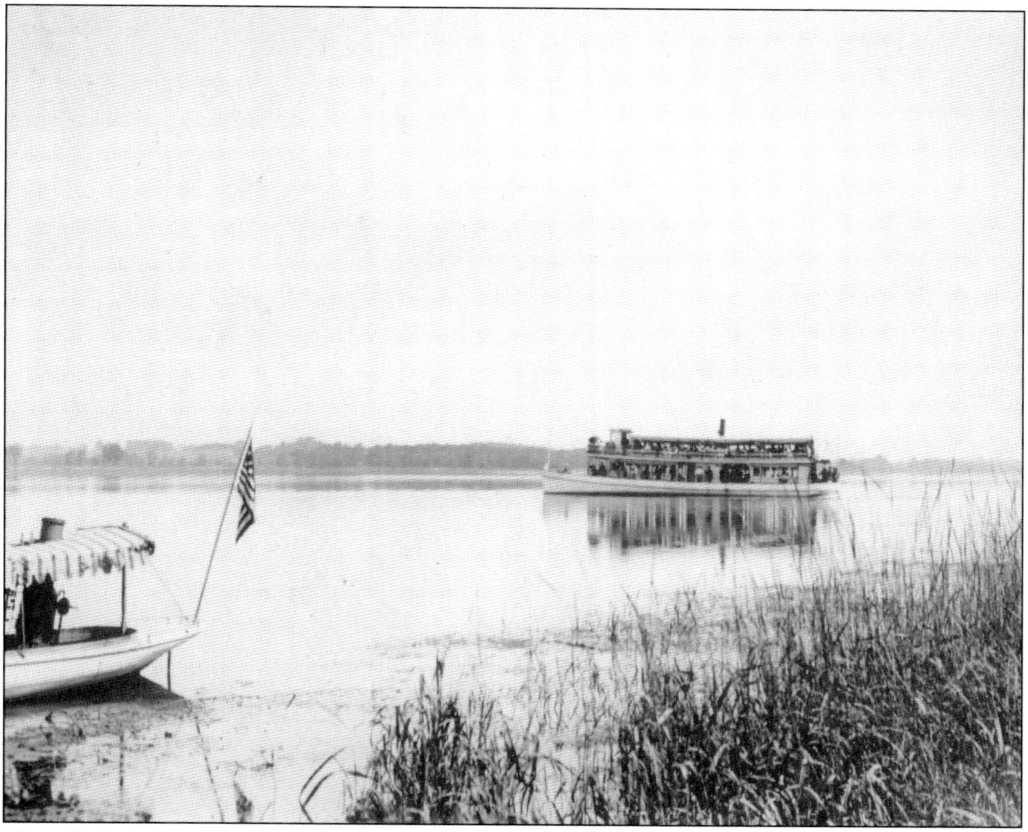

Though the *Sylvia* is easily the best-remembered steamboat to ply the Connecticut River in service to Riverside, she was by no means the only one. Equally loved in its time was the *Mascot*, seen underway in 1896. In service locally until 1900, she is believed to have later served the banana trade in South America. The launch partially seen to the left is possibly Henry Smith's *Calla II*.

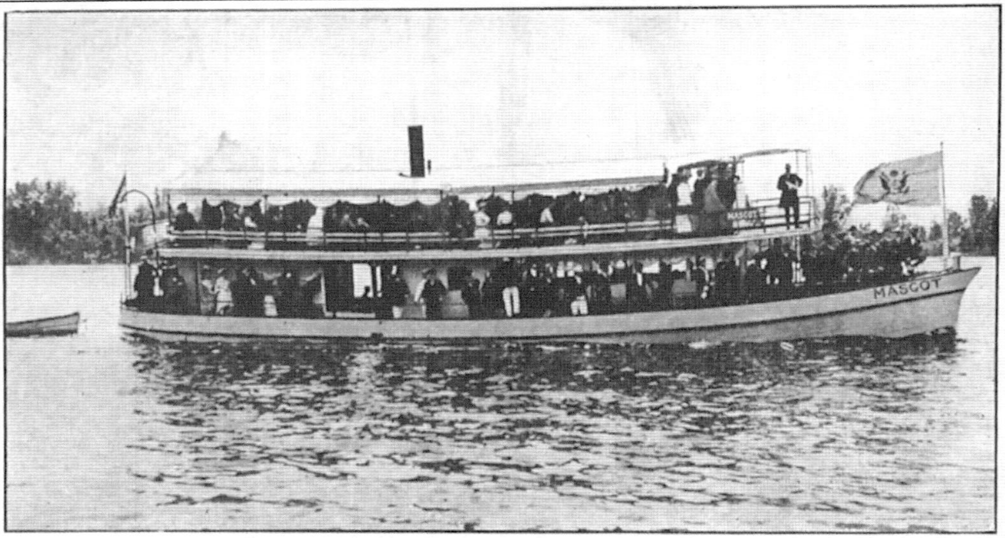

(0505) Arrival of President McKinley from Holyoke, at time of reception tendered him June, 1899, at Springfield, Mass.

Smith's *Mascot* of 1885 became locally famous when she transported Pres. William McKinley from Holyoke to Springfield on Wednesday, June 21, 1899. More than 6,000 people lined the riverbank to wave their greetings along the eight-mile voyage.

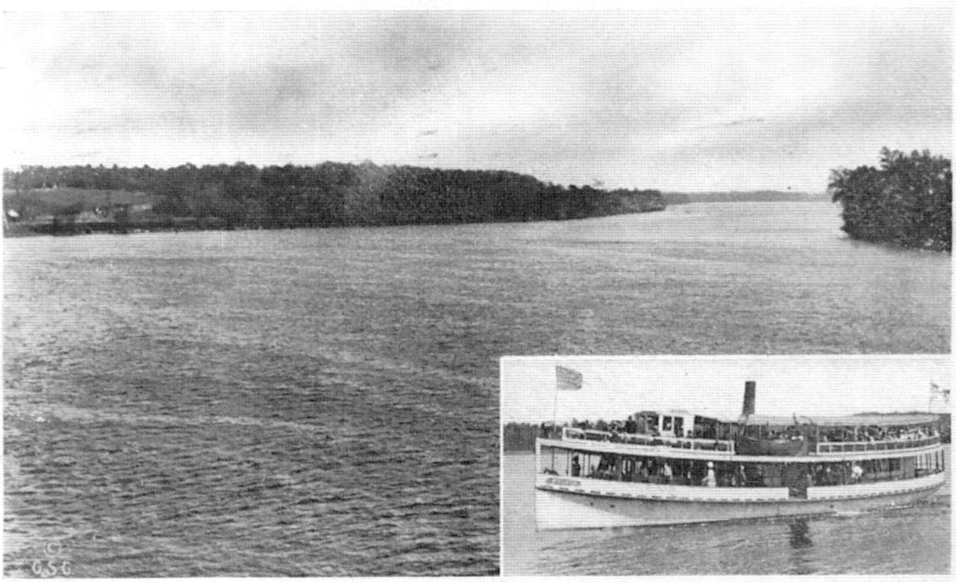

SPRINGFIELD, MASSACHUSETTS. Three miles of the Connecticut River below South End Bridge and STEAMER SYLVIA returning from RIVERSIDE GROVE where 40,000 people go in a single day. A-625

A controversy arose as the *Sylvia* was readied for launch in April 1900: the Women's Christian Temperance Union drafted a resolution requesting Captain Smith to substitute water or flowers for the champagne he intended to use in christening his new vessel. Newspaper accounts reported, matter-of-factly, "It is understood that Captain Smith will refuse to do this."

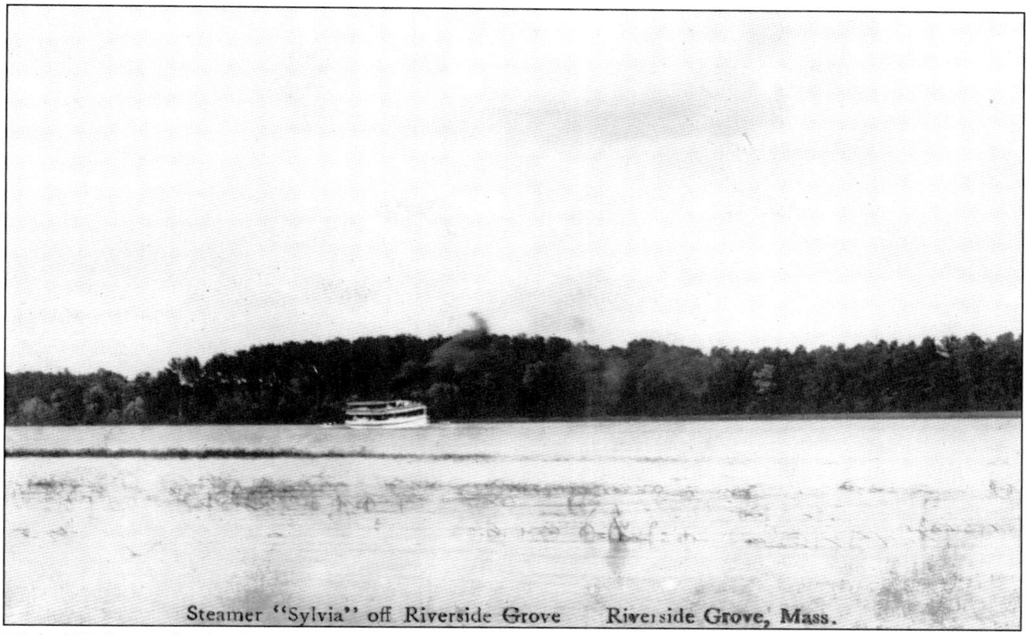


Mabel Kelsey, who had suggested the name of the craft, broke a bottle of wine across the bow of the *Sylvia* at precisely 4:30 p.m. on Thursday, April 26, 1900, before a crowd of 5,000 people at the dry dock at the foot of Clinton Street in Springfield. It was said that Springfield schools were closed that day so that children could witness a true launching.

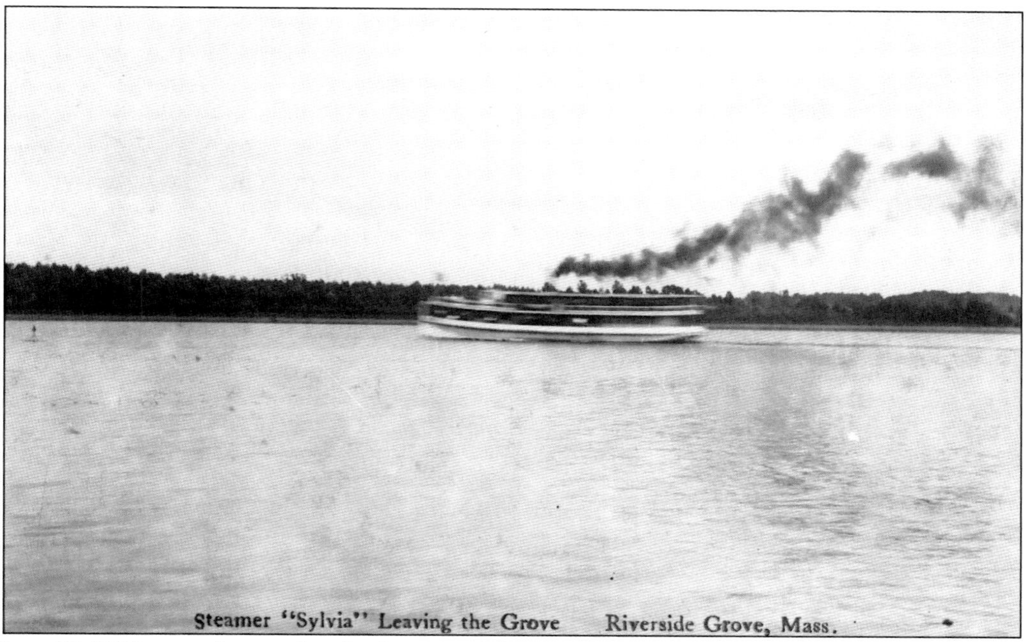


June 10, 1900, was advertised as the first trip of the new steamer *Sylvia*, although the day before she carried the Daughters of Caledonia from Holyoke to Riverside Grove. The voyage from Springfield to Holyoke took just 40 minutes, a trip that used to take the *Mascot* an hour and 10 minutes.

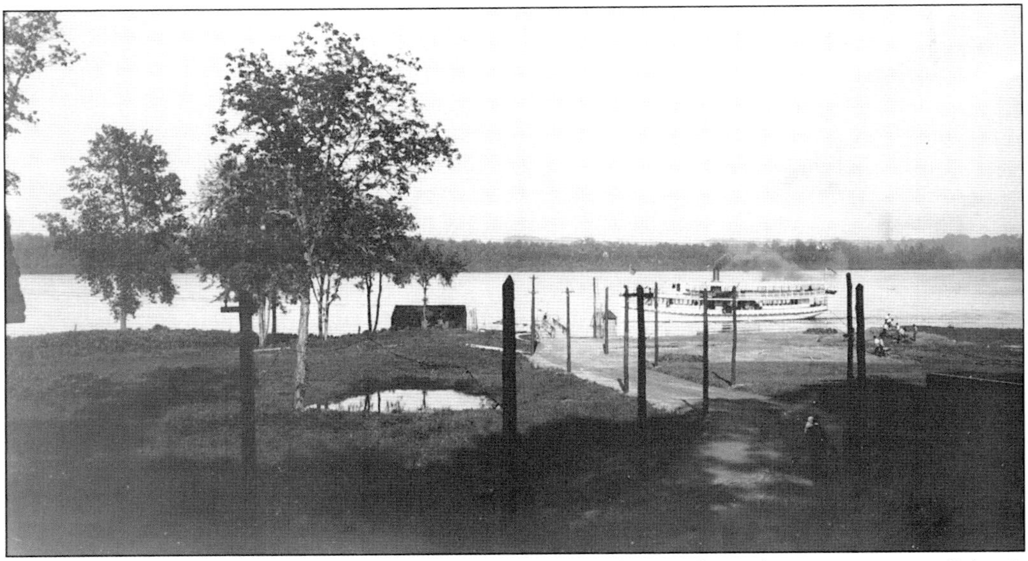

In 1907, Sunday shore dinners were offered to the public, with preference given to Sylvia's passengers. A sailing announcement in the *Springfield Daily Republican* offered: "Nice sail, no dust, fine breeze, music on the boat. The regular shore dinner served at 2:00 p.m. consisting of clams, lobsters, watermelons, and all accessories, at 74¢ per plate. Patrons of boat have first choice of dinner tickets, for sale at 1:0 p.m. boat. Fare 15¢ for round trip."

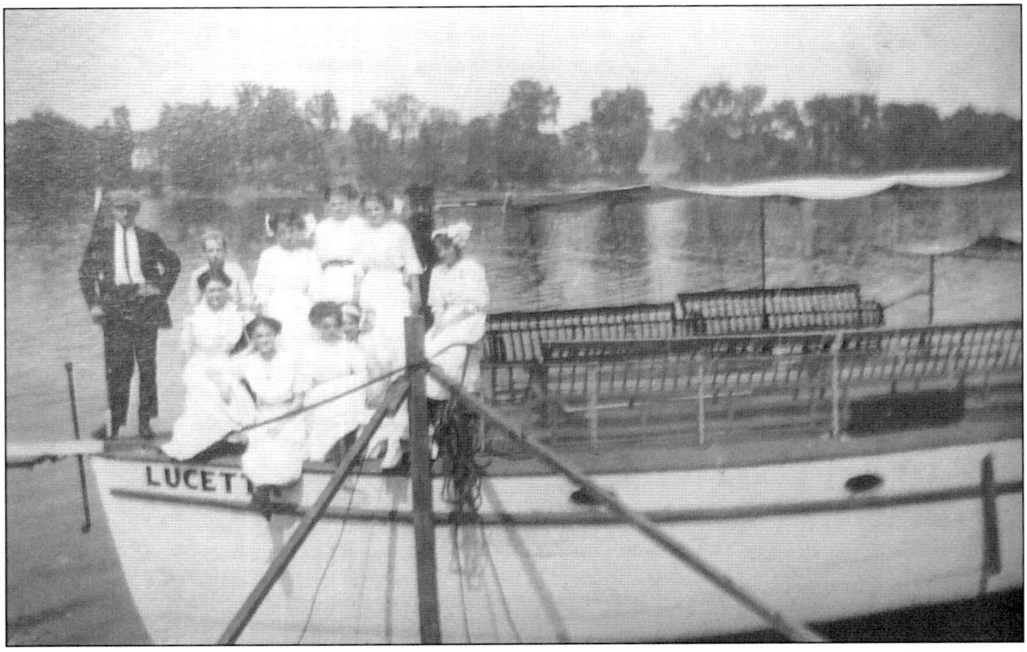


By 1911, the *Sylvia* had been in the water for a decade. That May, steamboat inspectors determined that her seams needed to be re-caulked before her license would be renewed. Taking the *Sylvia* out of service was an unexpected inconvenience, and the motor launch *Lucetta* was pressed into service. A much smaller craft, the *Lucetta* nonetheless provided happy passage for many park goers, including Helen Ewald (later Schilling) pictured at the far right. (Courtesy of Geraldine Schilling-Nordal.)

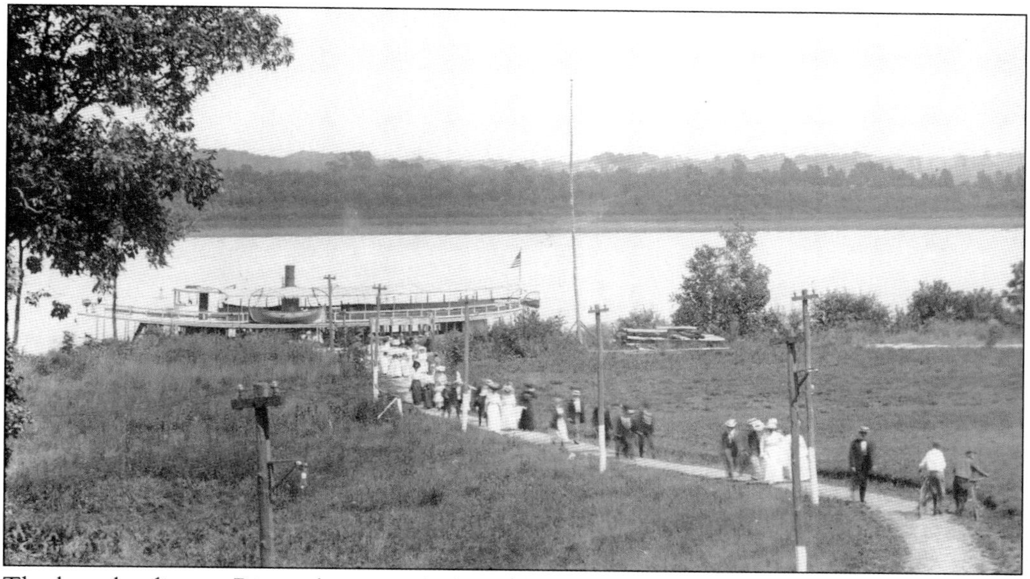

The boat landing at Riverside is seen before the park's purchase by Henry J. Perkins in 1911 (above) and after the construction of a pier into the river to ease arrivals and departures around 1913 (below). This is the scene that greeted countless visitors to the grove and park who arrived by boat over the years, including the Knights of the Golden Rule, the Ancient Order of Foresters, the Daughters of Pocahontas, Merrick Methodist Sunday School, the Order of Red Men, the Manchester Unity Odd Ladies Association, Wesleyan University's 1893 senior class, the Springfield Schuetzenverein, the Brotherhood of Railway Trainmen, the Springfield Automobile Club, the Hartford Road Drivers Association, the Springfield Board of Trade, Hendee Manufacturing (Indian Motocycle), and the employees of Brown Thomson, G. Fox, Massachusetts Mutual Life Insurance Company, among many others.

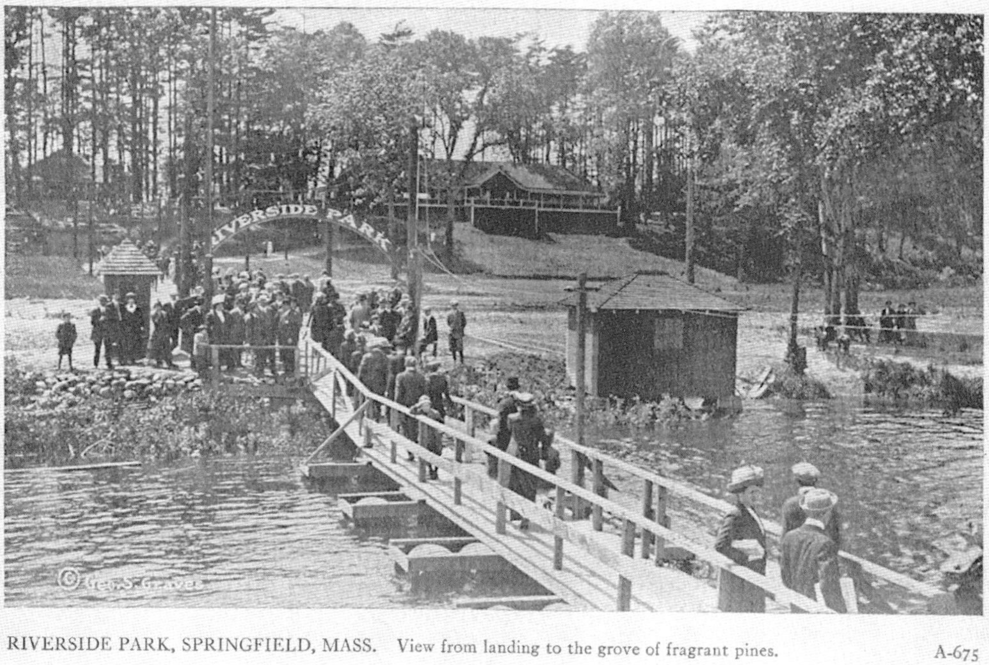


RIVERSIDE PARK, SPRINGFIELD, MASS. View from landing to the grove of fragrant pines. A-675

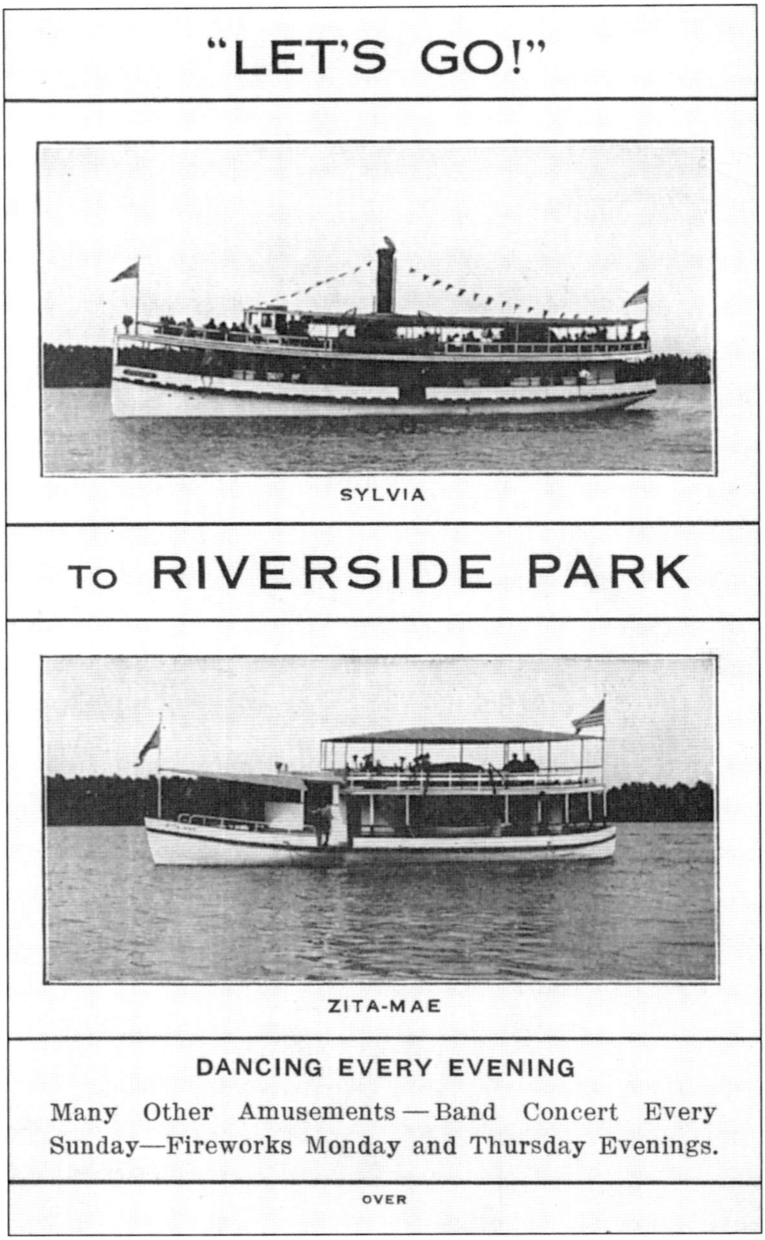


The improvements implemented at the park and grove by new owner Henry J. Perkins resulted in vastly increased attendance, and in 1913, the steamboat *Sylvia* was joined on the river by the gasoline cruiser *Zita-Mae*. The 65-foot *Zita-Mae* was fitted out at the John E. Mar & Company shipyard in New Haven and could carry 250 passengers. Her speed of 12 miles per hour matched the speed of the *Sylvia*. The two vessels alternated departures from Springfield and Riverside daily, every 90 minutes (on the hour on Sundays). In 1913, the *Sylvia* received a new collapsible life raft in addition to the two steel lifeboats usually carried, the result of a ruling by the steamboat inspection service after the sinking of the *Titanic* the year before. However, the *Sylvia* and *Zita-Mae* were not the only method of getting to Riverside via the river. On August 12, 1915, Sidney Dean and Bernard Caffrey swam to the park from the North End Bridge in Springfield. The six-mile swim took them 2 hours and 40 minutes.

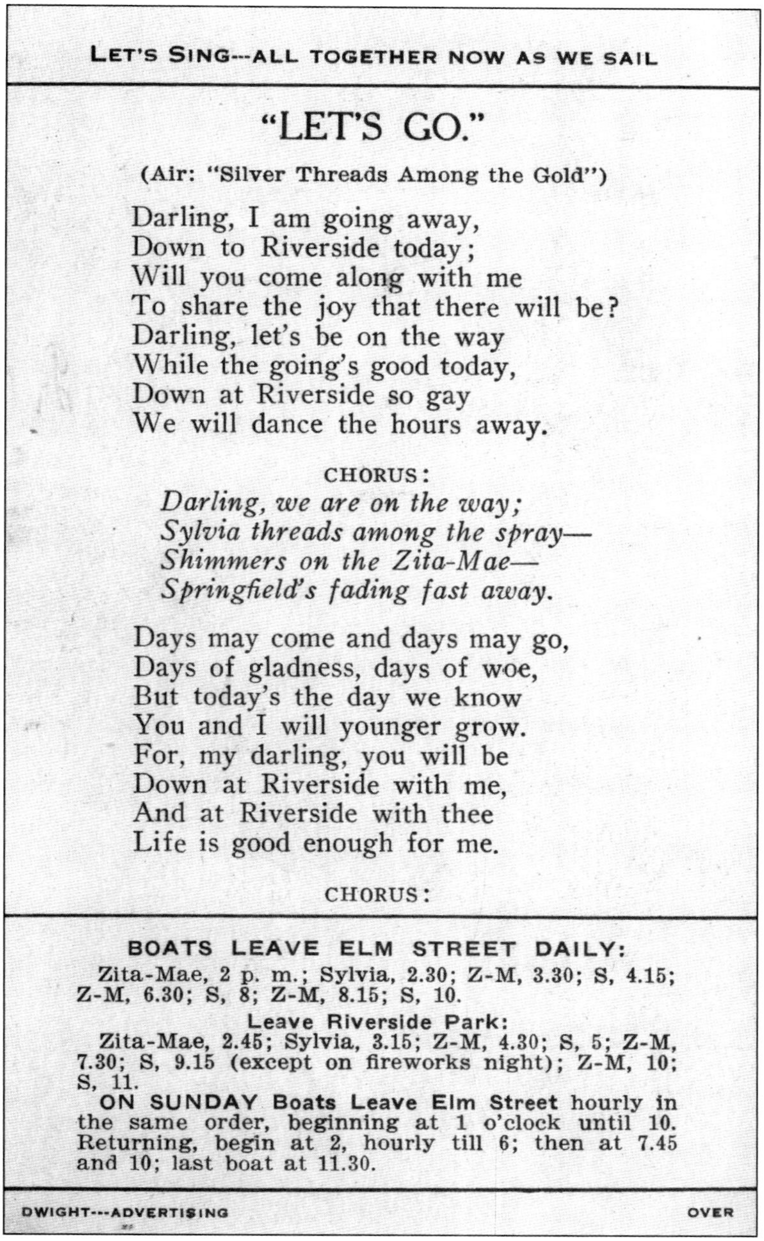

LET'S SING—ALL TOGETHER NOW AS WE SAIL

## "LET'S GO."

**(Air: "Silver Threads Among the Gold")**

Darling, I am going away,
Down to Riverside today;
Will you come along with me
To share the joy that there will be?
Darling, let's be on the way
While the going's good today,
Down at Riverside so gay
We will dance the hours away.

CHORUS:

*Darling, we are on the way;*
*Sylvia threads among the spray—*
*Shimmers on the Zita-Mae—*
*Springfield's fading fast away.*

Days may come and days may go,
Days of gladness, days of woe,
But today's the day we know
You and I will younger grow.
For, my darling, you will be
Down at Riverside with me,
And at Riverside with thee
Life is good enough for me.

CHORUS:

**BOATS LEAVE ELM STREET DAILY:**
Zita-Mae, 2 p. m.; Sylvia, 2.30; Z-M, 3.30; S, 4.15; Z-M, 6.30; S, 8; Z-M, 8.15; S, 10.

**Leave Riverside Park:**
Zita-Mae, 2.45; Sylvia, 3.15; Z-M, 4.30; S, 5; Z-M, 7.30; S, 9.15 (except on fireworks night); Z-M, 10; S, 11.

**ON SUNDAY Boats Leave Elm Street** hourly in the same order, beginning at 1 o'clock until 10. Returning, begin at 2, hourly till 6; then at 7.45 and 10; last boat at 11.30.

DWIGHT—ADVERTISING OVER

The promotional card featuring the *Sylvia* and her running mate, *Zita-Mae*, feature the boats on the front and the sailing schedule and the lyrics to the song "Let's Go" on the reverse. Apparently, passengers were encouraged to sing on the voyage. Singing on the *Zita-Mae* was short-lived, however. On August 27, 1916, the vessel struck a submerged object near the mouth of the Agawam River and a hole was ripped in the hull. *Zita-Mae* reached the Elm Street dock after a five-minute "wild dash" and promptly sank. None of the more than 200 passengers on board was injured. The mishap was referenced on the *Daily Republican* sports page a few days later. It reported, "The city league schedule has a hole in it this afternoon. So has the bottom of the *Zita-Mae*. The latter can be repaired, but with only five clubs left, the former can never be repaired." It is unknown if the *Zita-Mae* ever sailed again; after a brief note of the boat's schedule in September 1916, no mention of the vessel could be found.

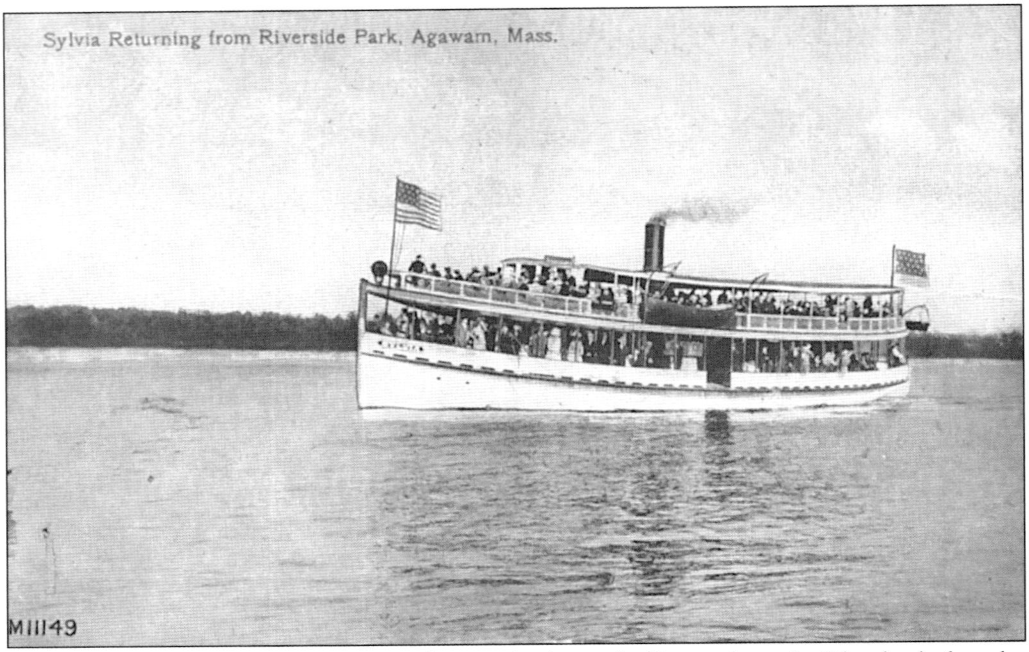


The year 1913 was an interesting time for vessels plying the Riverside trade. The day before the *Zita-Mae* accident, the *Sylvia* went aground at Riverside due to low water. On July 14, the launch *Palaids*, formerly the *Hobo* out of Thompsonville, Connecticut, sank after "rowdies" on board caused the majority of passengers to move to one side, then the other, forcing the boat's gunwales under and the vessel to take on water.

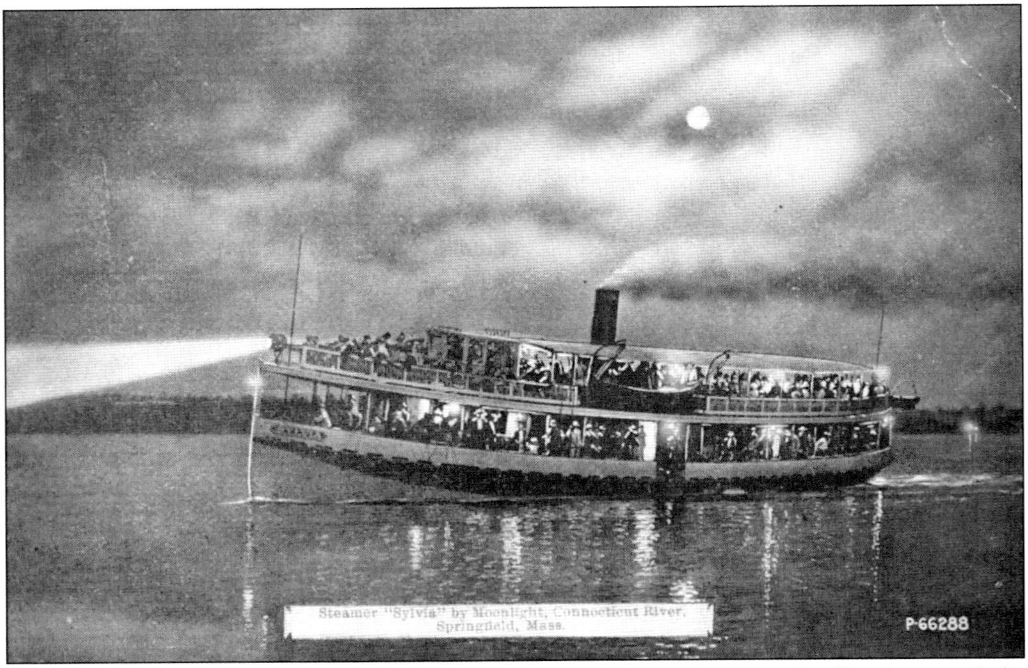


Moonlight excursions were very popular in the early 1900s. Capt. E.H. Smith offered a moonlight excursion and dance on Tuesday, July 24, 1906. The *Sylvia* left the landing at the foot of Elm Street at 8:00 p.m. Fare, including dancing to Coate's Orchestra, was 35¢.

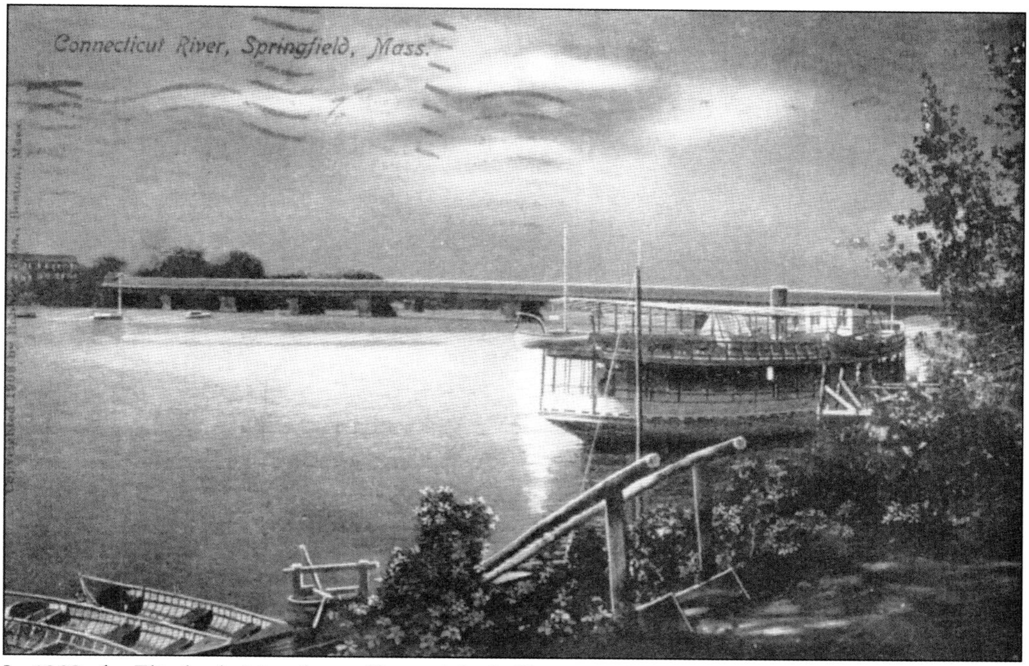


In 1902, the Elizabeth, New Jersey, Young Men's Christian Association prohibited hugging during its annual moonlight excursion. Appointed to police the boat to prevent any "iniquitous hugging" were 20 men. A newspaper notice predicted, "If, as the indications are, these 20 men are the only ones to go on the excursion, the rule is likely to be strictly observed."

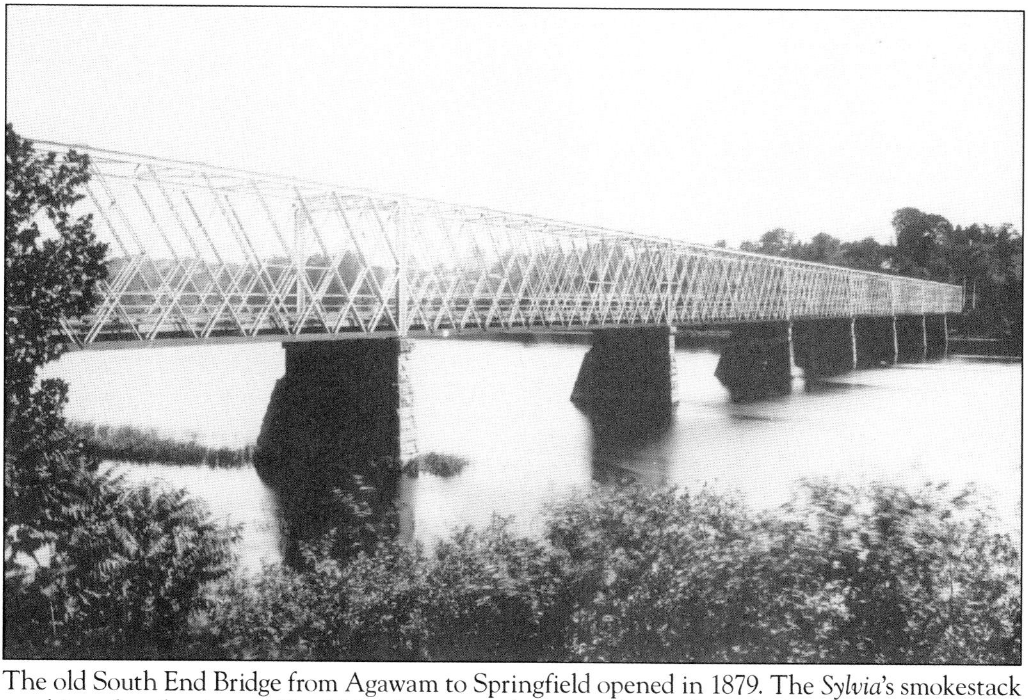

The old South End Bridge from Agawam to Springfield opened in 1879. The *Sylvia*'s smokestack was hinged so that it could be folded down in order to pass beneath, and after years of complaints by Captain Smith, the bridge was raised 15 feet in 1903. A modern span replaced it in 1954. In the early 1900s, hoodlums on the bridge often showered boat traffic with dirt and stones.

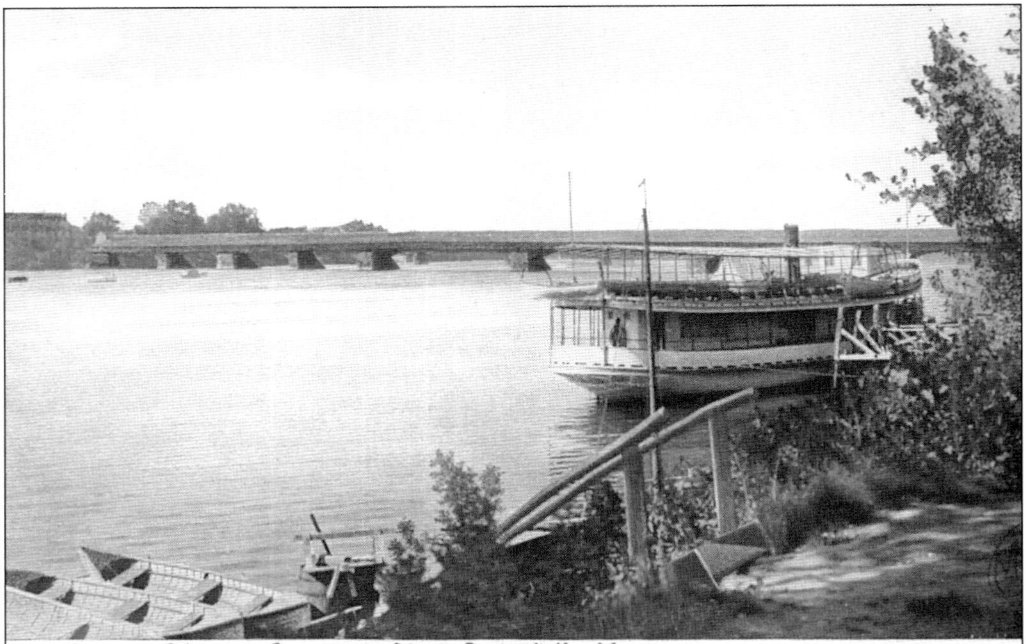

Steamer Silvia on Connecticut River, Springfield, Mass.
Johnson's Bookstore, Springfield, Mass.

After nearly a century of service, Springfield's old wooden toll bridge (pictured) was replaced by the Hampden County Memorial Bridge in 1922. By that time, the *Sylvia* was facing serious competition from the trolley and automobile as the preferred route to Riverside; within a few years, the *Sylvia* would be retired from service.

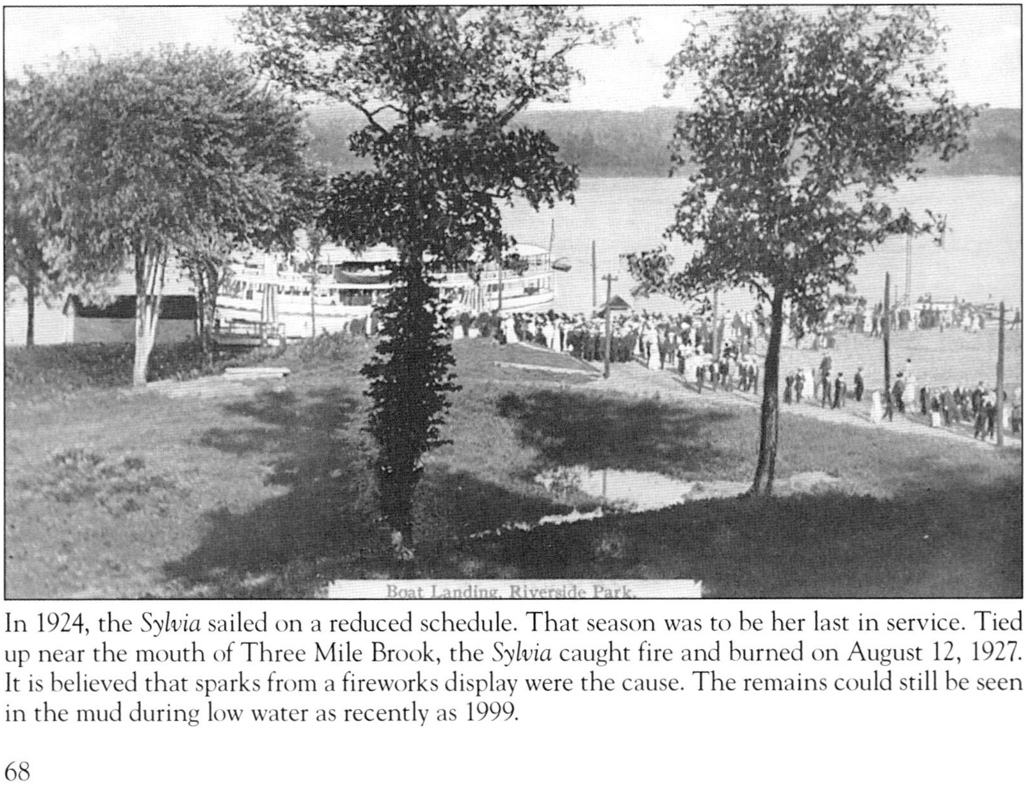

Boat Landing, Riverside Park.

In 1924, the *Sylvia* sailed on a reduced schedule. That season was to be her last in service. Tied up near the mouth of Three Mile Brook, the *Sylvia* caught fire and burned on August 12, 1927. It is believed that sparks from a fireworks display were the cause. The remains could still be seen in the mud during low water as recently as 1999.

*Six*

# Playground of the Connecticut Valley

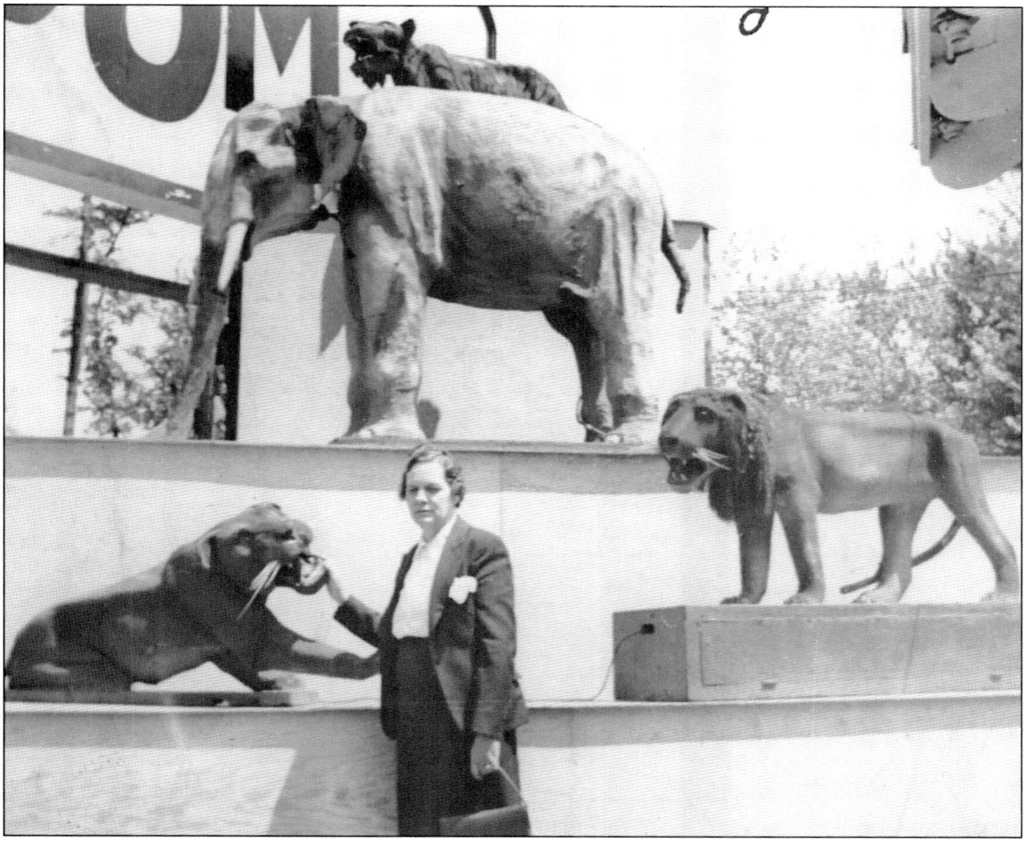

The public enthusiastically welcomed the reopening of the long-shuttered Riverside Park. More than 18,000 people attended its gala opening festivities on May 29 and 30, 1940. To put this in perspective, the opening of Disneyland in Anaheim, California, 15 years later, drew just over 28,000 people. Billed as the Playground of the Connecticut Valley, the park included among its new attractions the 12-acre Animal Kingdom, which featured more than 100 animals.

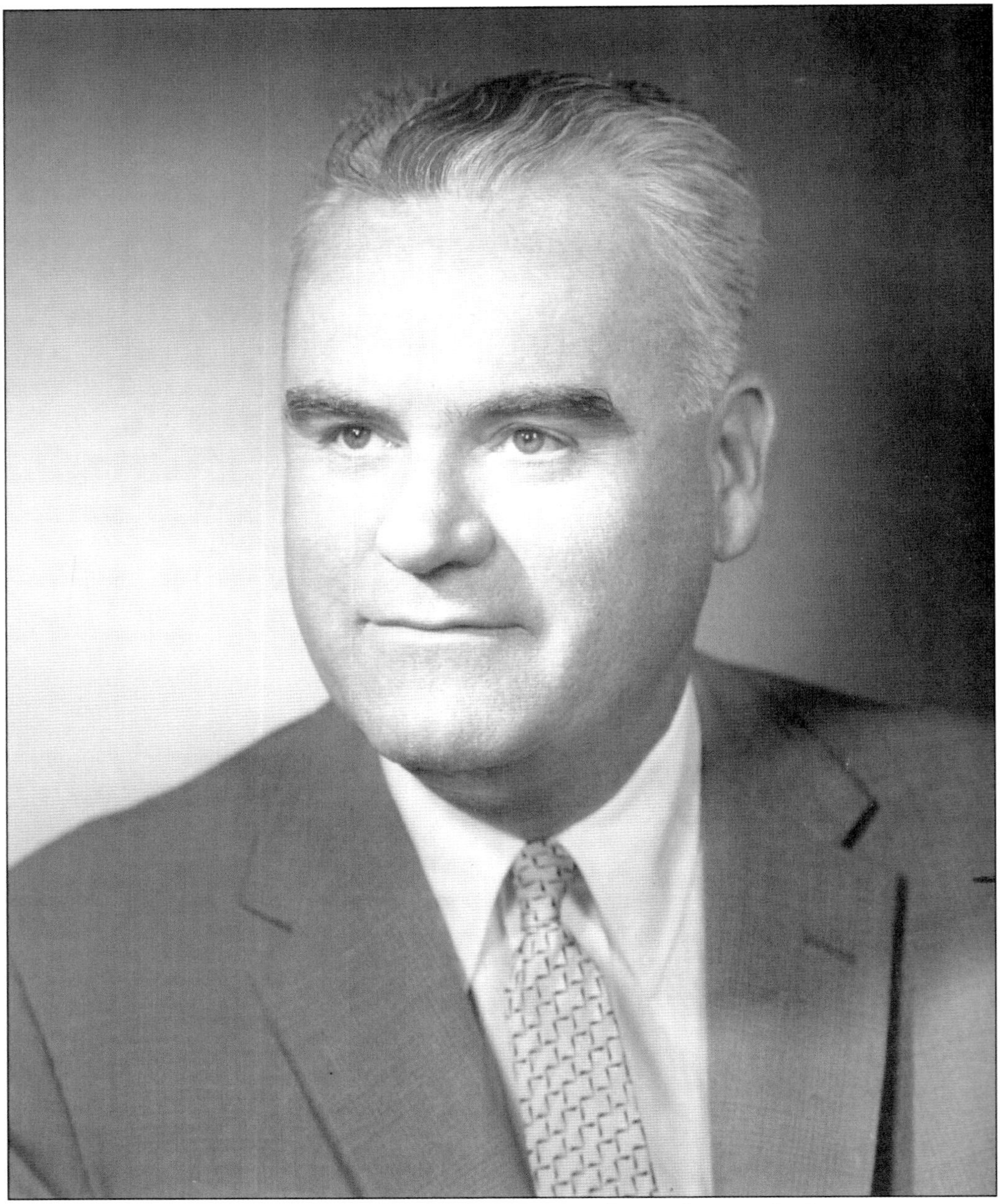

Edward J. Carroll Sr. rescued Riverside Park from ruins and turned it into the largest amusement park in New England. Carroll purchased the property in October 1939 for $31,000 and immediately embarked on renovations in anticipation of a May 1940 opening. With the 1939 New York World's Fair and, later, Walt Disney's Disneyland as inspiration, Carroll is credited, in the words of his son Edward J. Carroll Jr., with "turning a collection of concessions into a cohesive theme park." Carroll Sr. oversaw the expansion of Riverside Park during the golden age of amusement parks, when the number went from just 400 parks nationwide in 1935 to 1,500 by 1963. A true showman, Carroll served two terms (1951 and 1952) as president of the International Association of Amusement Parks and Attractions (IAAPA), then known as the National Association of Amusement Parks, Pools, and Beaches. Edward J. Carroll Sr. died in 1979. He was posthumously elected to the IAAPA Hall of Fame in 1991. (Courtesy of *The Republican*, Springfield, Massachusetts.)

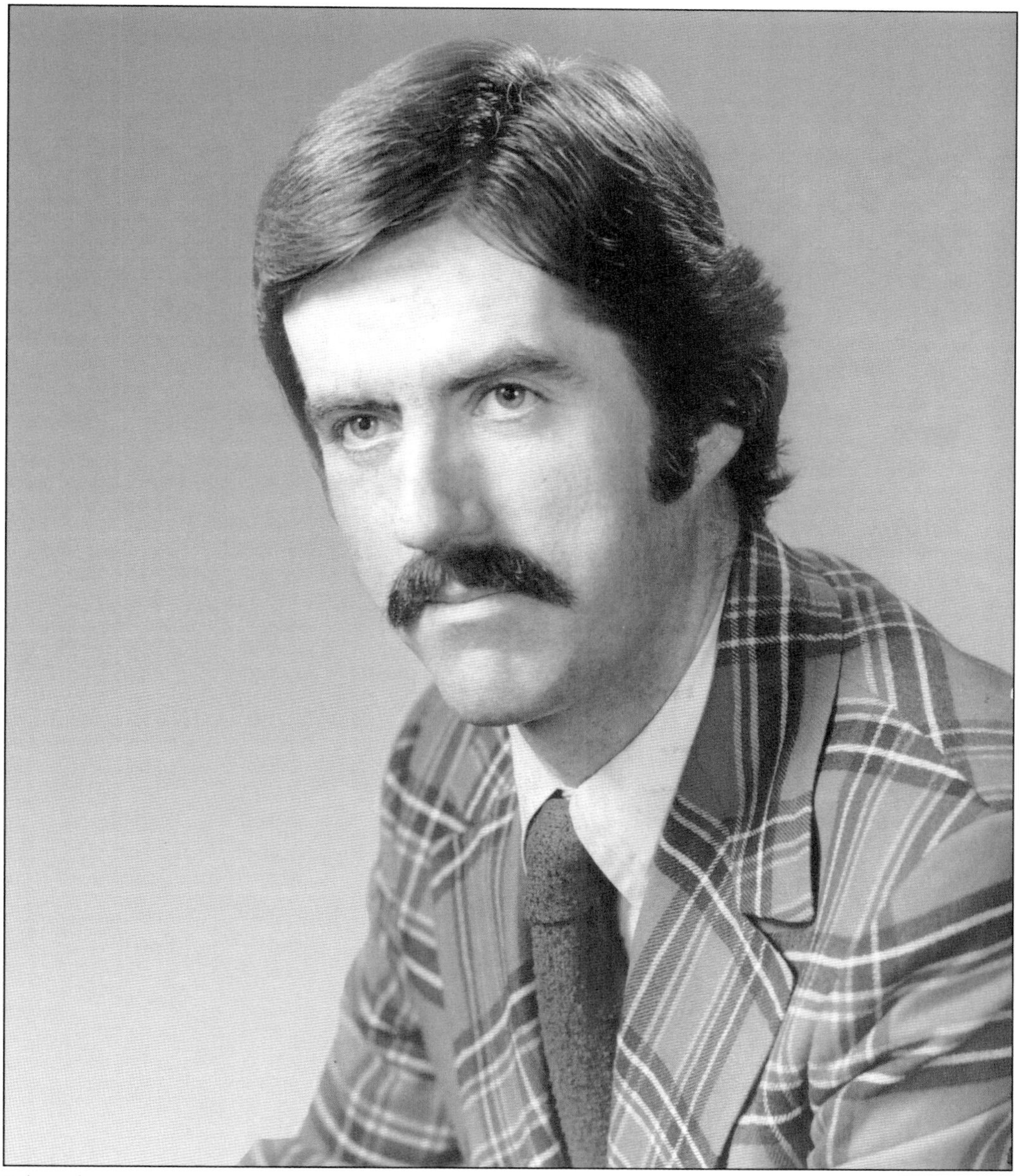

Edward J. Carroll Jr. was already general manager of the family enterprise when his father died in 1979. Father and son differed in management styles. Carroll Sr. walked the midway daily. As the 1980s began, Carroll Jr. anticipated more time in the office due to planning, marketing, and financial matters. The new focus would be capacity and marketing, not the addition of rides, games, or food stands. Nonetheless, the Cyclone roller coaster opened in 1983 and became a huge draw. By the mid-1990s, Riverside had grown as large as possible under family ownership. Responding to an offer by Premier Parks in 1996, the Carrolls held a family meeting and decided to sell, a choice Carroll Jr. calls "the right decision at the right time." Remembering his years at Riverside as "really a lot of fun," Carroll Jr. continues to serve the amusement park industry as a consultant. Both Carrolls were past presidents of the New England Association of Amusement Parks and Attractions and members of its Hall of Fame. The Carroll family was inducted into Springfield Technical Community College's Western Massachusetts Entrepreneurship Hall of Fame in 2002. (Courtesy of *The Republican*, Springfield, Massachusetts.)

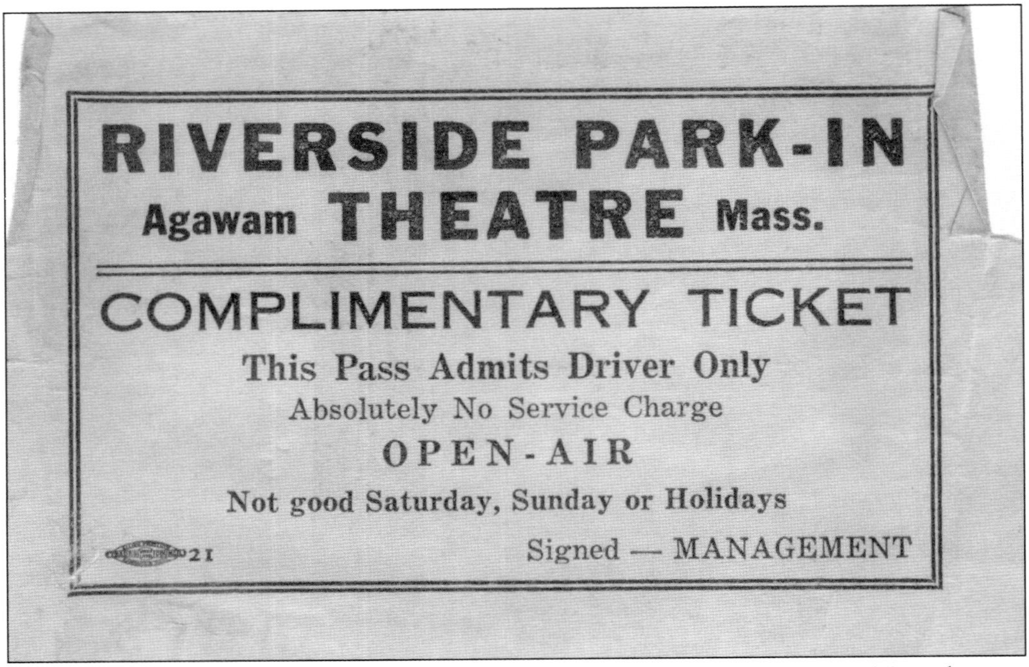


The Riverside Park-In opened in July 1937, the first drive-in movie theater in western Massachusetts. Initially, double features of second- and third-run movies were shown along with newsreels. In 1938, Ed Carroll Sr. moved to Agawam to manage the theater. Not particularly pleased with the films distributors regularly made available to drive-ins (Carroll called them dandies), he immediately set about improving the quality of the theater's offerings. The following year, he purchased neighboring Riverside Park and spent the next four decades building a first-class attraction. Verne Spear, who provided the ticket stub (below) and complimentary ticket (above) seen here, remembers taking a date to the Park-In in his 1935 Essex. Spear, now 93, recalls his companion, a New York City nightclub dancer from East Springfield, Massachusetts, who weighed just 95 pounds and needed a cushion to sit on in order to see over the car's dash. (Both, courtesy of Verne Spear.)

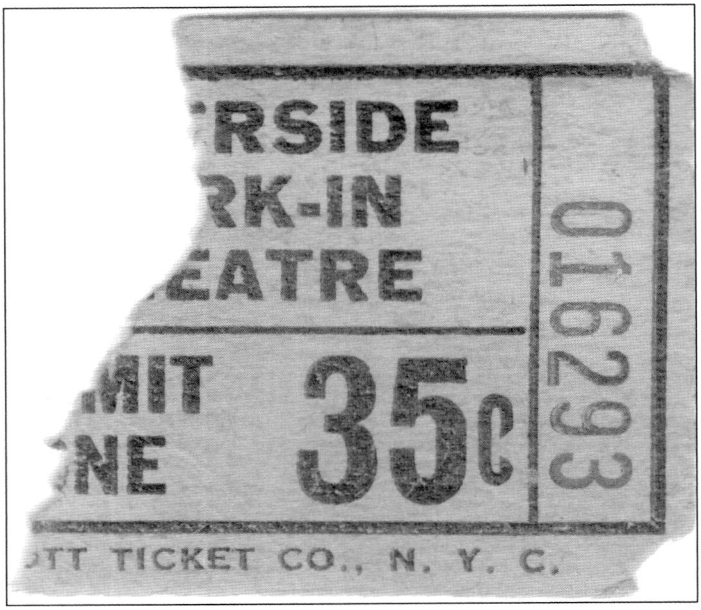

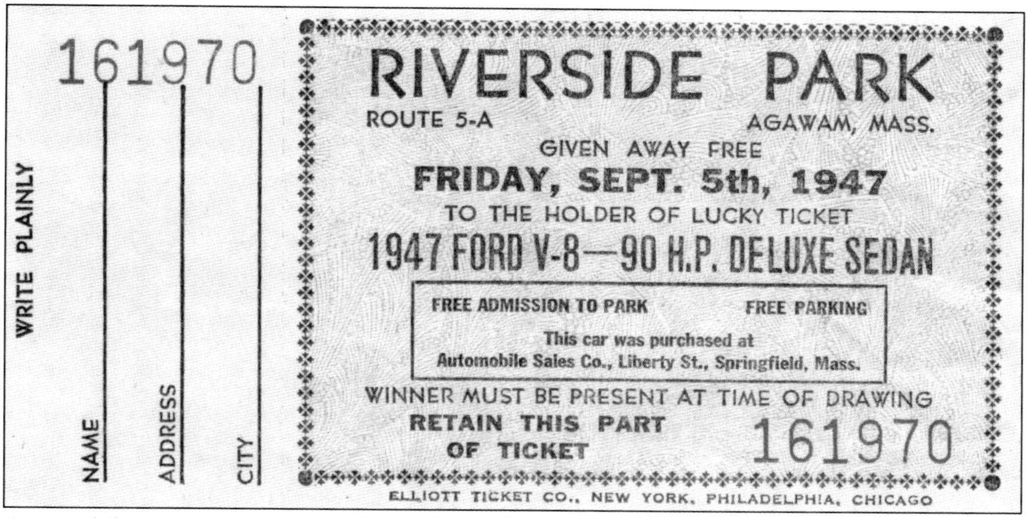


Automobile giveaways were popular at Riverside. In 1928, John Walkowski of Westfield won a Chevrolet. John Berard of Agawam won a roadster in August 1931. His wife had won an identical vehicle the month before. In 1947, Loretta Albano won a Ford DeLuxe Sedan. Albano, who had never owned a car and did not know how to drive, had purchased her winning ticket, one of 19 others she held, the night of the drawing.

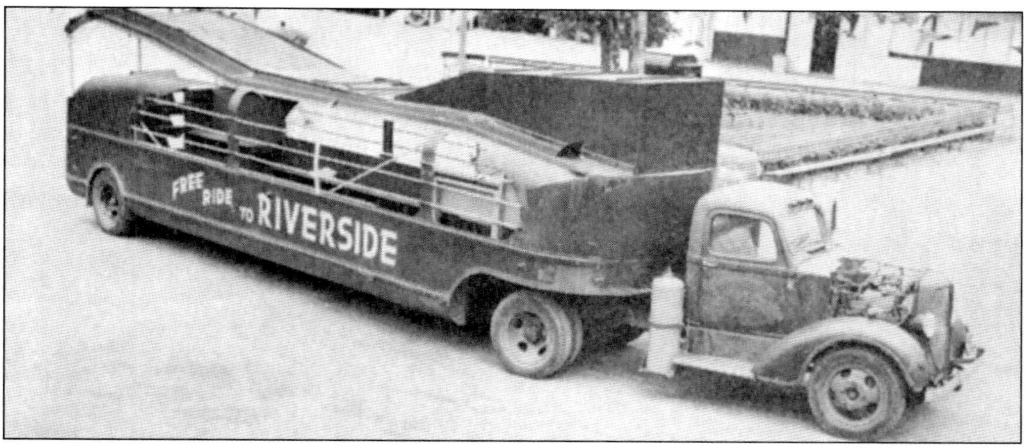


During World War II, gasoline rationing and virtually nonexistent public transportation posed a serious threat to Riverside attendance levels. Ed Carroll Sr. and park engineer Vernon Trigger developed the Transmobile, a converted tractor-trailer automobile carrier that ran on propane. Three 100-passenger Transmobiles were built and provided free transportation from downtown Springfield to the park. The unique vehicles often carried more than 3,000 passengers a day to Riverside.

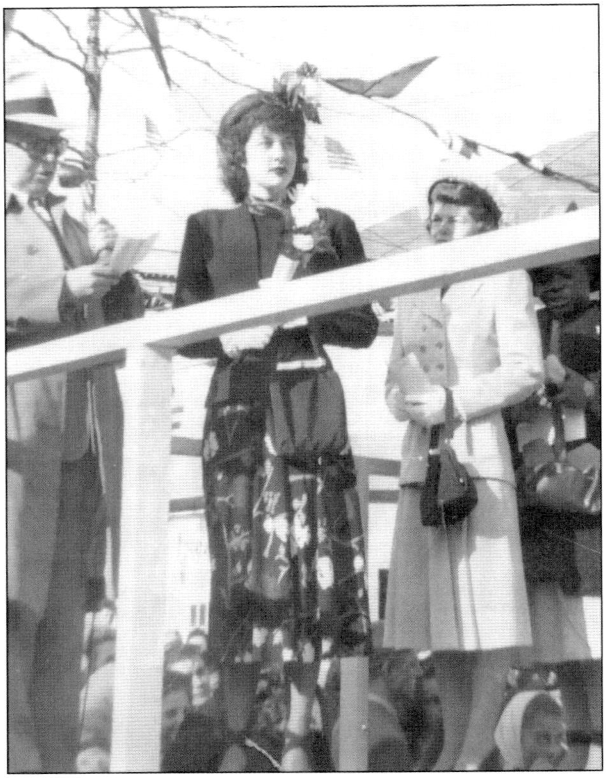

Riverside traditionally opened on Easter Sunday with an Easter parade. The title of Miss Riverside, given to the best-dressed woman seen on the midway, did not always go to a "miss." The married Margaret Mastroianni won the title in 1946. The following year, the award went to the unmarried Pauline Cormier (center). Among the judges were "fashion people" from local department stores Forbes & Wallace and Steiger's. (Courtesy of Pauline Cormier.)

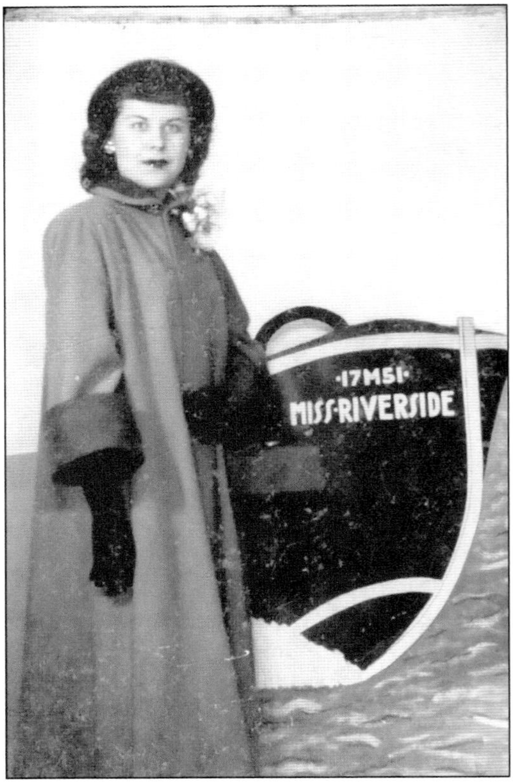


The title of Miss Riverside 1951 was shared between two women—Dorothy Fenton and Shirley Paradysz. Paradysz (pictured) worked at the Massachusetts Mutual Life Insurance Company. Fellow MassMutual employee Irene Wicker won the title the previous year. Another married woman, Lillian Peloquin, was Miss Riverside 1953. Her outfit consisted of a brown ensemble with matching accessories and a small mink fur piece. (Courtesy of Shirley [Paradysz] Williams.)

The *Sylvia* was a distant memory, but the *Miss Riverside* speedboat photograph backdrop was a popular keepsake for visitors to Riverside in the 1940s and 1950s. Here, April Lamora is seen at the helm. April had a long association with Riverside; she spent many years skating at the Rollaway and cheering on the drivers at the Riverside Speedway. (Courtesy of April [Lamora] Brunelle.)

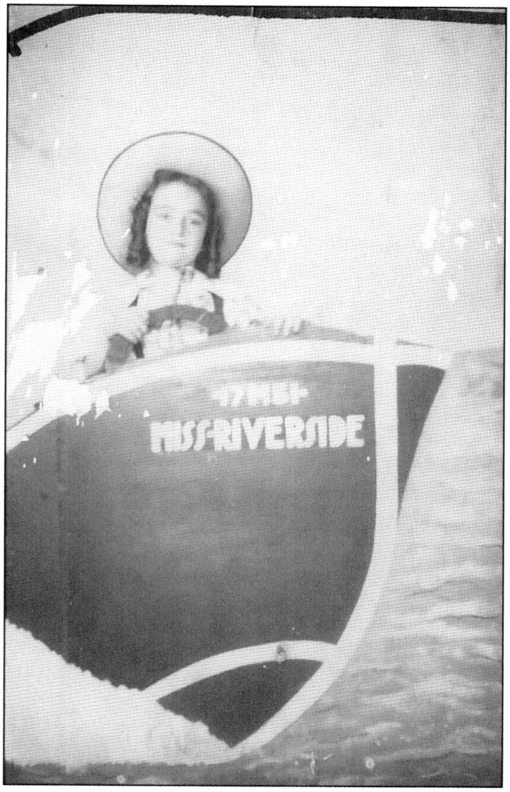


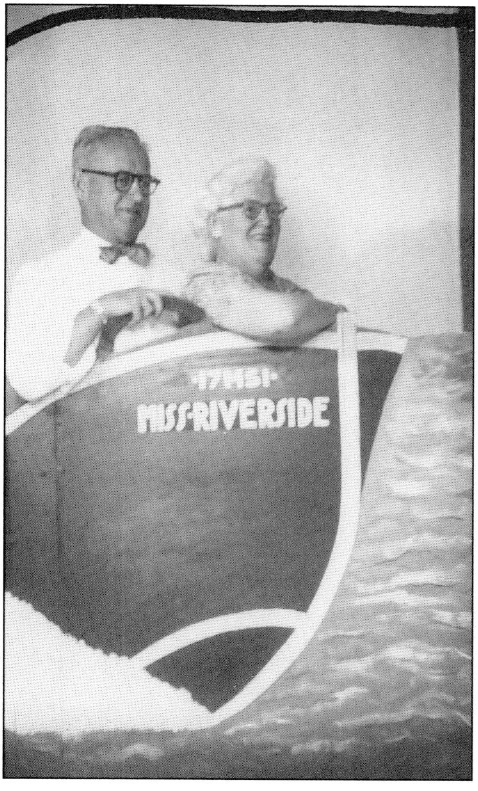


This unidentified couple certainly appears to be enjoying a visit to the park. For 100 years, Riverside Park has attracted young and old and promised them a fun time, a tradition that the current owners of the property, Six Flags New England, seem intent on upholding. (Courtesy of John DeVecchi.)

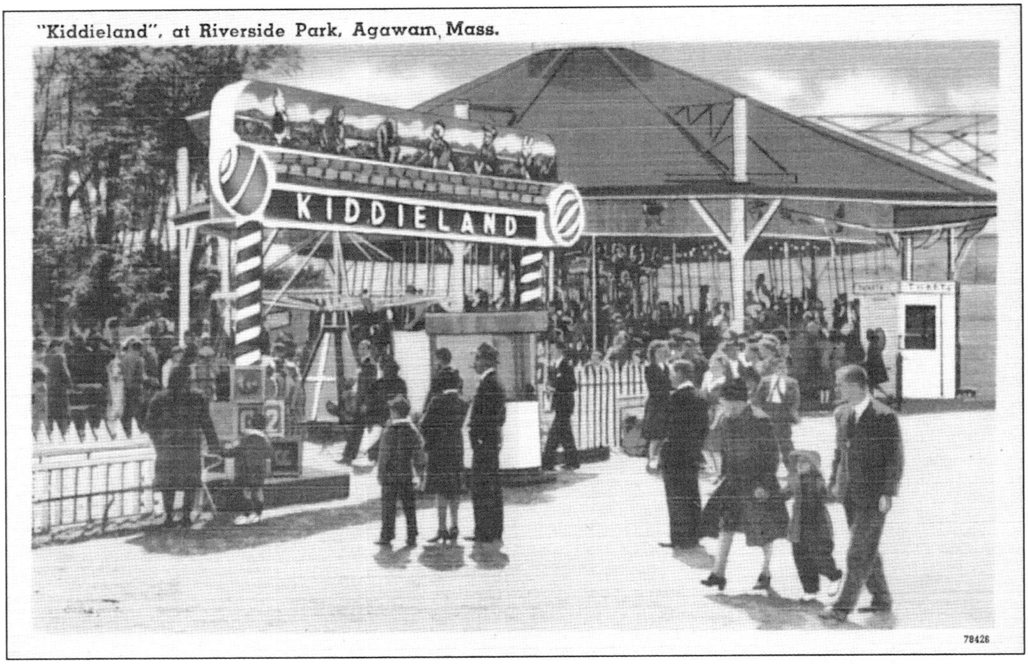


Families were an important part of the postwar Riverside audience, and Kiddieland was an area specifically tailored for the younger crowd. In those years, Wednesdays were kiddie days. There were free tickets for rides, pony rides for children, and reduced prices for adults after 1:00 p.m. Business was brisk enough that extra bus service was added on Wednesday afternoons.

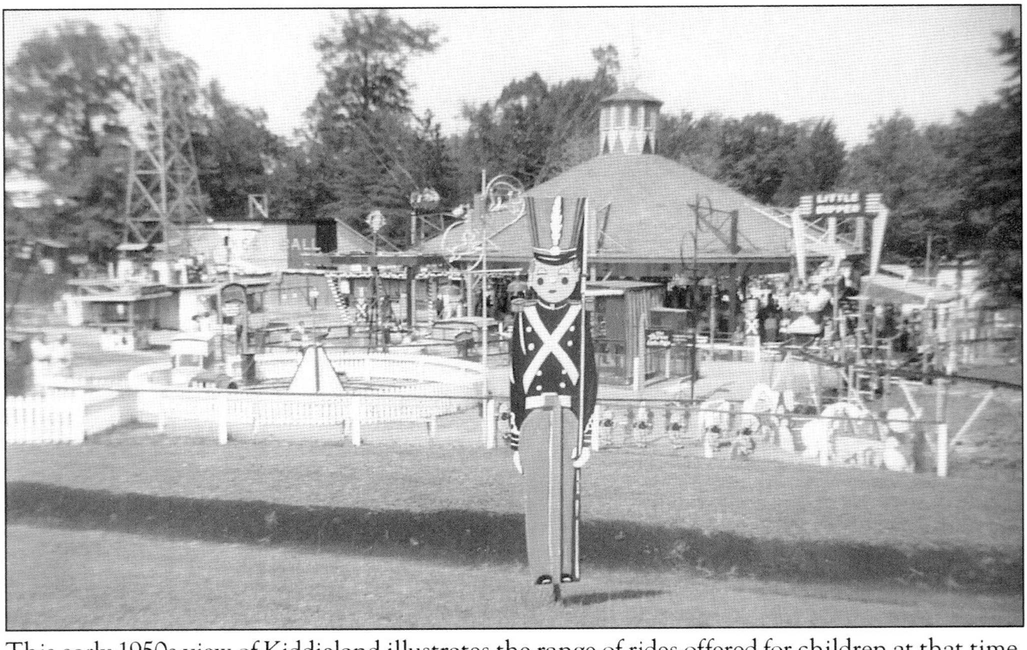


This early-1950s view of Kiddieland illustrates the range of rides offered for children at that time. On the right is the Little Dipper miniature roller coaster, which a 1948 *Springfield Daily News* article announced as the "First Kiddie Roller Coaster Ever Erected in the East." Beyond the miniature train ride are the Skee-Ball attraction and the carousel building. In the foreground, a wooden soldier photograph prop stands at attention.

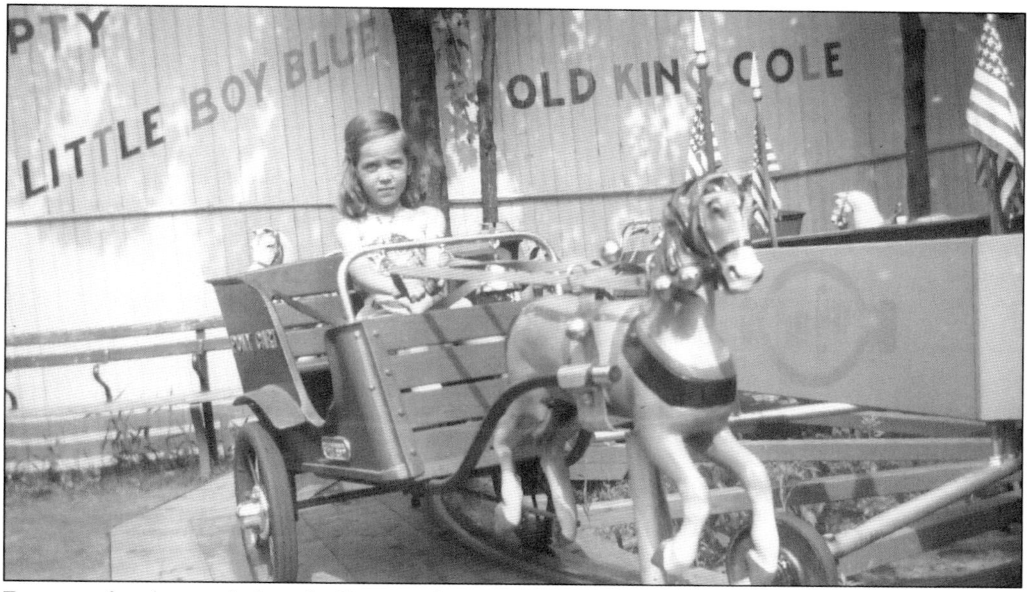


For many families, including the Dynias of Agawam, a trip to Riverside was a summertime tradition. Ted and Helen Dynia brought their four children—Emily, Richard, Lynn, and Joseph—to the park for years. The author's mother, Emily (Dynia) Cecchi, is pictured on the pony carts in the summer of 1951.

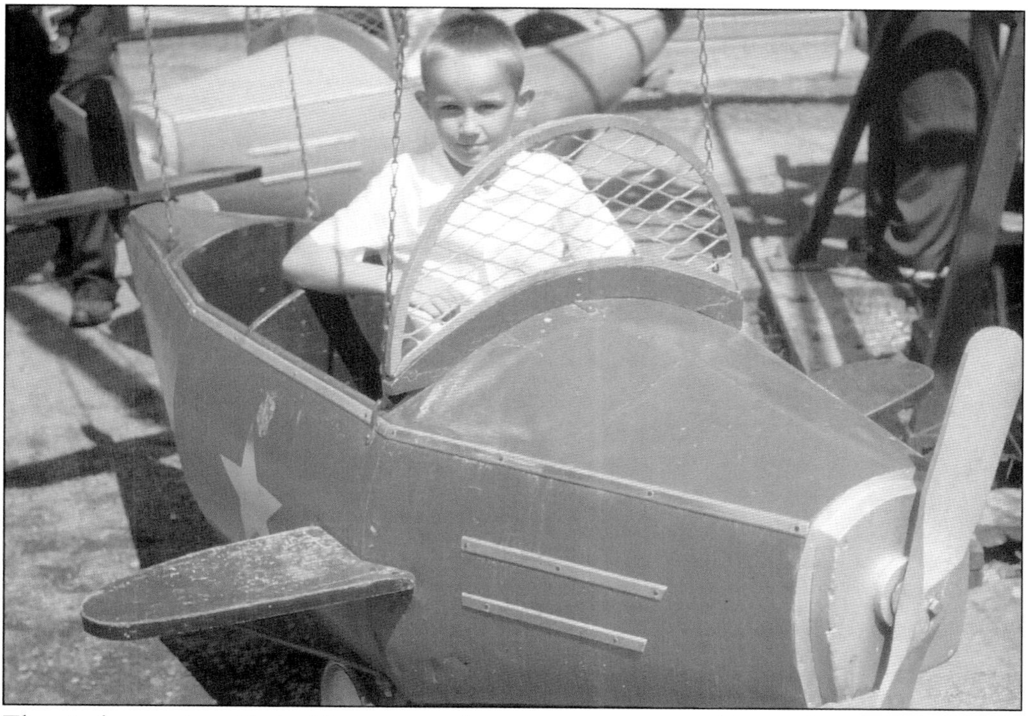

The airplane swing ride had been a popular attraction in several forms for many decades at Riverside. Here, David Kruger enjoys the ride in 1952. This image is one of a series of incredible color slides provided by Kruger that were taken by his father, Joseph Kruger. Seeing those color images of the park from the late 1940s and early 1950s was one of the highlights of putting this book together. (Courtesy of David Kruger.)

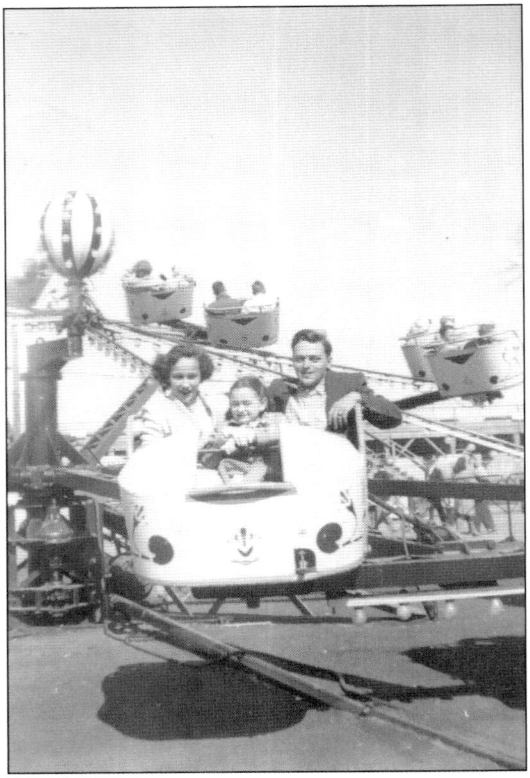

Joining thousands of others at Riverside Park on Easter Sunday in 1952 are, from left to right, Pat McCarroll, April Lamora, and Malcolm McCarroll. That year, Easter fell on April 13. From this black-and-white snapshot, the bright sunshine and the cool, crisp, early-spring air can almost be felt. No matter the weather, opening day was an event not to be missed. (Courtesy of April [Lamora] Brunelle.)

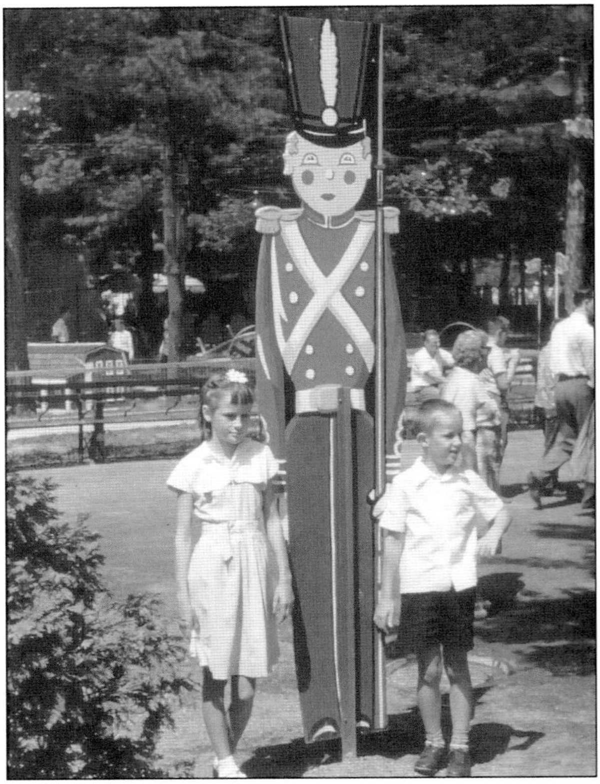

Joseph Kruger, of Turners Falls, Massachusetts, took this photograph of his son David and daughter Jo Ann with the wooden soldier in the summer of 1952. Notice how well dressed David and Jo Ann are. (Courtesy of David Kruger.)

Jo Ann (center) and David Kruger are pictured in front of a Disney characters mural in 1952. Years before Disneyland opened, Riverside Park featured images of popular Disney and comic-book characters, a practice theme parks have since emulated and developed to the extreme. A lawsuit filed by Disney against Riverside Park in 1962 for copyright infringement was settled out of court. (Courtesy of David Kruger.)

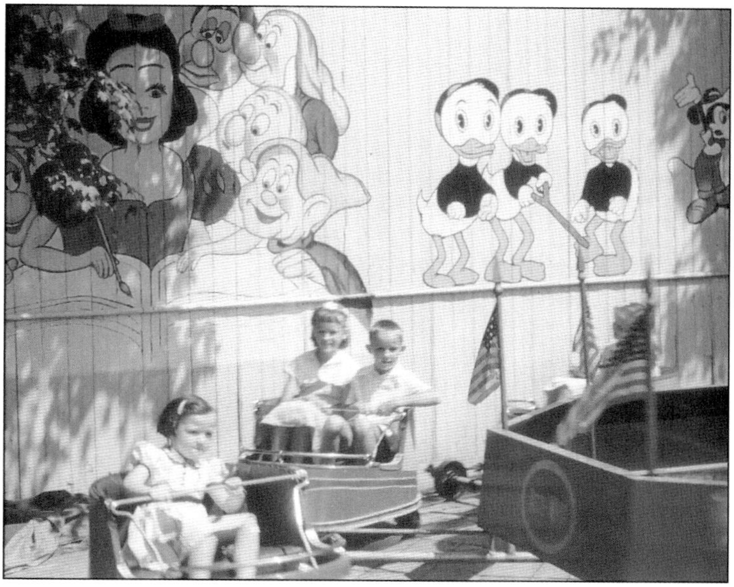

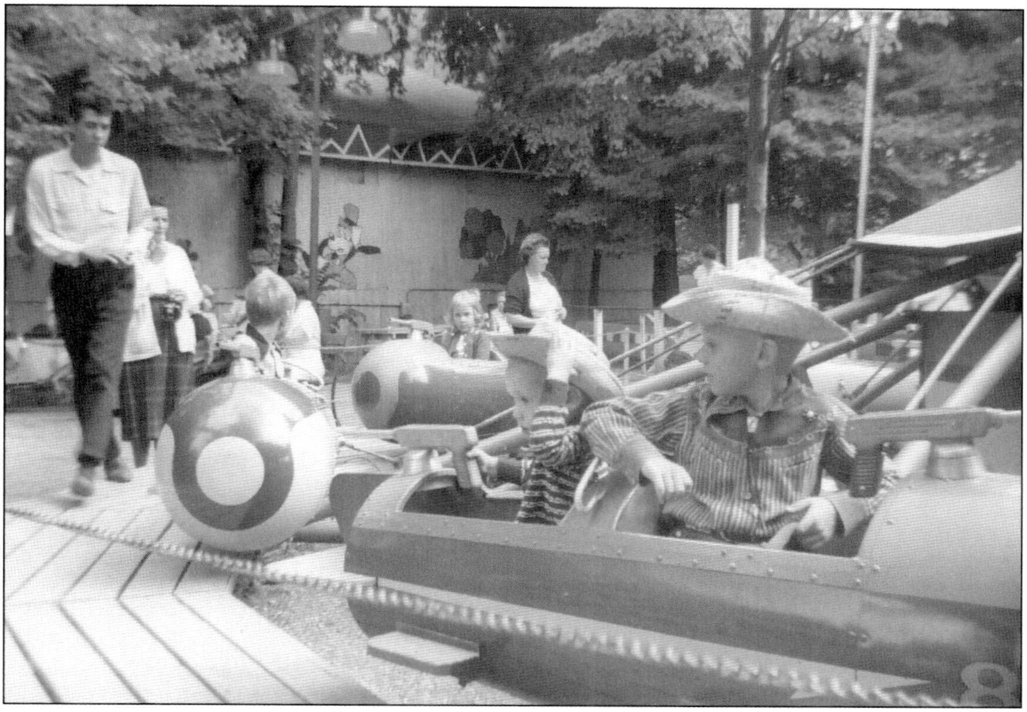

The author's uncles Richard Dynia (front) and Joseph Dynia (back) are pictured in cowboy hats on the jet fighter ride in 1956. Richard's outfit embodies many young boys' obsession with the Wild West during the mid-1950s, when television shows such as *The Roy Rogers Show*, *The Gene Autry Show*, *Gunsmoke*, and *The Lone Ranger* as well as hundreds of big-screen Westerns were at their most popular.

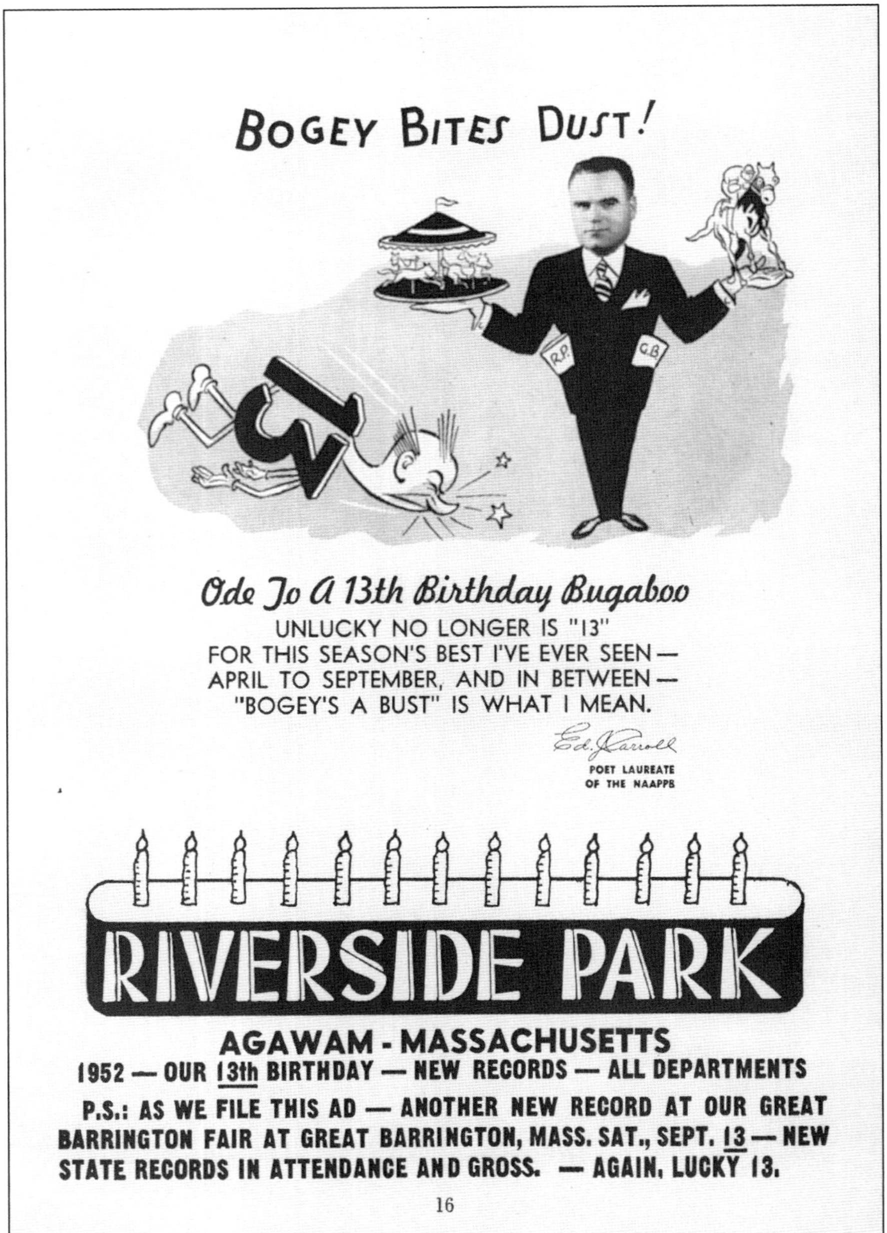


By the mid-1950s, Ed Carroll's $31,000 gamble was paying off. In 1952, Carroll was serving his second term as president of the National Association of Amusement Parks, Pools, and Beaches. He ran this advertisement in trade publications on the occasion of the 13th anniversary of his purchase of the park. Carroll wanted to make it known that Riverside Park had set new records in every department. The next 13 years would see the park experience even more growth. The advertisement also references the Great Barrington Fair, in Great Barrington, Massachusetts, which Carroll purchased in 1941. He bought it from the Barrington Fair Association, successor to the Housatonic Agricultural Society, which had run the fair from 1841 to 1936. As he did with Riverside, Carroll purchased a tired and rundown facility and immediately upgraded the entire operation. The fairgrounds were under his management until 1976.

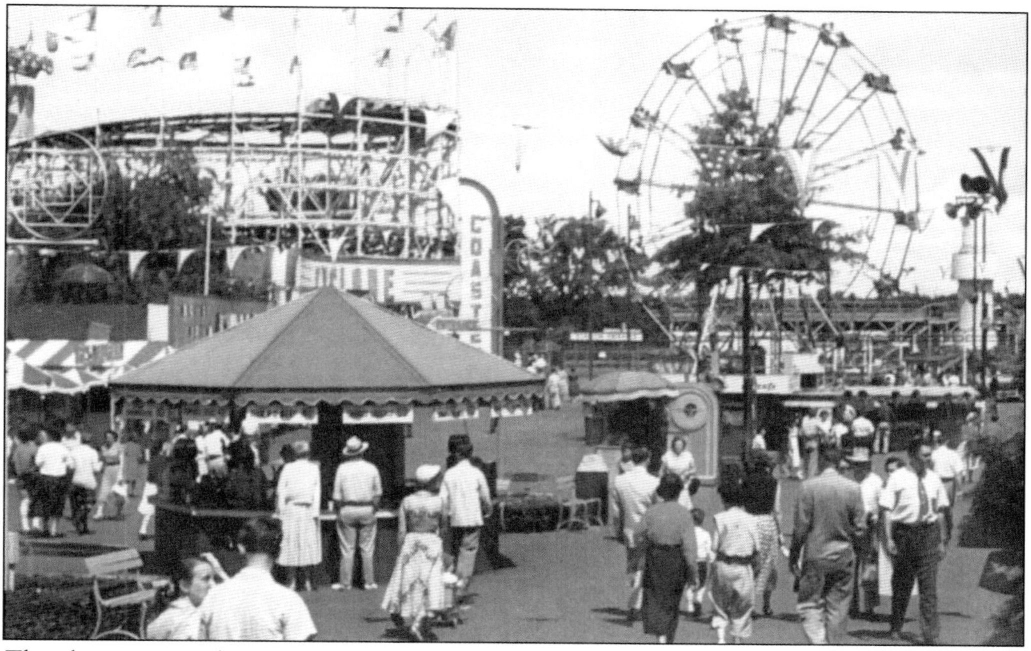

The plans, cars, and tracks of the original Cyclone roller coaster were purchased from the 1939 New York World's Fair. Carroll wrangled nearly $18,000 worth of lumber on credit from Boston magnate Jake Grossman and hired Joseph Drambour to build the ride. Drambour's father, who sailed on the ship carrying the Statue of Liberty to America, assisted his son. The Cyclone opened in 1941; shortly thereafter, it was renamed the Thunderbolt.

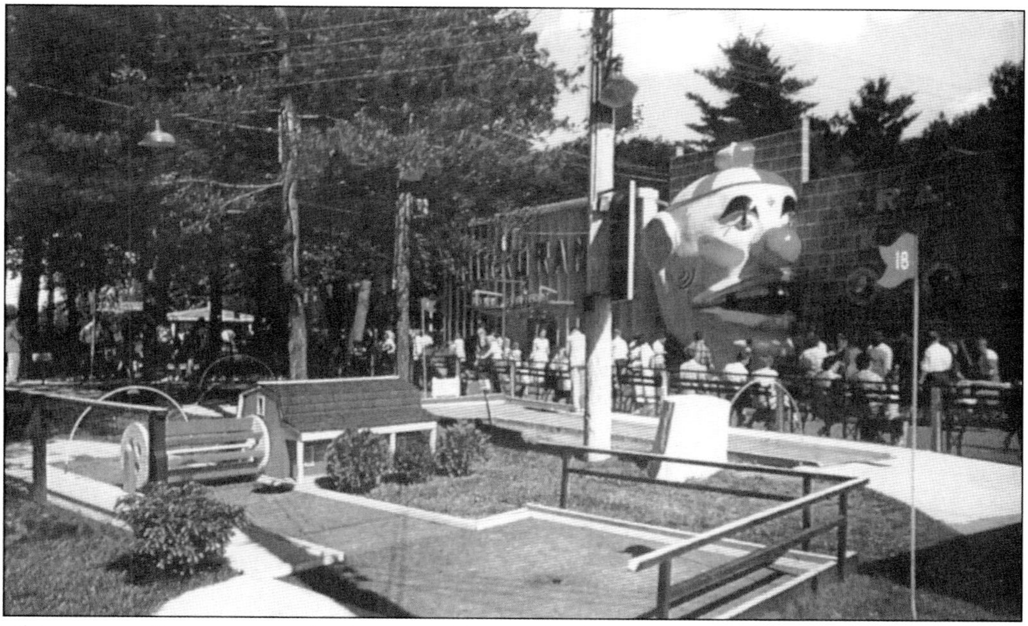

This postcard's caption reads, "Massive Clown Head, miniature Golf Course, and exclusive 'Mirrorama' feature—Riverside Park, Agawam, Mass. 'Playground of the Connecticut Valley,' located on Route 5-A between Springfield and Hartford. 60 thrilling amusement features including auto racing, outdoor stage shows, with TV and movie stars, dance gardens, private picnic and clambake groves, etc. Free admission and free parking. Edward J. Carroll is owner-mgr."

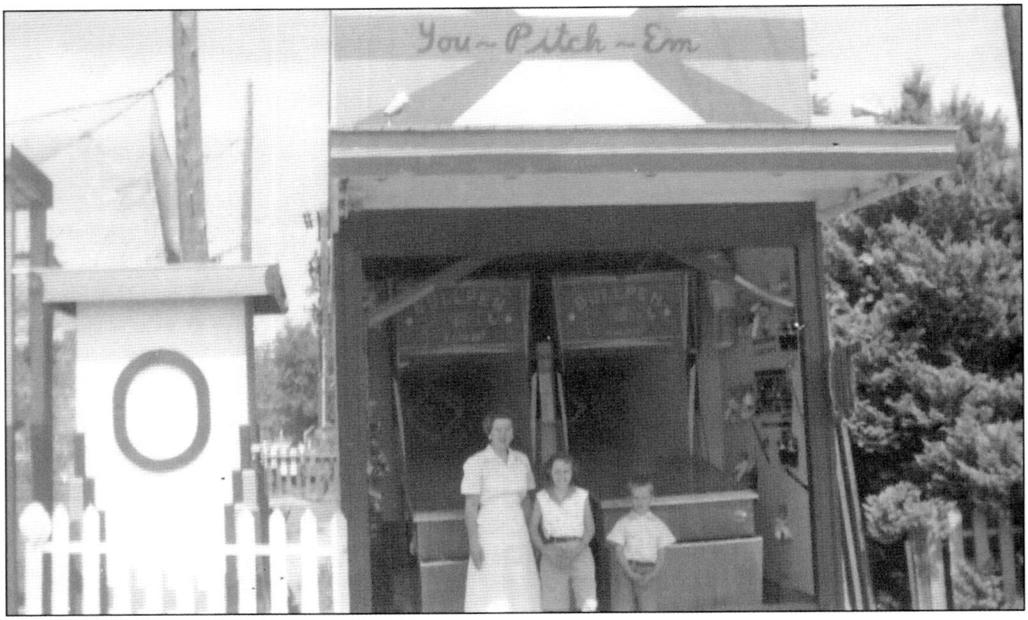


The Gilligan family owned three concession stands at Riverside Park. The 1956 photograph above shows Louise M. Gilligan and two of her four children, Audrey and Don, in front of the You-Pitch-Em stand. In the 1956 photograph below, Robert J. Gilligan stands near his wife's Ford in front of his Bat-A-Ball booth. Gilligan was a salesman for a coffee company during the day and worked most evenings and every weekend during the season running his three concessions, which also included a Skee-Ball stand. The Gilligans lived in a small cottage on the park property when they moved to the area in the mid-1940s. In 1949, they built a new house in East Forest Park. They sold their booths in the early 1960s in order to set up a new concession stand at Holyoke's Mountain Park. (Both, courtesy of William J. Gilligan.)

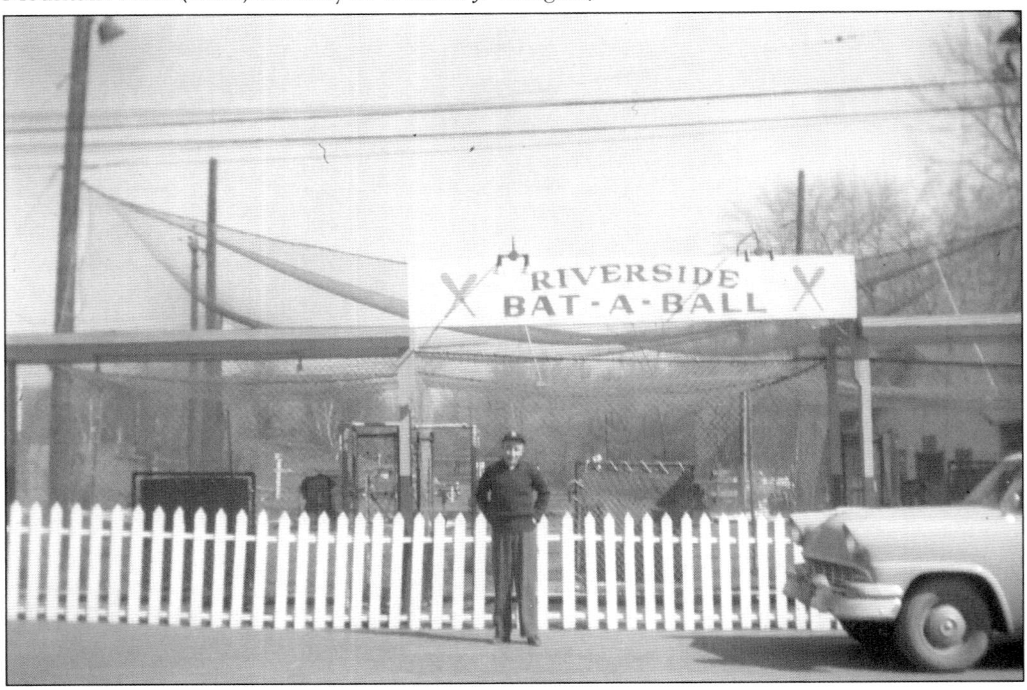

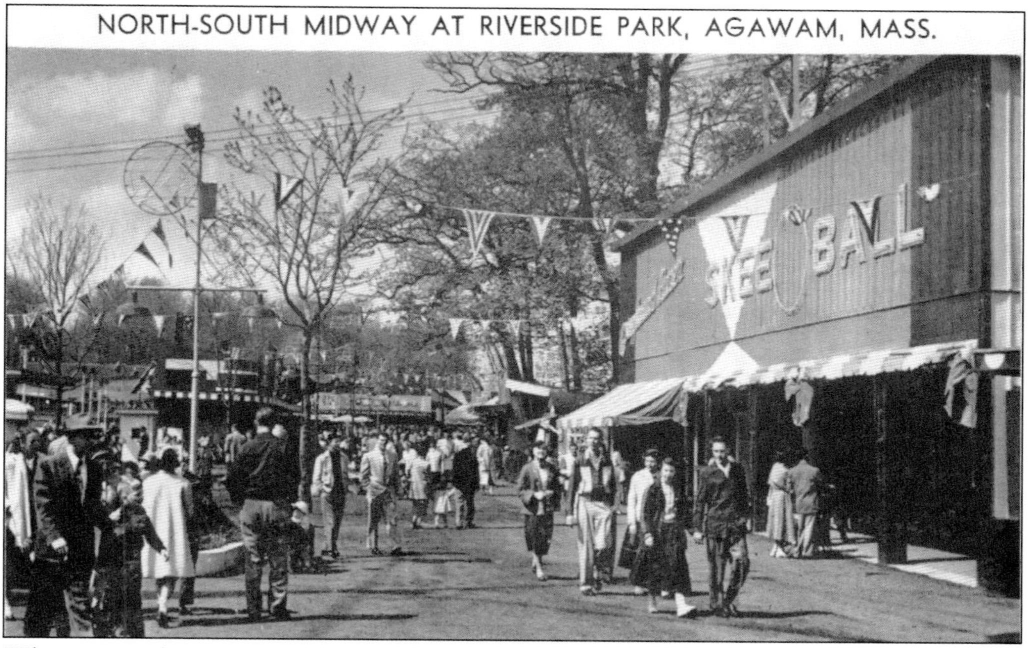


"This picture shows just a small section of the vast amusement area at Riverside Park, Agawam, Mass., located on Route 5-A between Springfield & Hartford. Riverside is one of New England's great amusement parks, with many thrilling rides, kiddieland, auto races, free shows, etc.," reads the caption of this 1950s-era postcard.

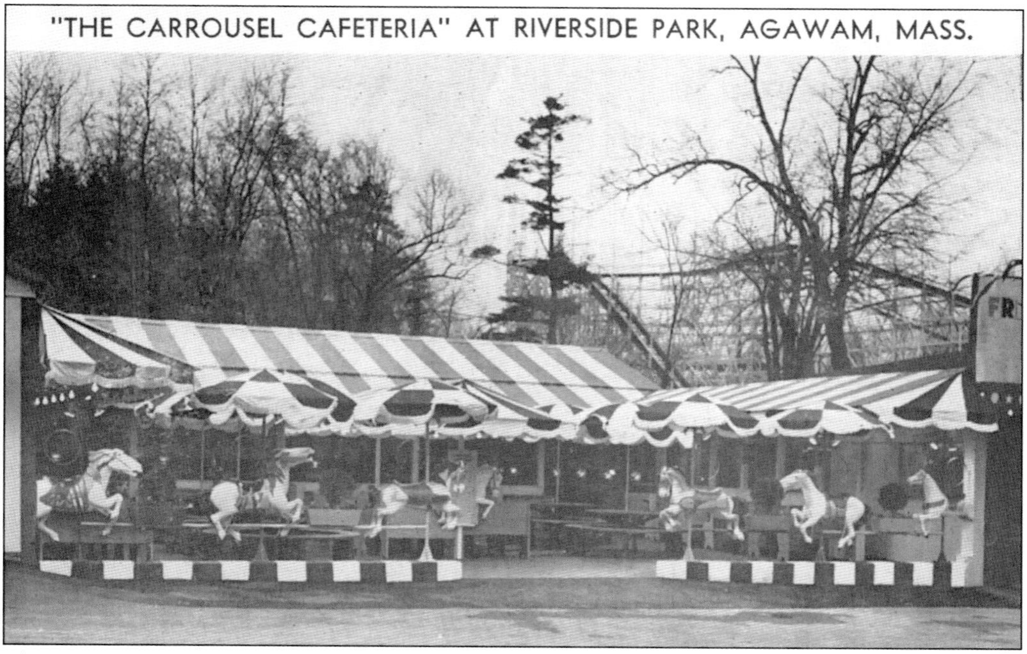


The Carrousel Cafeteria is described on this 1950s postcard as being "a brand new feature on the gay midway at Riverside Park, Agawam, Mass., located on Route 5-A between Springfield & Hartford. Seating 300 in colorful surroundings, the cafeteria-restaurant serves many choice menus. It is also used for private parties. This is just one of 60 features at this great New England amusement center."

RIVERSIDE PARK, AGAWAM, MASS.

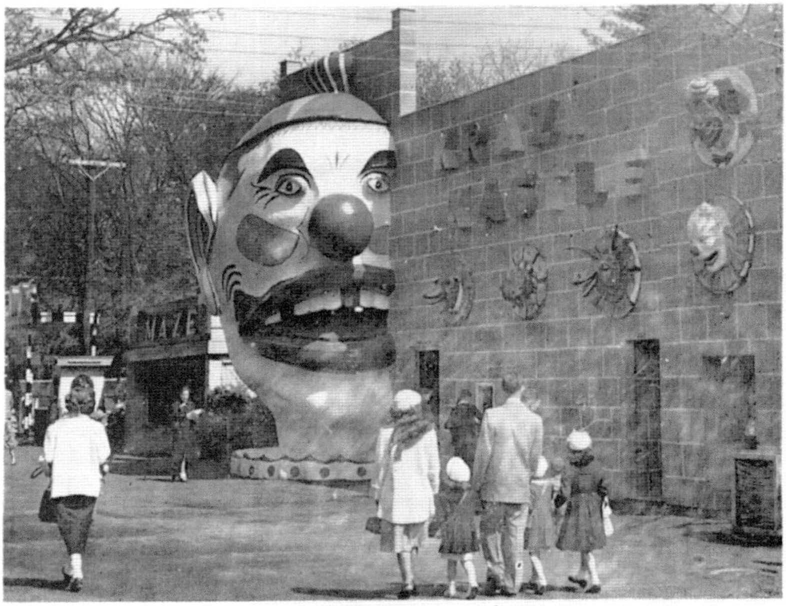


Large Clown Head on Midway

The caption on this postcard reads, "Picture shows the huge clown head, built in 1954, at Riverside Park, Agawam, Mass., located on Route 5-A between Springfield & Hartford. Riverside Park is one of the greatest amusement parks in the East with many thrilling rides, picnic groves, free shows, fireworks, auto racing, and many other attractions." Most people the author spoke to remember being terrified of this clown head as children.

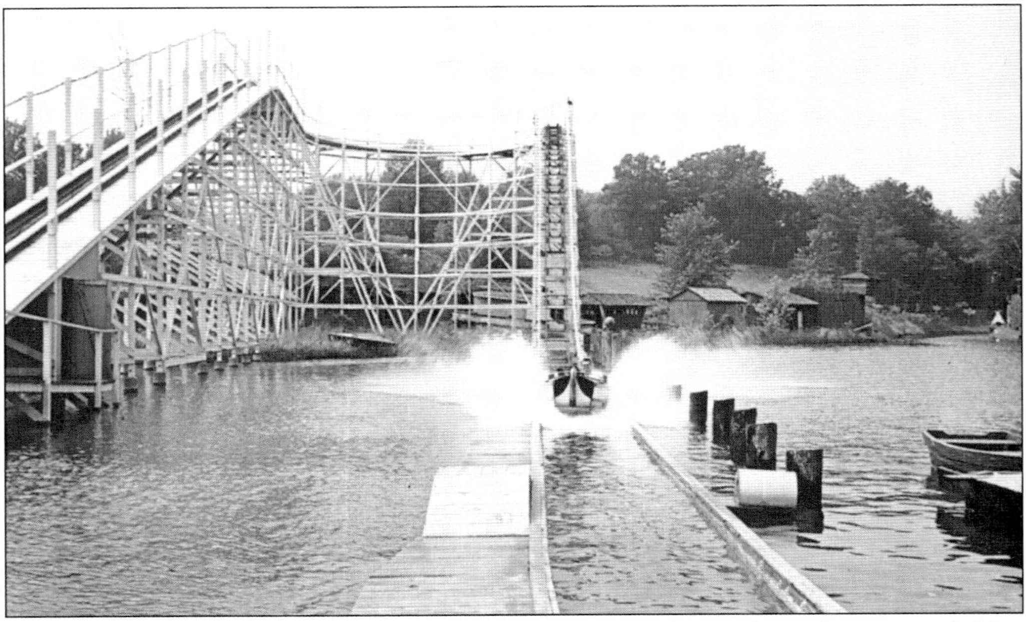

"Shoot-the-Chute: on the popular Water Sled Ride at Riverside. Popular with young and old at this famous amusement park between Hartford, Conn. and Springfield, Mass.," reads this postcard from the 1960s. From the Panama Canal ride of the early 20th century to the water parks of the 21st century, water rides have always been popular attractions.

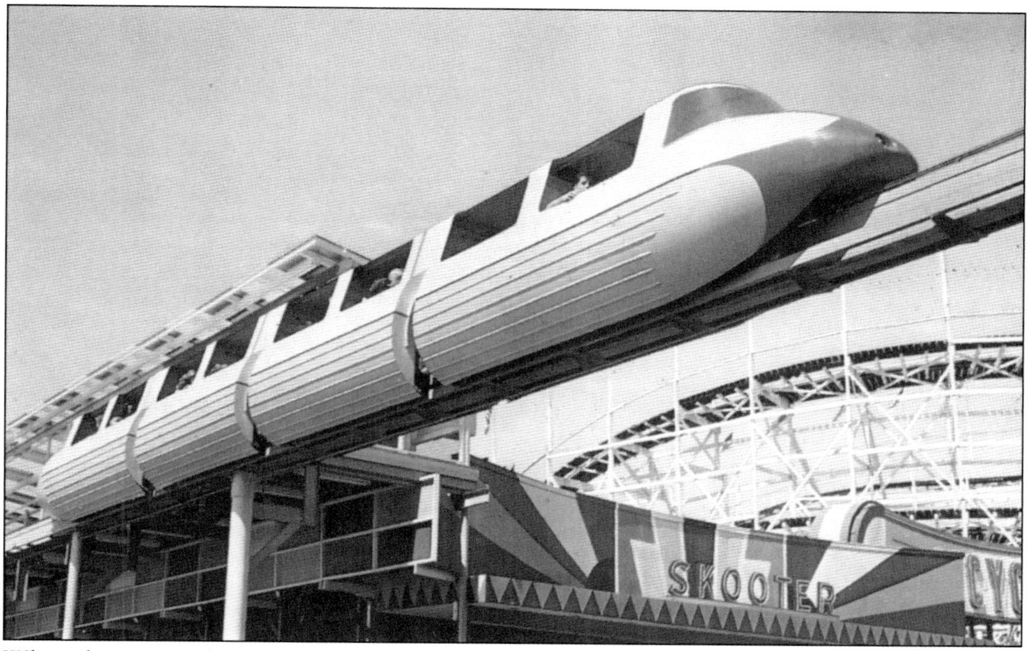


When the monorail at Riverside Park was built in 1959, it was the only monorail in an amusement park outside of Disneyland in Anaheim and only moved forward and backward on a small track. Later, David Weiner, general manager of United Engineers, worked with Ed Carroll to expand the track to make a complete loop around the park.

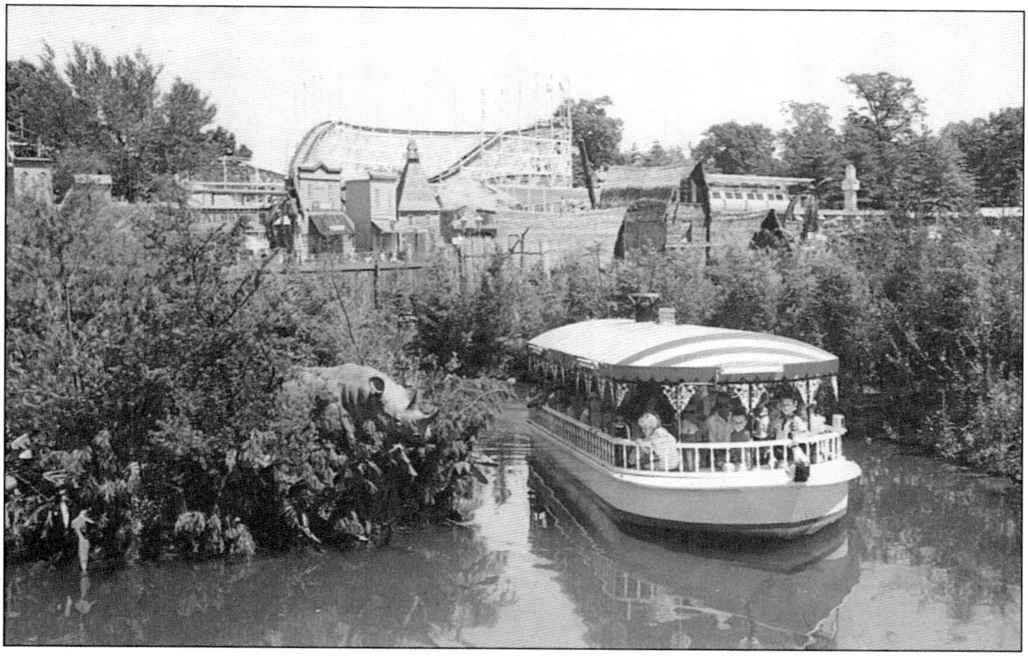

Another Disneyesque attraction built in 1959 was the Jungle Cruise, billed as a cruise up the Amazon River with alligators, head hunters, rhinoceros, and hippopotamus. This ride was heavily influenced by the Jungle Cruise ride at Disneyland that opened in 1955. Another recognizable feature at the park were the pylons at the main entrance, which were from the 1964 New York World's Fair.

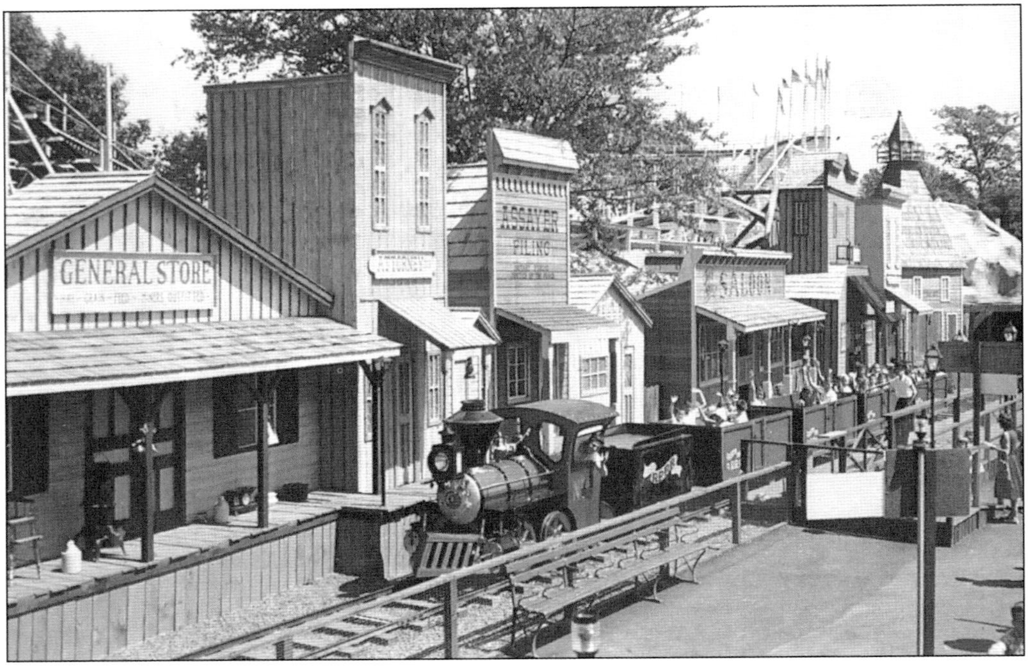


The national Western craze that began in the 1950s continued into the 1960s. Television shows such as *Bonanza*, *The Big Valley*, and *The Wild, Wild West* continued to capture America's imagination. The Old West Village and Eldorado Train Ride were built in 1960. The train left from the "ghost town of Eldorado" and travelled along the lake and into the tunnel to see the "seven wonders of Riverside." The ride was located next the Thunderbolt roller coaster. The train ride was destroyed by fire in September 1971 in an intense blaze that injured a fireman and two Riverside employees and put the Thunderbolt temporarily out of commission.

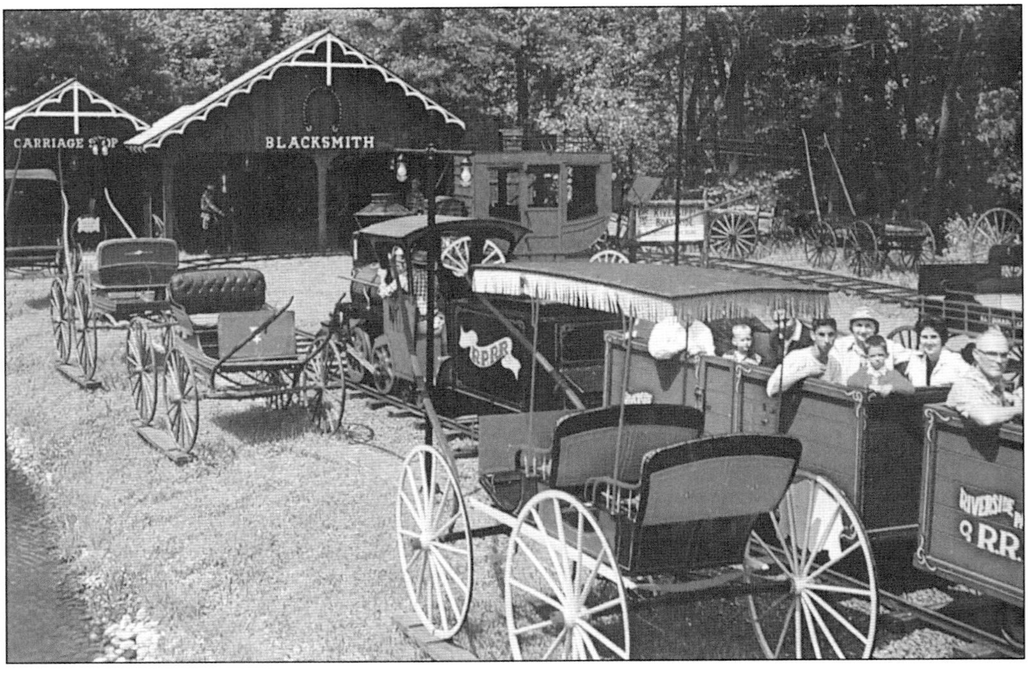

Raymond and Helen Hamel often took their sons to Riverside. Ronald (left) and David Hamel are pictured in April 1962. Riverside had its finger on the pulse of American culture; note the Rocket to the Moon poster. The space race was one thing that excited Americans as much as Westerns at that time. The previous year, Pres. John F. Kennedy challenged the country to put a man on the moon by the end of the 1960s. (Courtesy of David Hamel.)

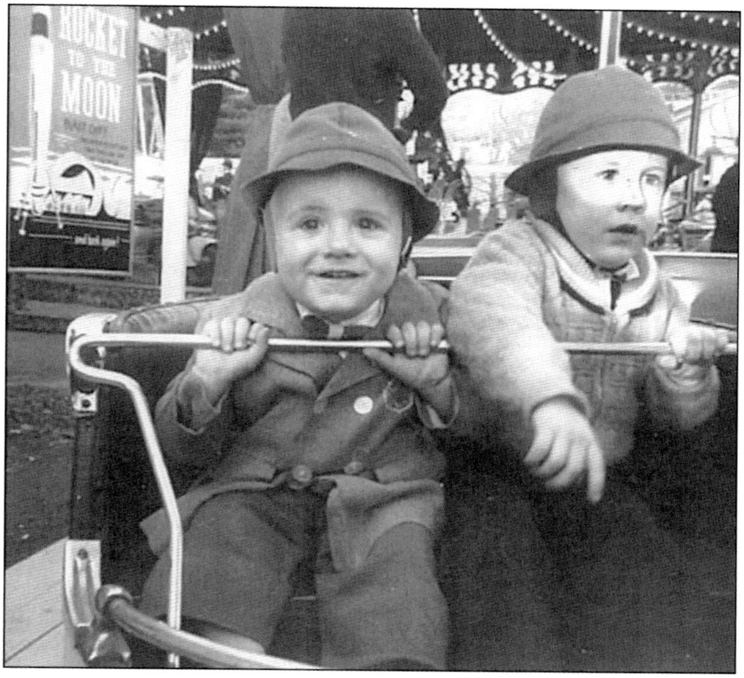


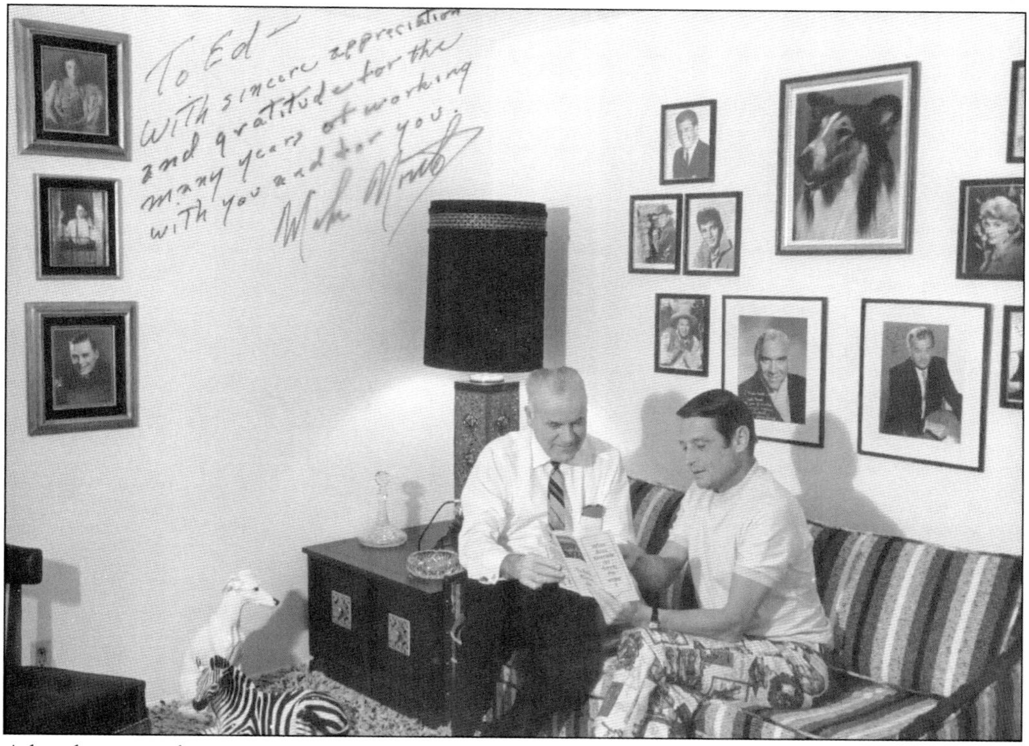


A big draw was the appearance of television and movie stars in the Riverside Free Show Area. Ed Carroll Sr. (left) often worked with Hollywood agent Michael North to book the biggest names of the day and said, "The trick is to get the acts while they are popular and before they price themselves out of your range. The thing to do is avoid the stinkers. You don't want to smell the joint up." (Courtesy of Edward J. Carroll Jr.)

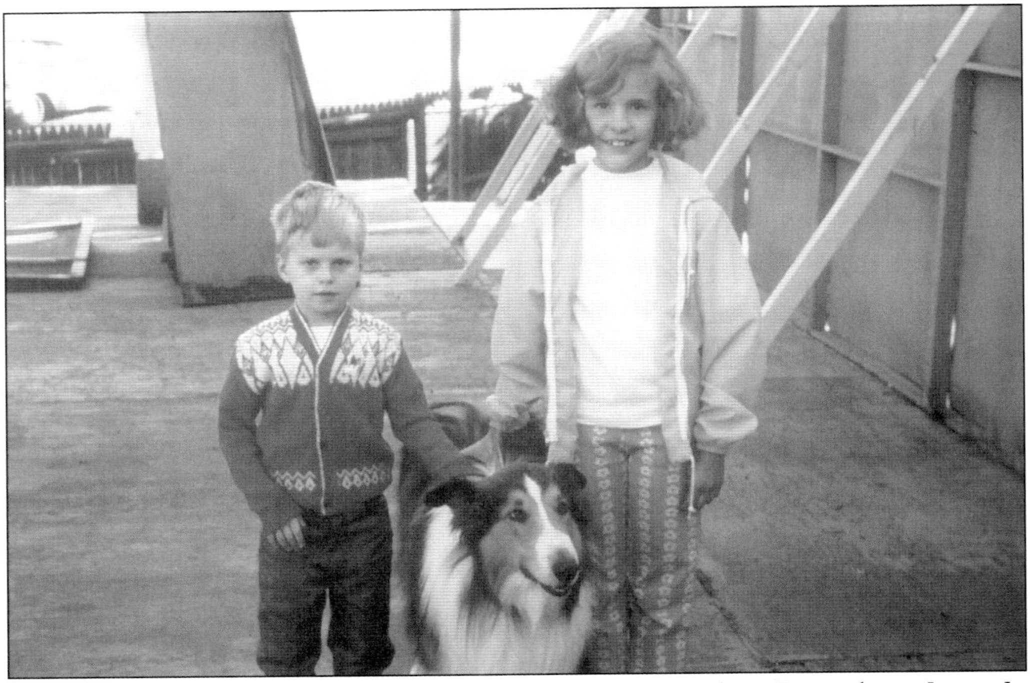

One star of television and movies whose appearance was very popular at Riverside was Lassie. In the above photograph, Richard Gebo (left) and an unidentified friend are seen backstage with Lassie after the canine star's appearance before capacity crowds in the Free Show Area in May 1970. Gebo's mother was convinced that her son was chosen for the personal visit due to his close resemblance to Jon Provost, who played Timmy Martin on the long-running television series *Lassie*. In the photograph below, Rudd Weatherwax, who trained four generations of Lassies, works with the dog during the show. A true movie star, Lassie flew in a first-class airline seat when traveling to various appearances. (Both, courtesy of Richard Gebo.)

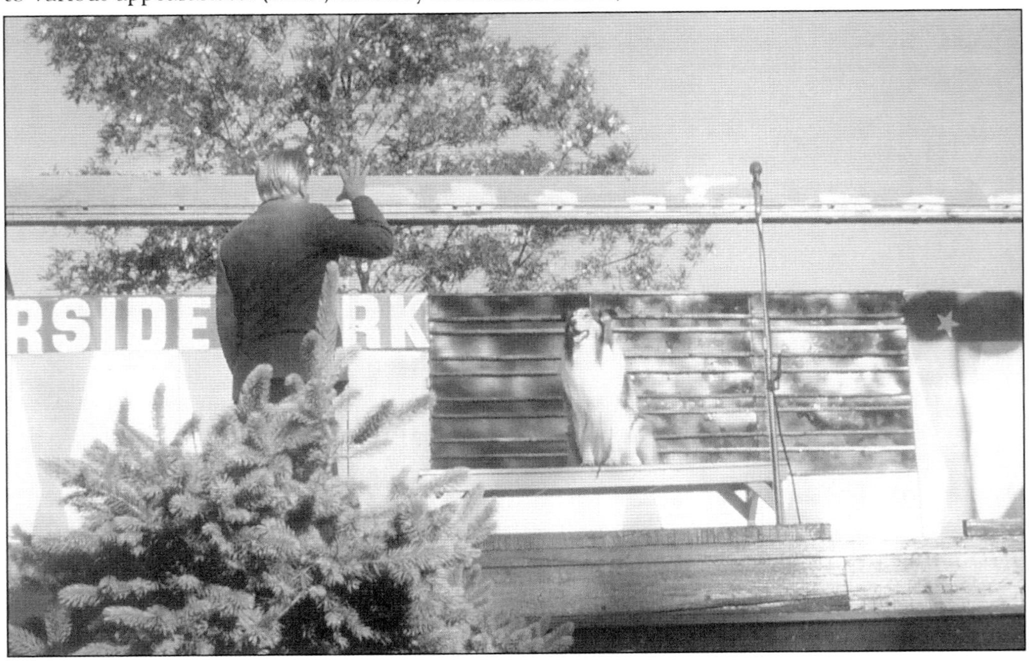

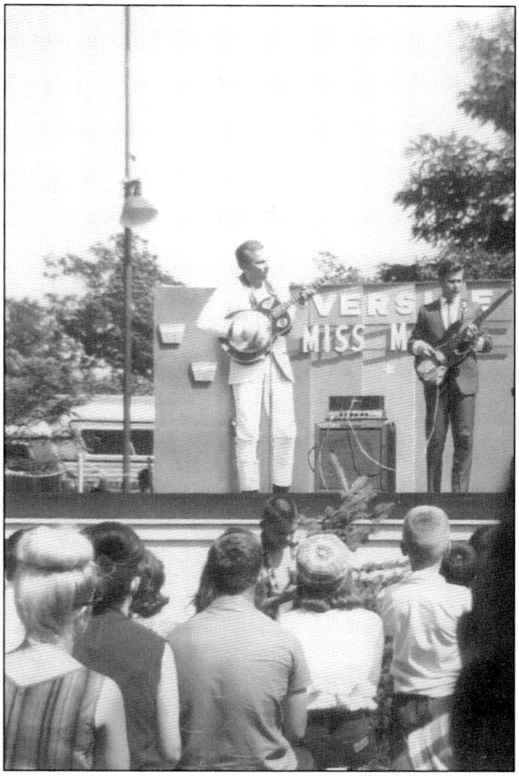

Through the late 1970s, admission and parking at Riverside were free, as were the acts presented in the Free Show Area. Ed Carroll Sr. believed this practice was crucial to attracting repeat visitors. "When they [guests] come out and see this wonderful talent for free, they have to be in a good mood and we hope they will stick around and spend a little money so we can keep bringing them these big names," he said. Along with music groups of the day (right), big names such as Lorne Greene (below), fellow *Bonanza* cast members Michael Landon and Dan Blocker, and others appeared on the Riverside Free Show stage. Ed Carroll Jr. remembers Michael Landon being a funny guy who "thought Riverside was a riot" and invited kids in the park to join him on the rides. (Both, courtesy of David St. John.)

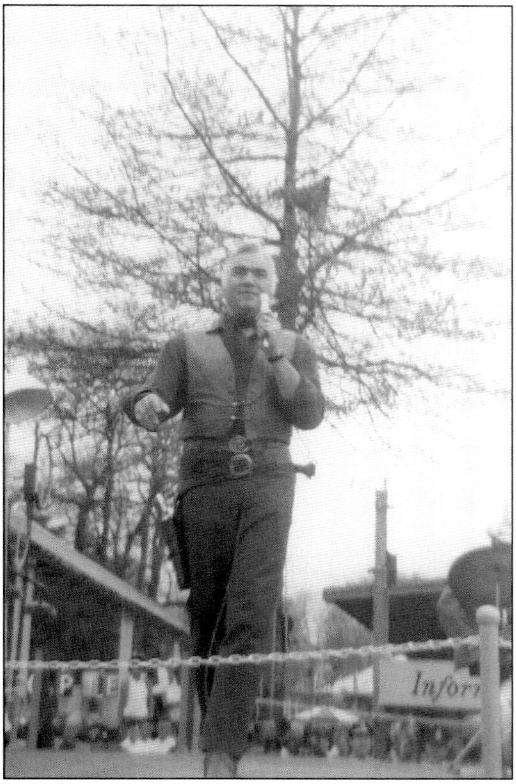

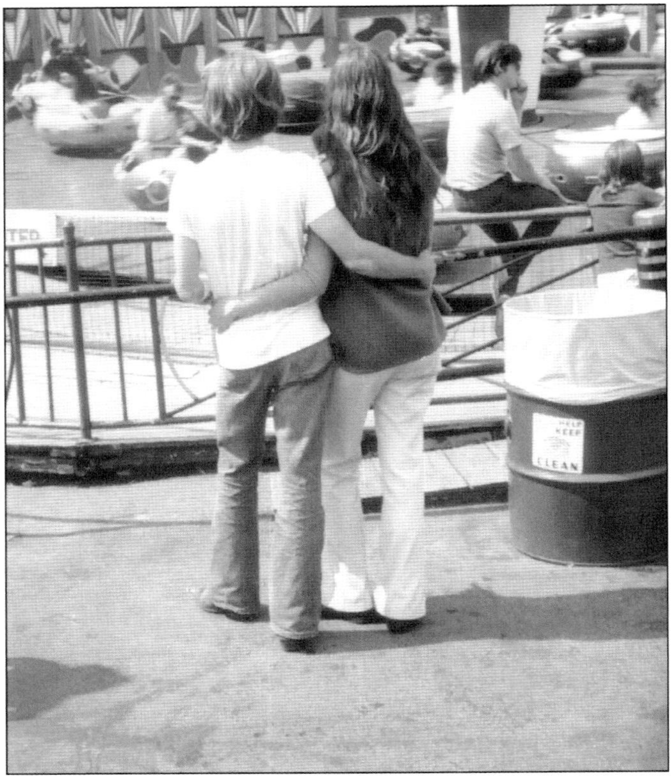

The 1960s and 1970s saw a large number of attractions built at Riverside Park. The Calypso, Round-Up, Whiz Bang, and Moon Rocket were added in 1963; 1968 saw the addition of the Meteor, Spider, and Twister, and the Rotor and Swiss Bobs joined the Riverside lineup in 1972. That same year, the Giant Wheel (a Ferris wheel) from the recently closed Palisades Amusement Park in New Jersey was reconstructed on the Riverside grounds. In 1971, in an effort to keep the park active during the offseason, a snowmobile area with a three-mile trail was proposed but never built. The Loop Coaster was added in 1977. (Both, courtesy of the Agawam Historical Association, Edith LaFrancis Collection.)

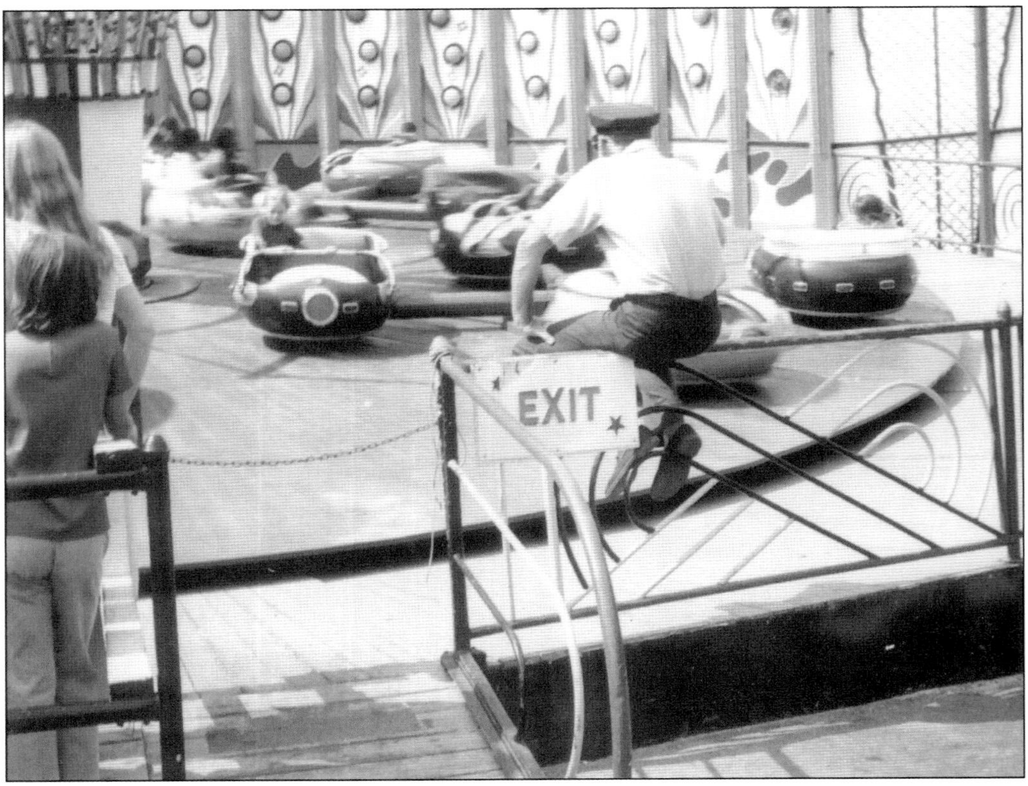

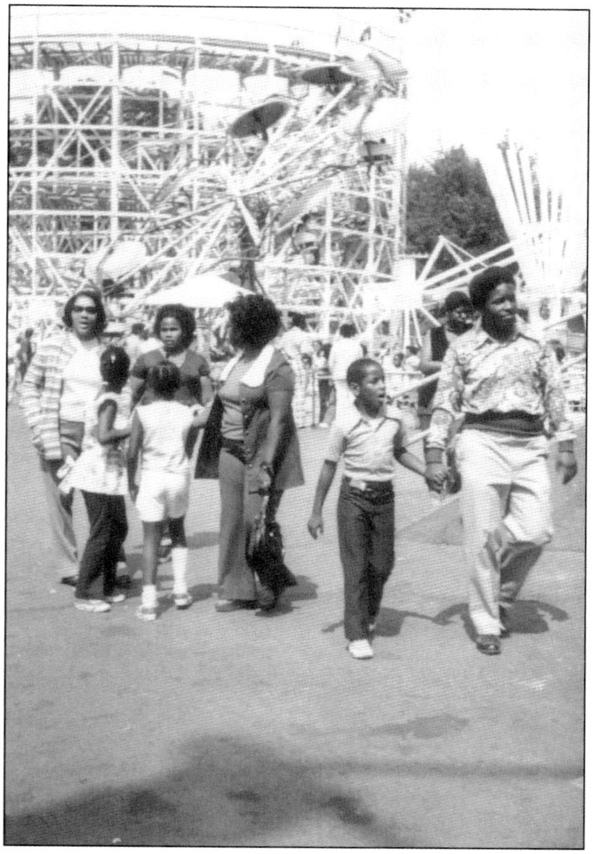

By the mid-1970s, there were 50 rides, 35 food stands, and 30 games of skill scattered across Riverside Park's 150 acres. By the late 1970s, the park even had its own mascot, Captain Rivi. An employee handbook from those years credits Riverside's success to four principles: safety, courtesy, cleanliness, and service. How a person looked was included under "service" and offered the following perk: "All hairstyles should be neat and clean. We provide a barber for you on Mondays. You pay one dollar. Riverside pays the rest." The handbook also revealed that "Riverside has a language all its own. We urge you to learn this language. It begins with please and thank you. Those two words unlock all the unhappy frowns you may come across. The other method of courteous attitude development is a smile. Smiles are contagious. Give everybody the disease." (Both, courtesy of the Agawam Historical Association, Edith LaFrancis Collection.)

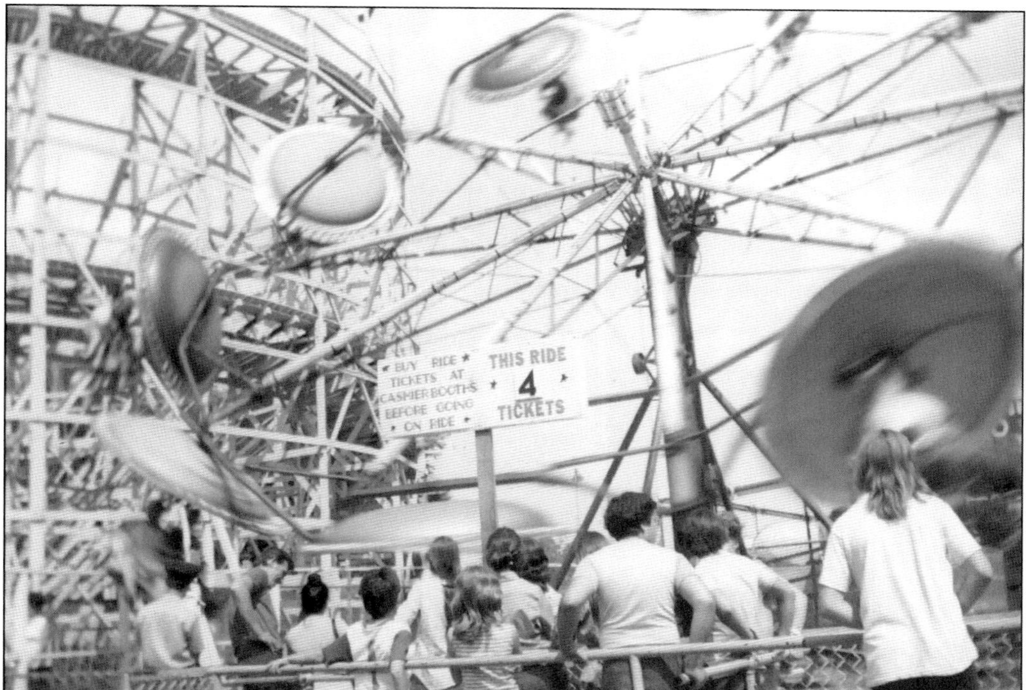

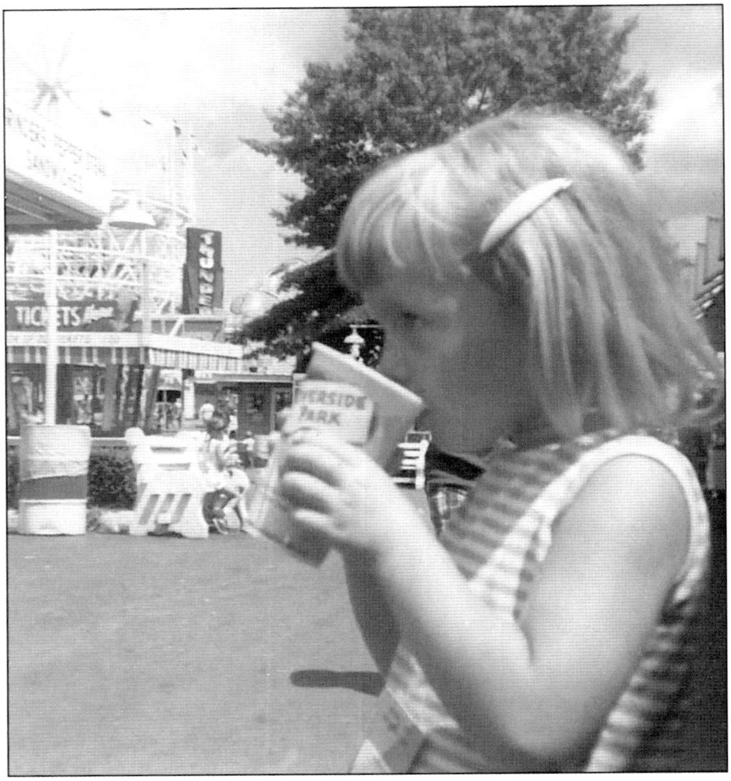

This photograph of Dawn Michelle Roche was taken in August 1970 by her father, Jim Roche. The Thunderbolt roller coaster can be seen in the background. Jim remembers Riverside to be a "warm, sweet, and traditional amusement park, not like the modern ones today"—a sentiment that is shared by many people who spent time at the old Riverside Park. "Each time we went it was an event, and we always stayed until evening, when the sun went down and it cooled off. The lights and organ music made it a magical place," according to Jim. (Courtesy of Jim Roche.)

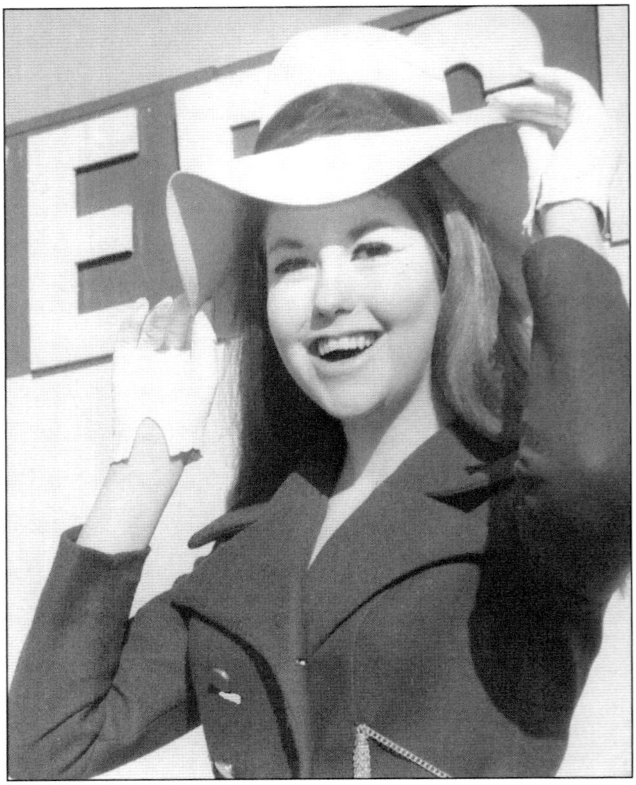

The tradition of selecting Miss Riverside was lost as society underwent massive cultural shifts during the 1960s and 1970s. Young women no longer wore bonnets on Easter Sunday and fewer still were interested in an Easter parade. In 1973, Catherine Krafft of Springfield was one of the last to hold the title of Miss Riverside. (Courtesy of *The Republican*, Springfield, Massachusetts.)

Riverside was long known as a place for romance—a reputation that extended to the workplace. Morris Lainer worked there from 1964 to 1974, ending as a relief ride operator. He recalls, "It was during this time I was relieving a cute little operator on the merry-go-round, Teresa, who would eventually be my wife." Teresa Serafin (pictured) was a ride operator from 1972 to 1979. She loved her job at Riverside. (Courtesy of Teresa Serafin and Morris Lainer.)

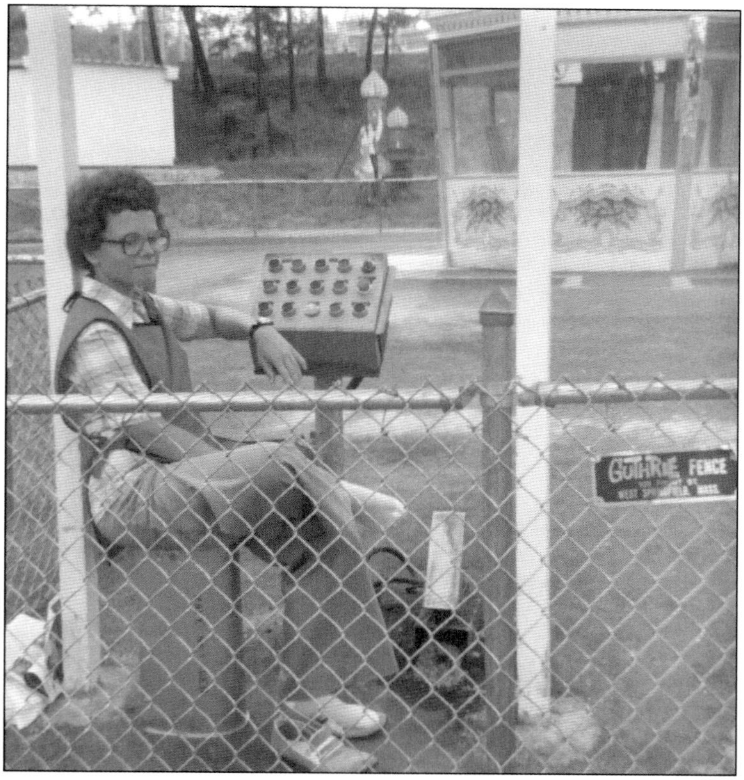


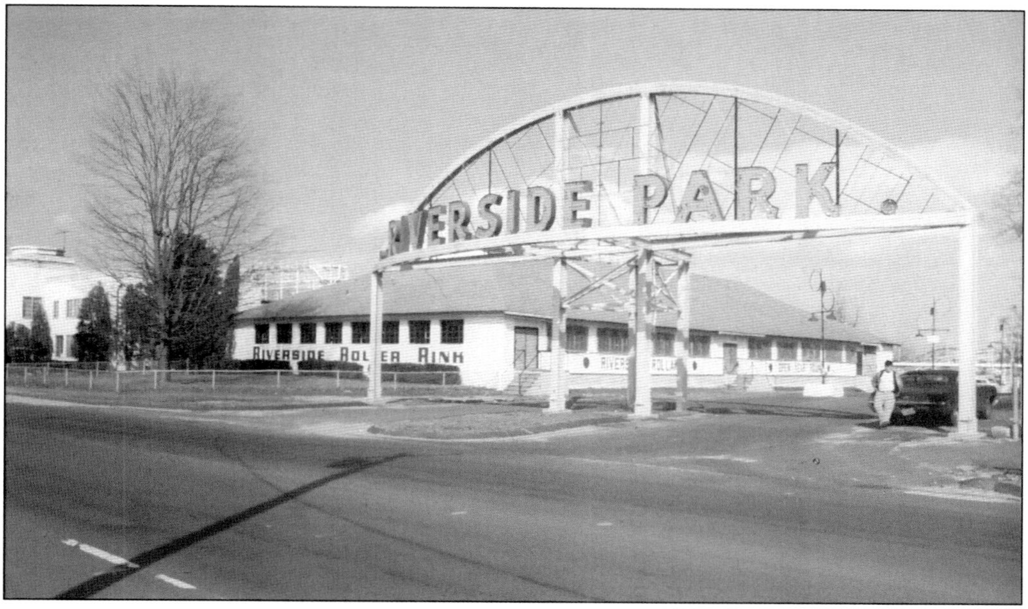


Visitors entered Riverside Park through the main gate at 1623 Main Street, Agawam. The former bowling alley building (seen at far left) had been converted to administrative offices and a maintenance area when it was destroyed by fire in 1987. The spectacular blaze, which could be seen for miles, caused $1 million in damage and destroyed "irreplaceable memorabilia" chronicling the history of the park, according to Tina Trerice, director of marketing at that time. (Courtesy of Les and Dale Melanson.)

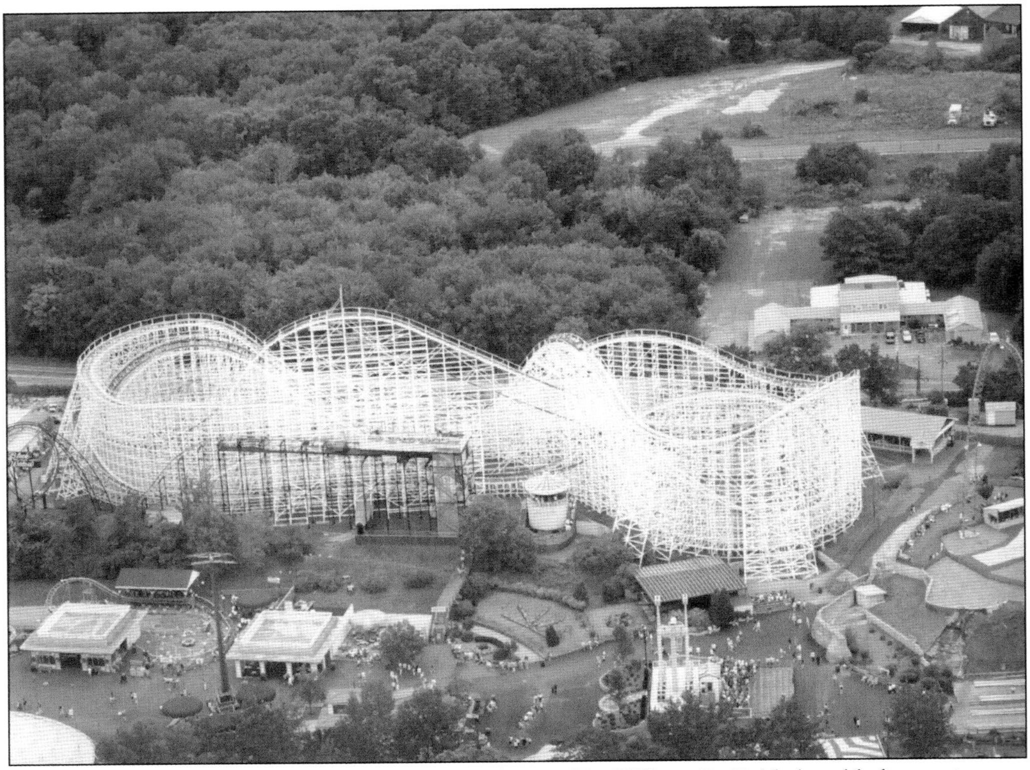

The construction of the Cyclone roller coaster, designed by William L. Cobb, heralded a renaissance for wooden coasters when it opened in 1983. Inspired by the original Cyclone at Coney Island and topping many best-of lists, the 3,600-foot-long coaster was known for its intense turns and drops. Slightly reconfigured, the Cyclone is still a major attraction at Six Flags New England. (Aerials by Don Couture, courtesy of Mike Donahue.)

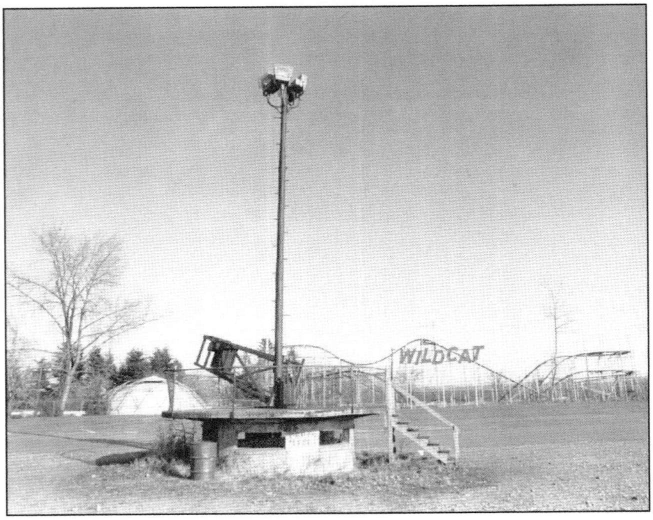


A close look at this light-pole base in the Riverside Park parking lot reveals it is the old diving platform from Lake Takadip. The platform survived well into the 1990s. According to newspaper accounts, when the Wildcat roller coaster was built in 1968, Riverside joined Palisades Park to become just the second park on the East Coast to have two roller coasters. The Wildcat was dismantled in the mid-1980s. (Photograph by Frank Usin, courtesy of *The Republican*, Springfield, Massachusetts.)

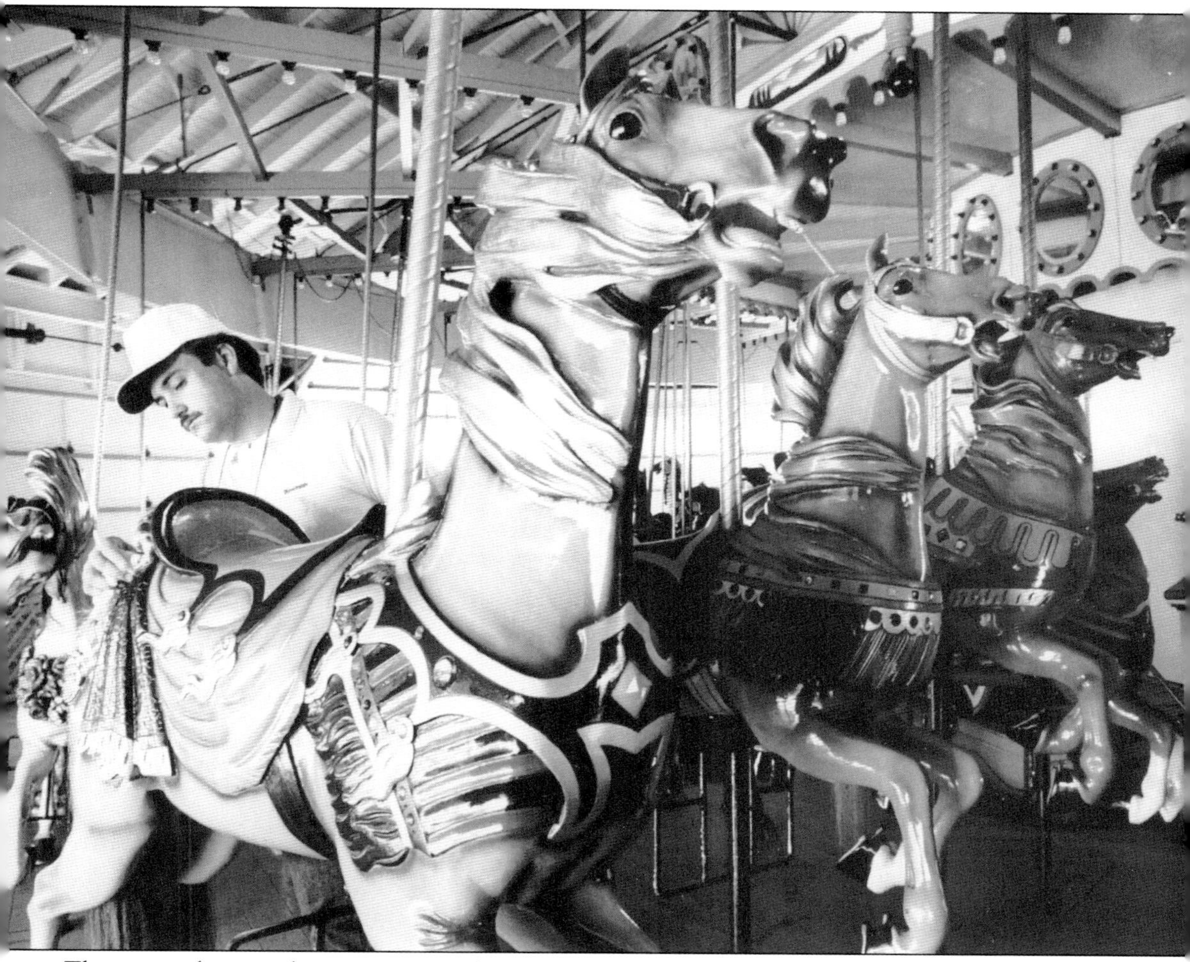

The carousel currently in use at Six Flags New England was purchased with 300 pairs of roller skates by Ed Carroll Sr. in 1940. Built by M.C. Illions and Sons and William F. Mangels in 1909 for Savin Rock Amusement Park in West Haven, Connecticut, the 72-animal Riverside carousel is unlike any other Illions machine. The signed American Beauty lead horse is the only known gelding on a carousel in the United States. Most carousels carry one or two armored horses—Riverside's holds three, including one in full armor. It also carries the following four rare menagerie animals: a lion, a tiger, and a pair of stags. Long known as the "Carousell," it underwent a $100,000 restoration in 1986. During the restoration, its original Wurlitzer 146-B military band organ was purchased and restored. At the time of its restoration, the carousel was valued at nearly $1 million. Though it is eligible for the National Register of Historic Places, no application has yet been submitted. In this 1988 photograph, then maintenance manager William Jatkevicius cleans one of the restored horses. (Photograph by John Suchoki, courtesy of *The Republican*, Springfield, Massachusetts.)

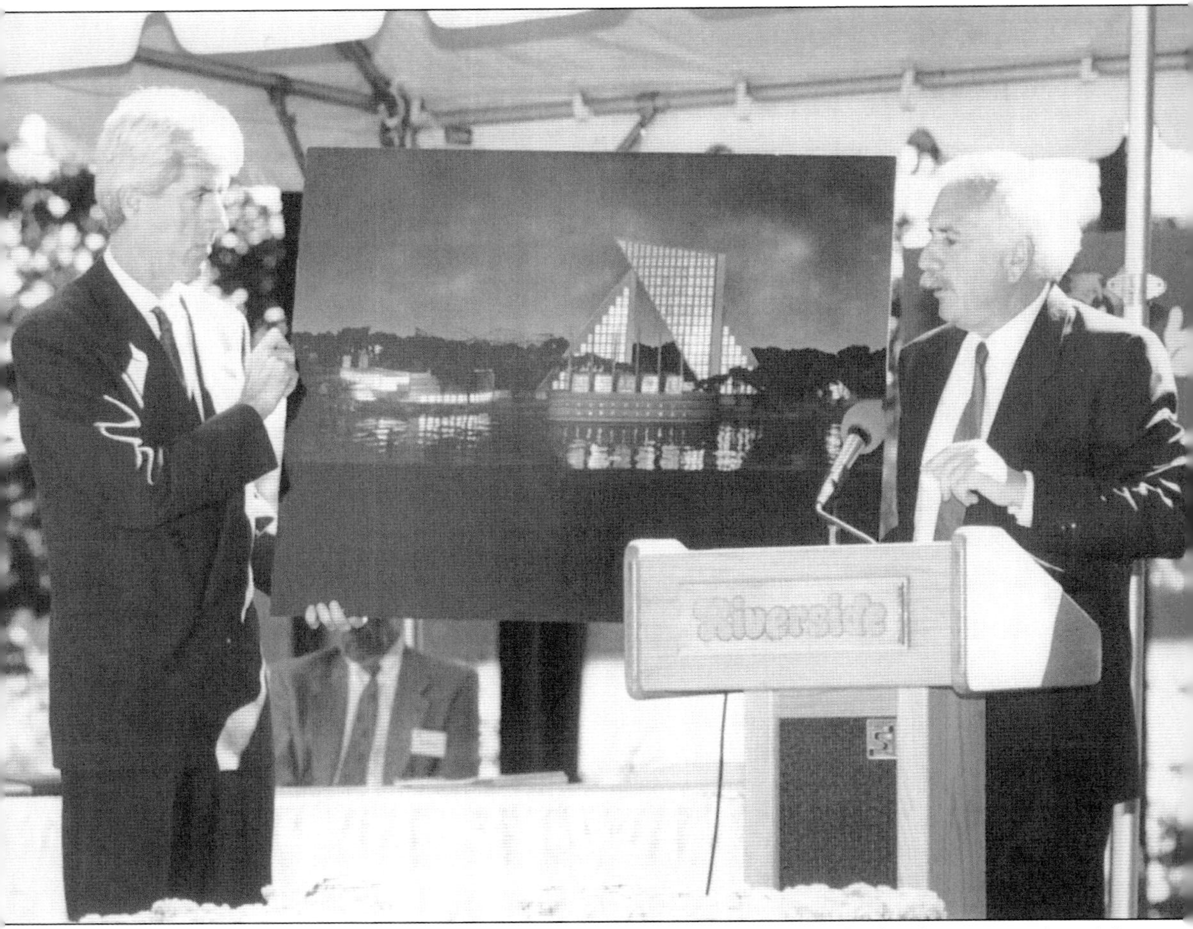


Riverside Park owner Edward J. Carroll Jr. and architect Moshe Safdie display drawings and models of a proposed riverboat casino and hotel at Riverside Park in August 1994. That November, a nonbinding referendum was placed on the ballot asking Agawam residents if casino gambling should be permitted at Riverside Park in the future. (At the time, and as of 2010, casino gambling was not legal in Massachusetts.) The controversial project generated intense debate among residents and town officials. Nearly 74 percent of Agawam voters turned out to cast their ballot, and the issue was soundly defeated by nearly 70 percent of voters (7,513 to 3,383). Members of the Agawam Historical Commission, fearing detrimental traffic increases within the proposed Agawam Center Historic District on Main Street, were among the first public officials to speak out against the proposed casino. In June 2001, after years of effort, Agawam Center was placed in the National Register of Historic Places. The district includes over 100 structures dating from the mid-18th through the mid-20th centuries. (Photograph by Don Treeger, courtesy of *The Republican*, Springfield, Massachusetts.)

# *Seven*

# God Bless Ed Carroll

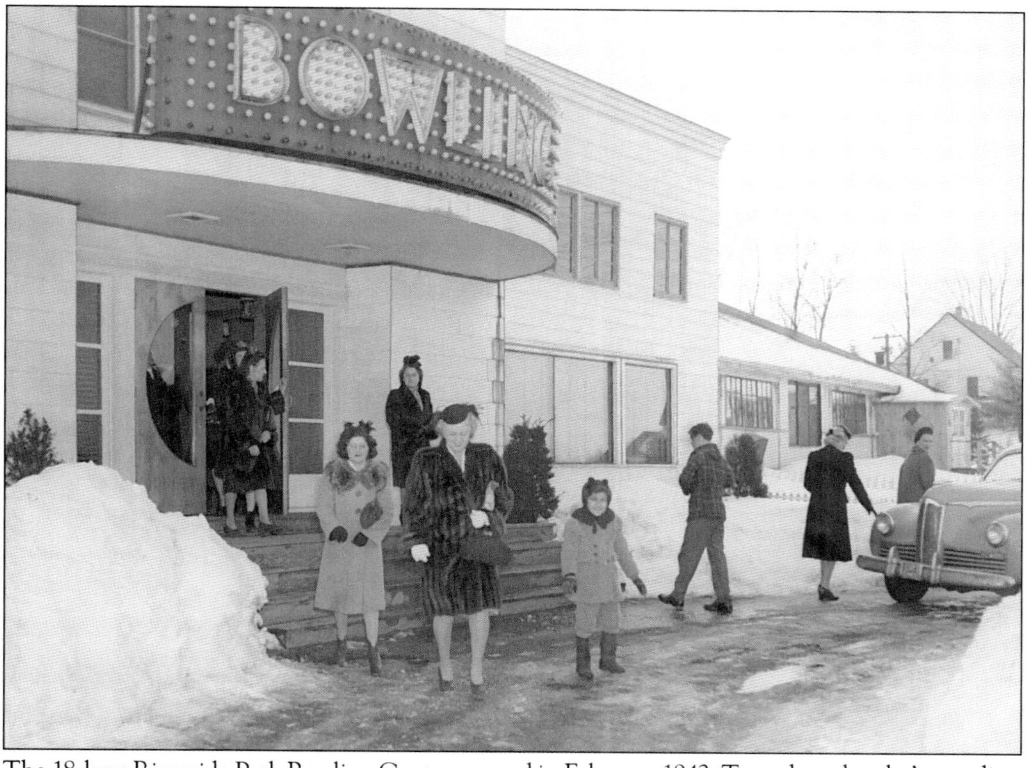


The 18-lane Riverside Park Bowling Center opened in February 1942. Touted as a bowler's paradise, the facility boasted private locker rooms with showers, a conference room for league groups, spectator galleries, and a 72-lamp lighting system hidden in a step-down ceiling described as the first of its kind. A two-story tower housed the executive offices of Edward J. Carroll Enterprises. Soon enough, the bowling alley would serve a higher purpose. (Photograph by Stephen N. Lemanis, courtesy of Mickey Bandarra.)

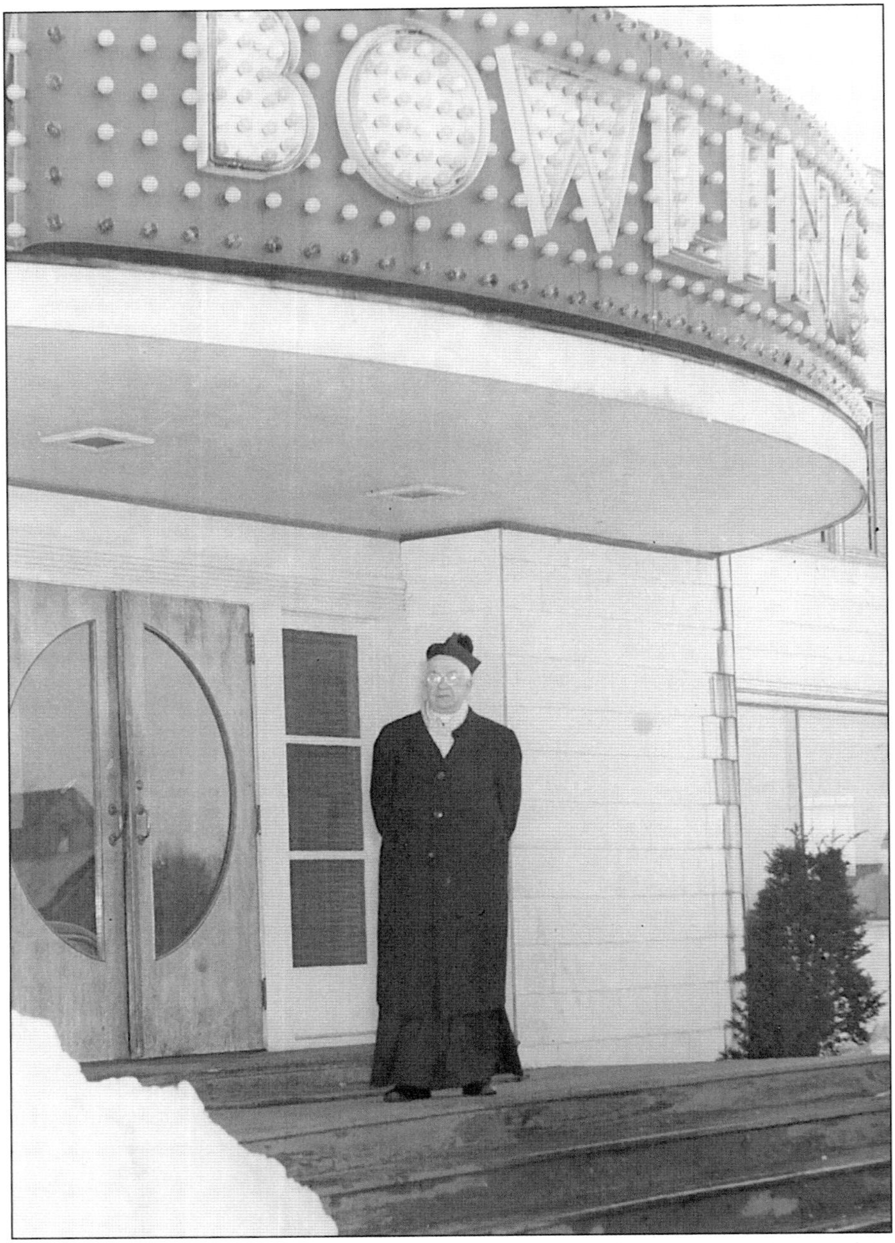


In the late 1930s, having no place of their own to worship, the Catholic population of Agawam Center decided to establish the Mission Church of the Immaculate Conception Parish of West Springfield. In 1938, Fr. John A. O'Connell celebrated the first Mass of the Mission Church in the old Agawam Town Hall, continuing on there until the building was demolished in 1939 to make way for the new Agawam Center (now Benjamin J. Phelps Elementary) School. Refused by the Baptist Church, the congregation next met in the Congregational church, with a monthly rent of $50. In late 1942, the Congregationalists doubled the rent, and the cash-strapped, 135-member Catholic congregation was forced to look for another home. Edward J. Carroll, who lived on River Road at that time, was a member of the Mission Church parish and offered his newly opened bowling alley as a Sunday morning meeting location. (Photograph by Stephen N. Lemanis, courtesy of Mickey Bandarra.)

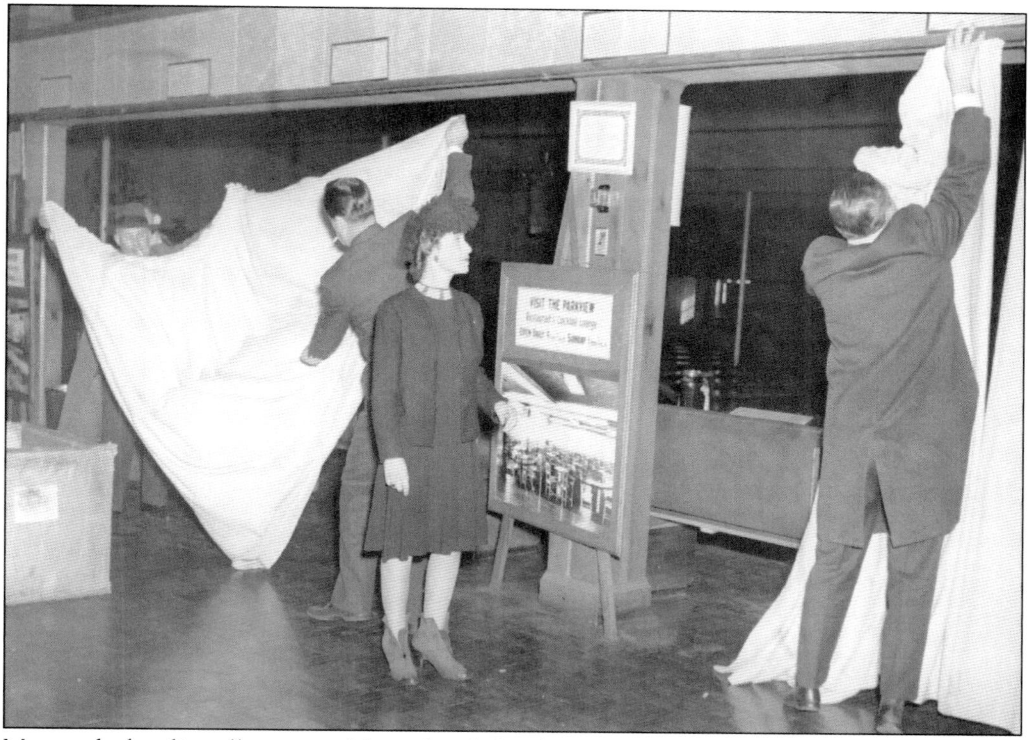

Mass at the bowling alleys was celebrated each Sunday at 9:00 a.m. Carroll provided folding chairs for the congregation and donated drapes to separate the bowling lanes from those attending Mass. An hour before the service, a small group, including Ann O'Keefe (above, center; below, far left) and James O'Keefe (below, third from left) would arrive to set up chairs, hang drapes, and arrange the altar. After Mass, it was all taken down and packed away until the following week. The bowling alleys opened for business at 1:00 p.m. Ed Carroll not only provided physically for his parish during its time of need but financially as well. In 1944, July 19 and 20 were among several Festival Nights at Riverside Park. On these evenings, the entire proceeds of designated sections of the midway were donated to the Mission Church building fund. (Both, photograph by Stephen N. Lemanis, courtesy of Mickey Bandarra.)

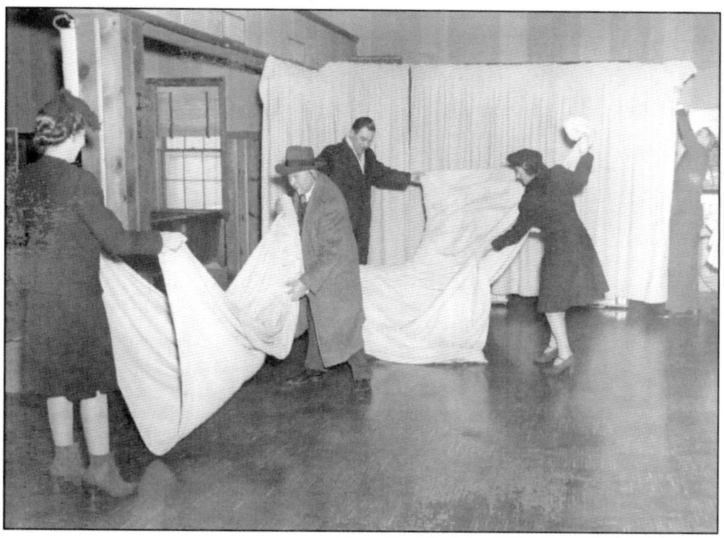

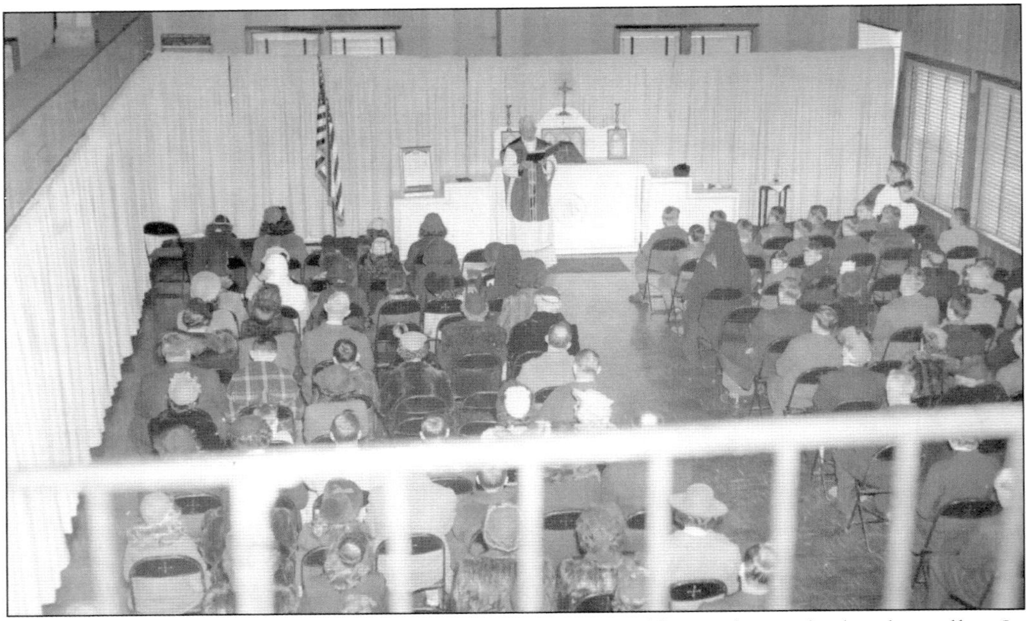

The congregation, now numbering 200 and growing, would soon leave the bowling alley. In October 1945, ground was broken at 833 Main Street on property that had been purchased two years earlier by the Catholic Women's Club. Mass was first celebrated in the new church on Easter Sunday in 1946, when the parish formally became St. John the Evangelist Parish. (Photograph by Stephen N. Lemanis, courtesy of Mickey Bandarra.)

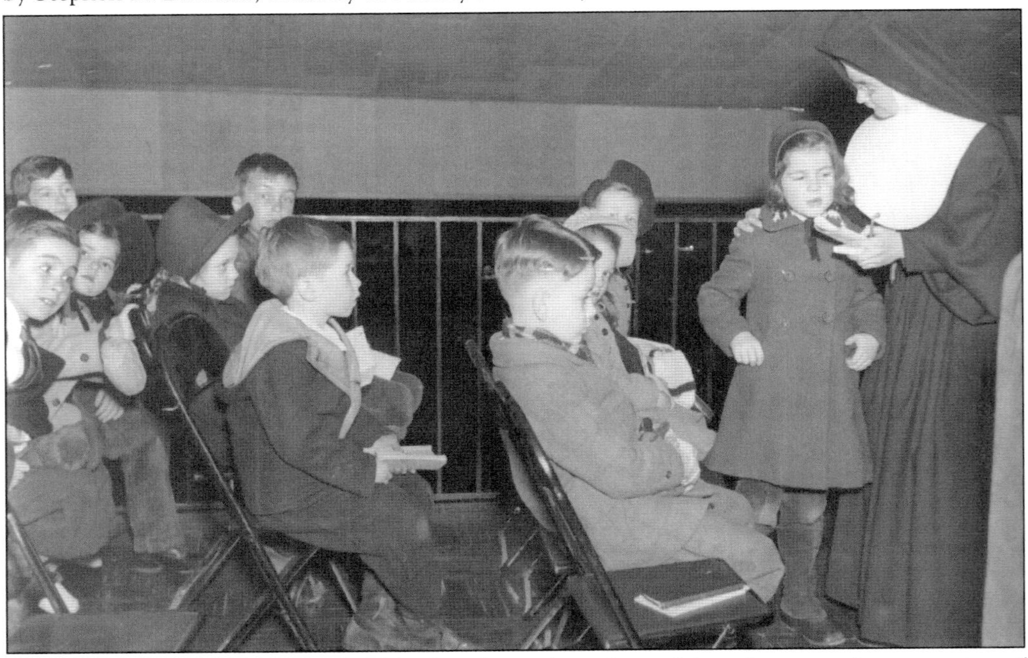

Each week after Mass, the Sisters of St. Joseph conducted catechism classes on the mezzanine of the bowling alley building. Members of this early-1940s class include Ronald LaFleur (back row, rear), Celine LaFleur (back row, middle), Eddie Caldon (middle row, foreground), Thomas O'Keefe (front row, foreground), Joan O'Connor (front row, rear), and Constance McGovern (standing). (Photograph by Stephen N. Lemanis, courtesy of Constance McGovern.)

# *Eight*

# The Rollaway

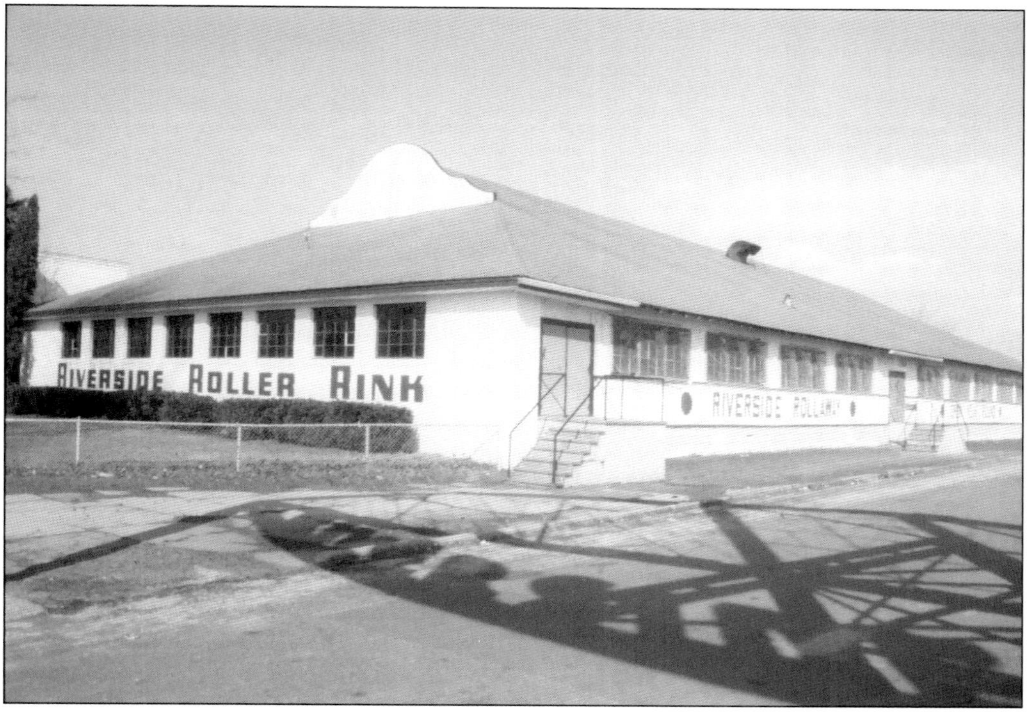


Known as the roller Rink de Luxe when it opened in May 1916 (the Lyman Street Rink in Springfield had already been renamed the Rollaway in 1912), the skating rink at Riverside Park was a popular destination for over six decades. The *Springfield Daily Republican* reported that the rink was remodeled in 1922 with a "grandstand section for those who wish to watch the others fall down." Roller-hockey games were held at the rink as early as 1932. (Courtesy of Les and Dale Melanson.)

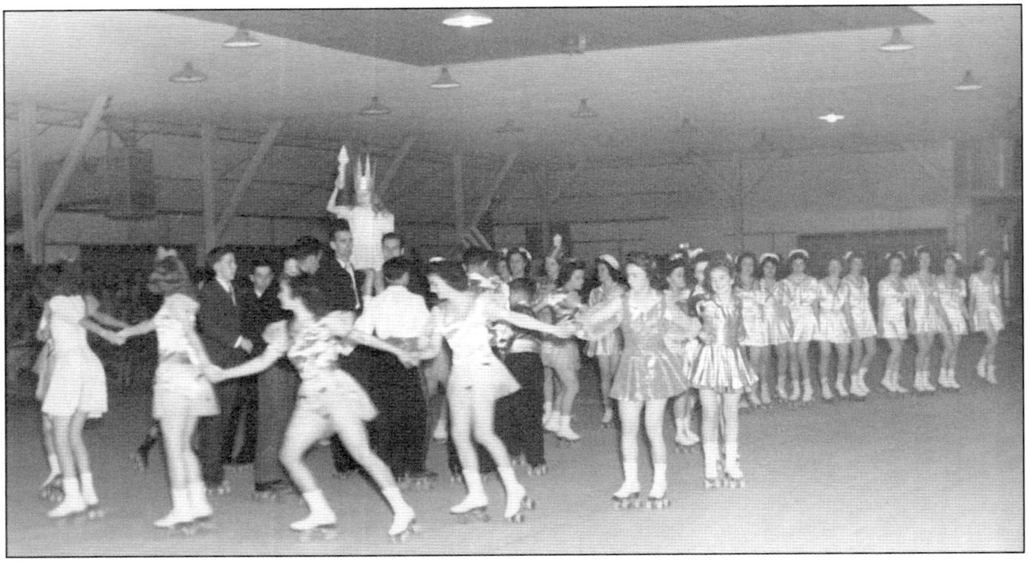

In October 1944, a Roller Revue was presented at the Riverside Rollaway by the Agawam American Legion Wilson Thompson Post. The revue opened with a march by the Capette Capers, of which Susan Cross (later Maiolo) was a member. The finale featured eight-year-old Ann Oberheim as the Statue of Liberty being carried on the shoulders of four young men, and it ended with the organist playing the national anthem. (Courtesy of Susan and David Maiolo.)

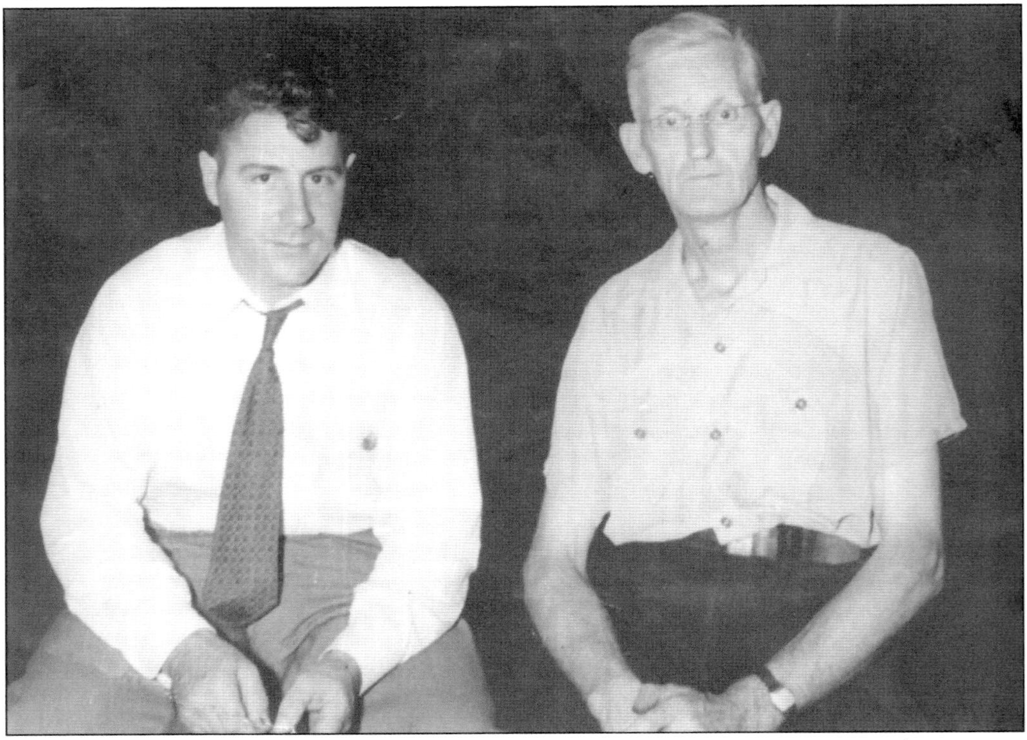

In this c. 1945 photograph are Frank Maiolo (left) and Harold "Pop" Briggs. Briggs was the manager at the Rollaway for many years prior to the 1940s. Maiolo managed the rink for a short time in the mid-1940s, moved to Rhode Island, then moved back to the area and managed the rink from 1949 until his death in 1966. (Courtesy of Susan and David Maiolo.)

Frank Maiolo was known for his offbeat promotions at the Rollaway. In this c. 1949 photograph, Bill Lenehan (left) and Eddie Ainsworth vie at the tip-off during a game of roller basketball. Frank Maiolo is in the background. In the 1950s, Lenehan would go on to become Massachusetts state figure skating champion. (Courtesy of Susan and David Maiolo.)

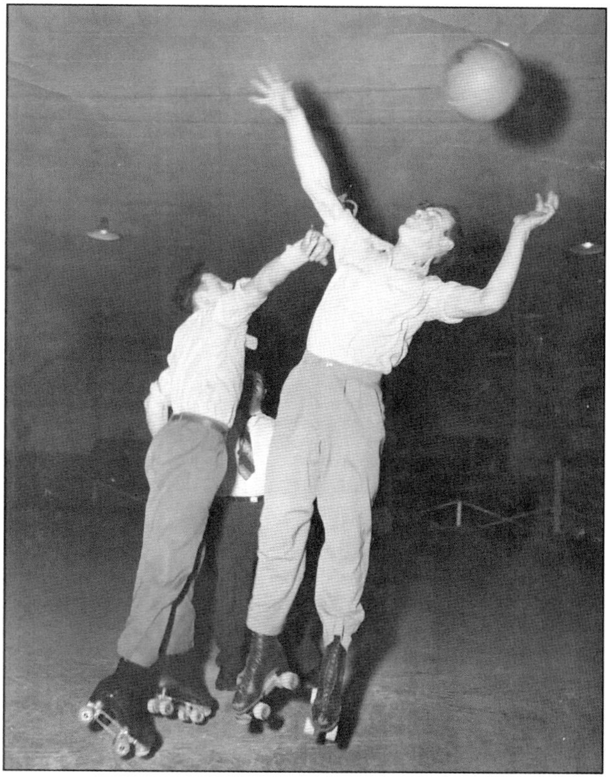

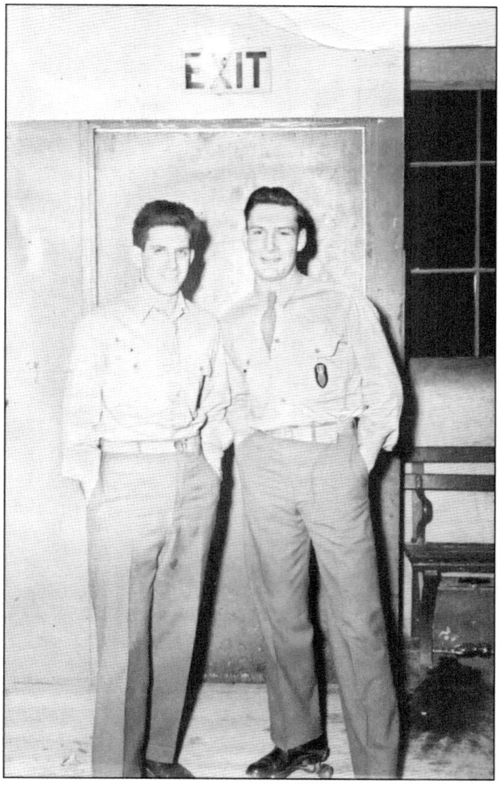


In uniform are Ed Duclos (left) of Agawam and Robert Lee of Springfield at the Riverside Rollaway while home on leave from training during the early years of World War II. "Everybody loved skating," remembers Ann LaPalme, Lee's sister, who spent a lot of time at the rink. Their father was Hal Lee, who played the organ at the Rollaway for many years. (Courtesy of Ann LaPalme.)

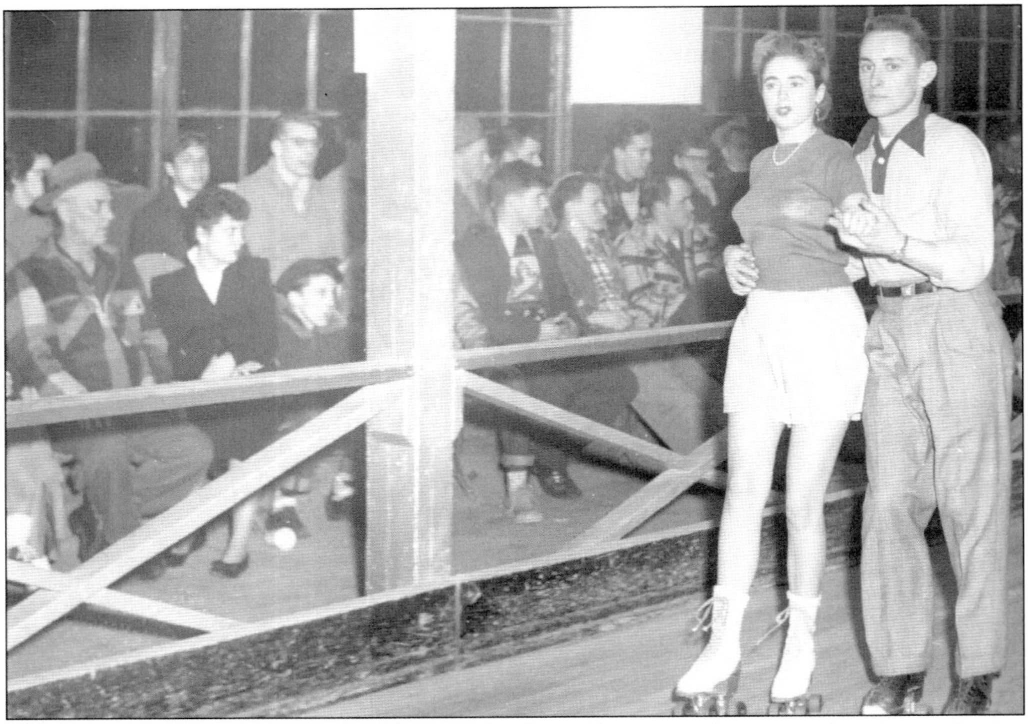

Skating was not popular only for those on the floor. Spectators far outnumber skaters in this photograph from the late 1940s or early 1950s of the "couple's skate." The rink was open six nights a week (closed Mondays) as well as Saturday and Sunday afternoons. (Photograph by Richard Russell, courtesy of Susan and David Maiolo.)

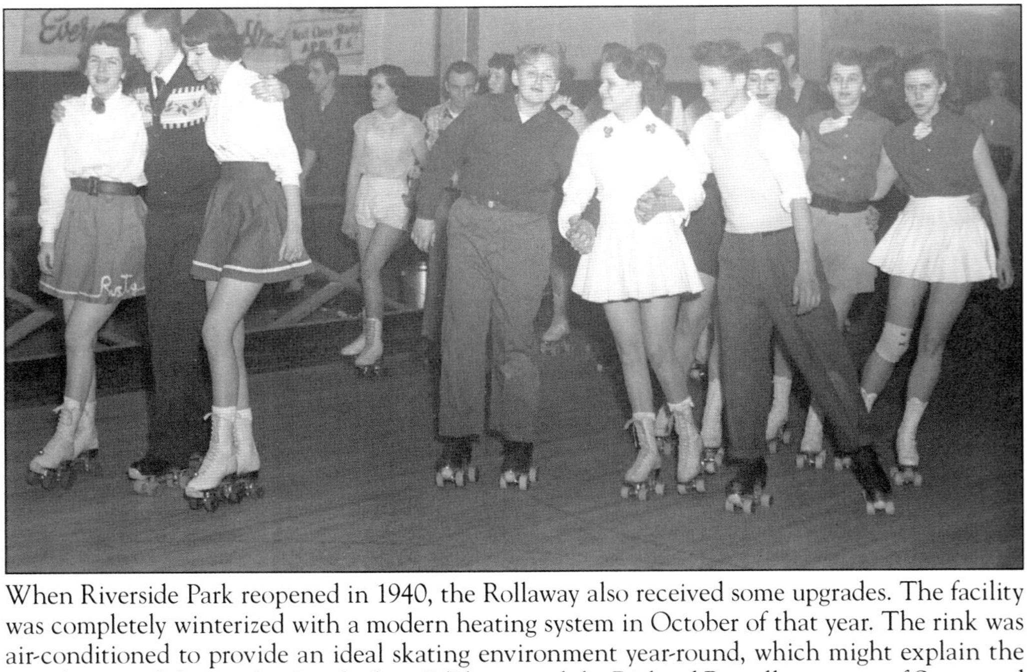

When Riverside Park reopened in 1940, the Rollaway also received some upgrades. The facility was completely winterized with a modern heating system in October of that year. The rink was air-conditioned to provide an ideal skating environment year-round, which might explain the crowd pictured during this "triple skate." (Photograph by Richard Russell, courtesy of Susan and David Maiolo.)

Hal Lee was the organist at the Riverside Rollaway during the 1940s and early 1950s. He loved to play music and was a member of a musical trio. He also played piano and organ in some of the large theaters in Springfield. Employed at Pratt & Whitney by day, Lee could be found on the Rollaway's organ stand each night. (Courtesy of Ann LaPalme.)

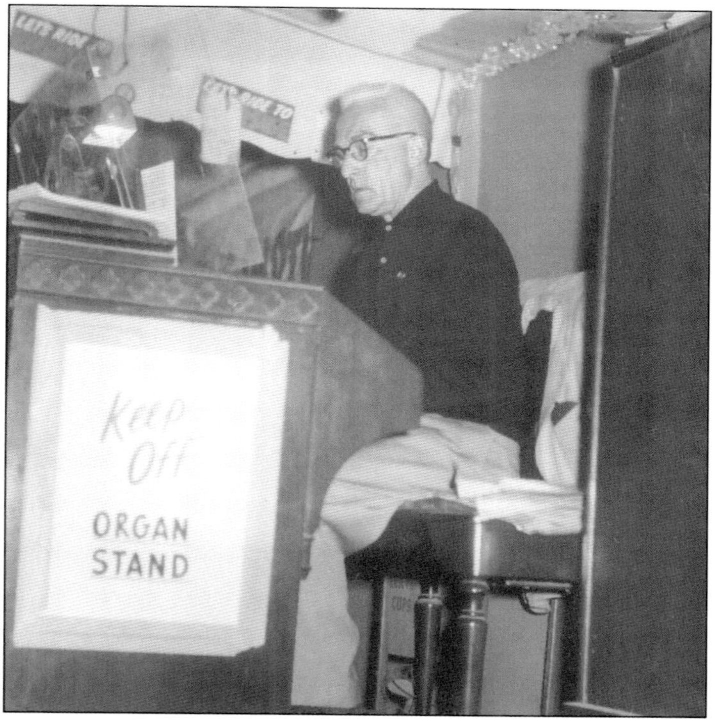


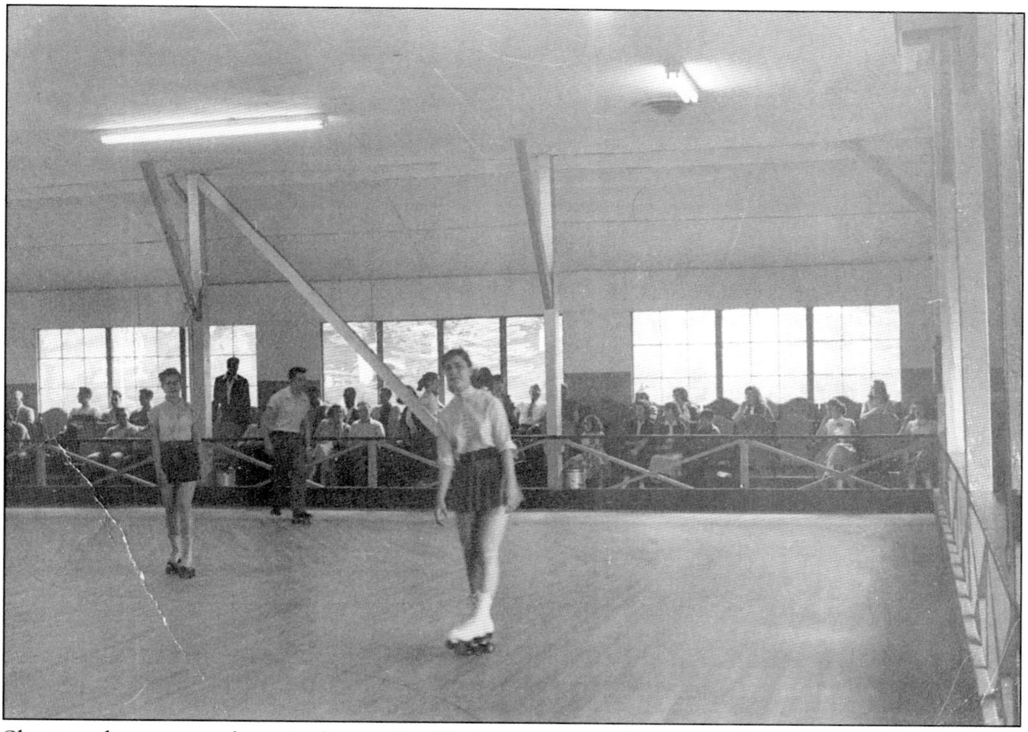

Skating the reverse skate in front of a filled spectator gallery on a Sunday afternoon in 1952 were Clara Carzello and Barbara Reynolds, both of Thompsonville, Connecticut. The recently installed fluorescent lighting system, which replaced the individual incandescent bulbs (page 102), is clearly visible in this photograph. (Courtesy of Clara Carzello Sanborn.)

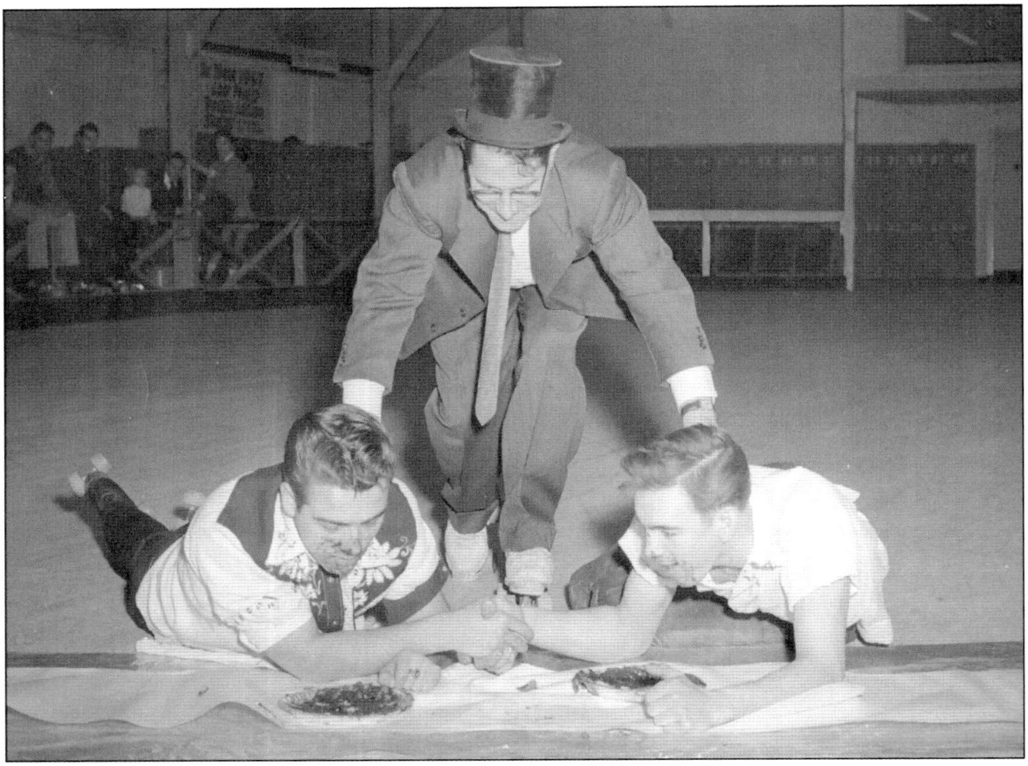

In garnering publicity, no stunt was too outlandish, as these photographs will attest. However, property owner Ed Carroll had his limits, and a wedding on skates planned in 1958 ruffled some feathers. A newspaper account from that time quotes Harry Storin, public relations director of Riverside Park, as saying, "The recent story of a proposed wedding at Riverside Rollaway is news to both Edward J. Carroll and myself. The roller rink at Riverside is a leased concession. Frank Maiolo has held that lease for many years and operates the rink as manager. It came as a complete surprise that such a promotion was planned. Needless to say, we would have thrown it out. We have tightened control of such offbeat ideas. We trust no one has been embarrassed in this situation, though frankly we have been, and we want no more of this kind of thinking." How times have changed! (Both, photograph by S.G. Shadbegian, courtesy of Susan and David Maiolo.)

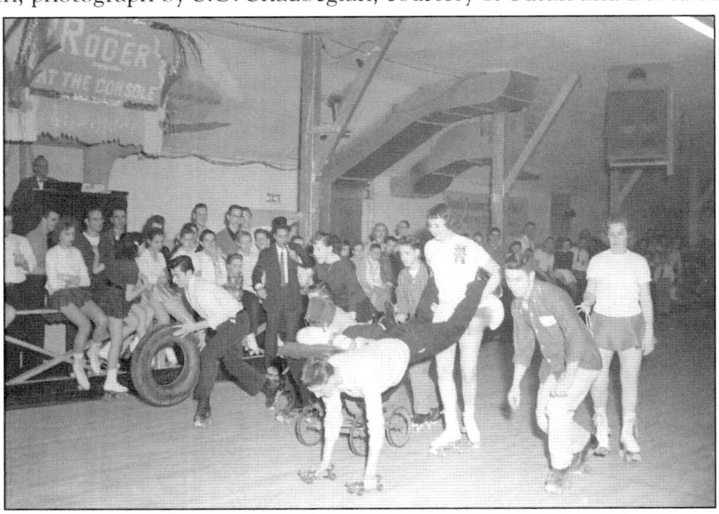

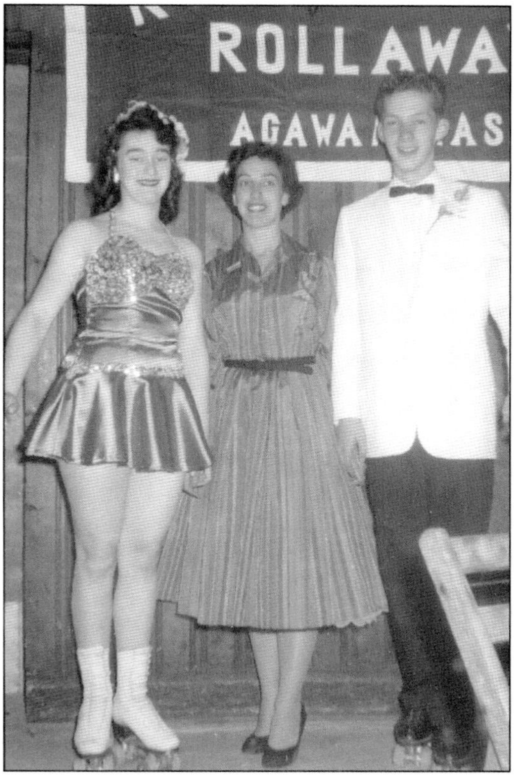


April Lamora (left), Rollaway skating professional Beverly Ross (center), and visiting pro Pinkie Packard are pictured at a 1959 skating competition presented by the Riverside Figure and Dance Club. The club creed stated the following: 1. I am a Club member; 2. I am no exception; 3. I skate for the love of the sport; 4. I am to abide by the rules of my home rink; and 5. I am a sportsman at all times. If I should fail I stand to be corrected. (Courtesy of April [Lamora] Brunelle.)

The author's grandfather, the late Erminio Cecchi, grew up on his father's farm less than 1.5 miles from the Riverside rink. In his younger days, he spent some time skating there in the offseason. This 1955 photograph includes Erminio (left), with the broken arm he suffered roller-skating as an adult. Also pictured are Robert Cecchi Sr., the author's father (center), and Carol Cecchi, the author's aunt. (Courtesy of Carol Cecchi Kaleialoha.)

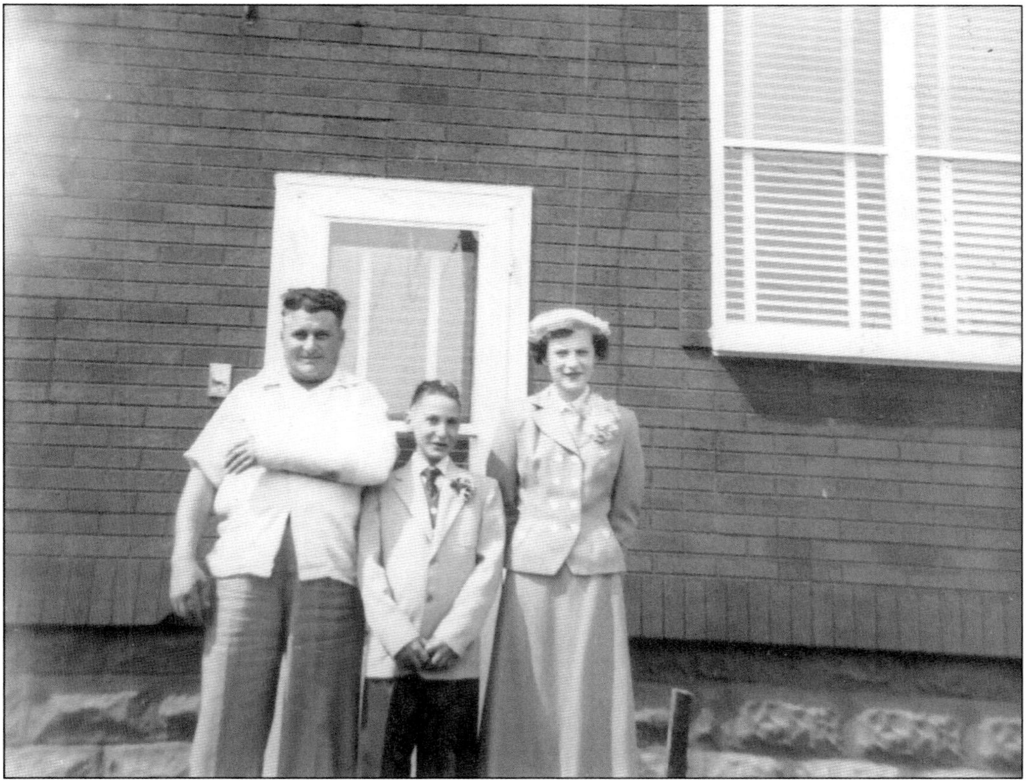

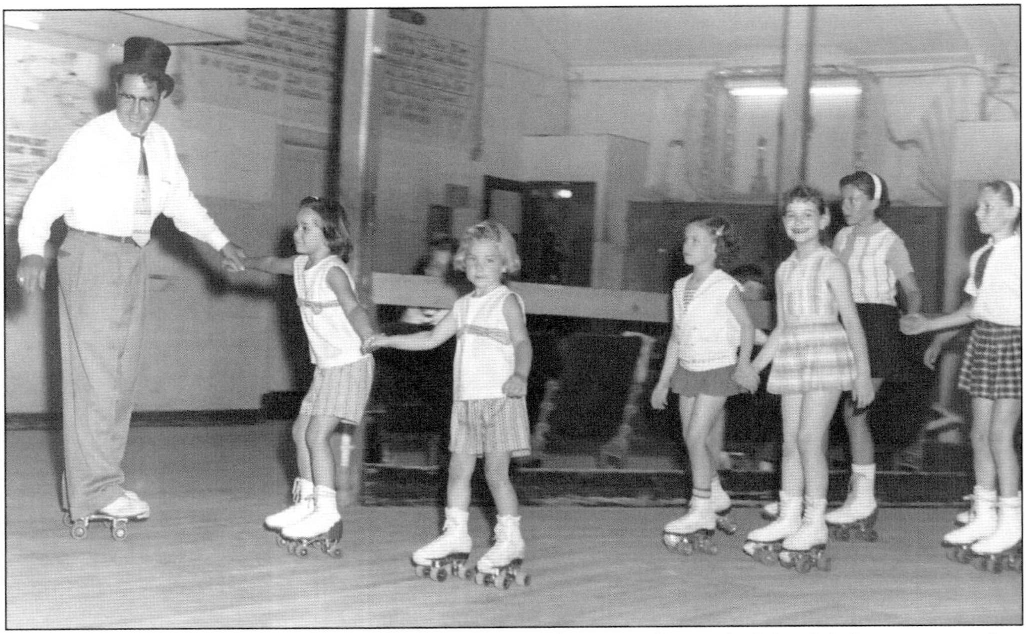

Frank Maiolo is pictured leading young skaters in the Grand March. Maiolo's heart was as big as his personality. He was very active in organizing events at the Rollaway to benefit charities such as the Massachusetts Heart Association Heart Fund, the American Cancer Society, and the Breath of Life, which in 1952 provided an iron lung for polio victims. A 1959 roller-skating show raised $6,000 for the Jimmy Fund. (Courtesy of Susan and David Maiolo.)

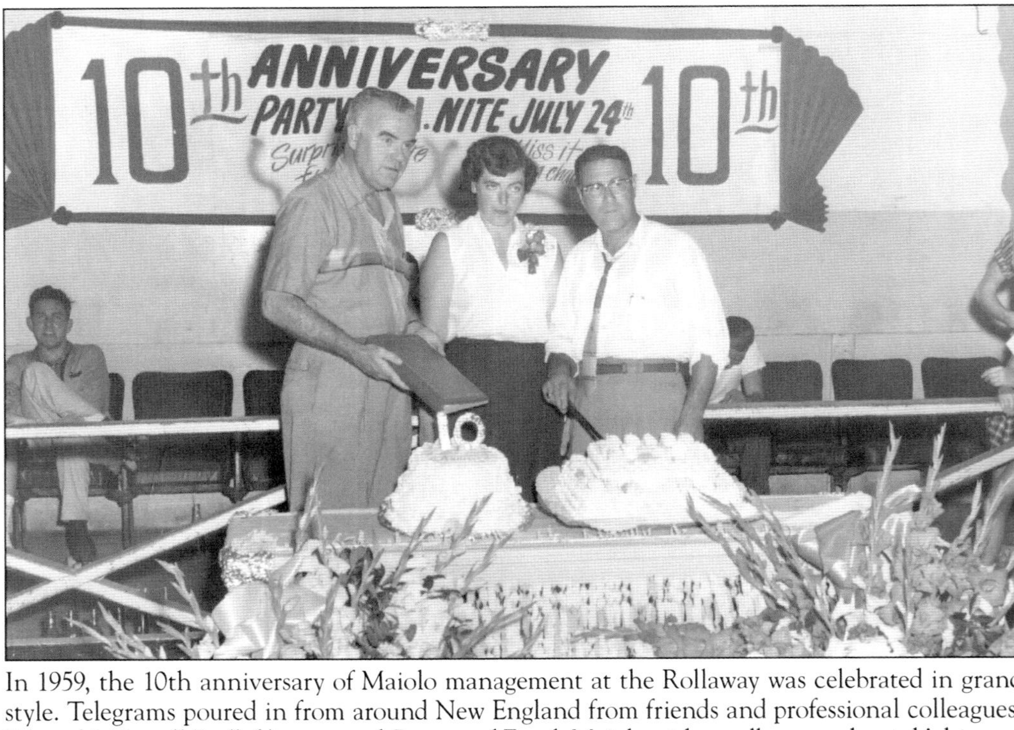


In 1959, the 10th anniversary of Maiolo management at the Rollaway was celebrated in grand style. Telegrams poured in from around New England from friends and professional colleagues. Edward J. Carroll Sr. (left) presented Susan and Frank Maiolo with an album on the rink's history. (Courtesy of Susan and David Maiolo.)

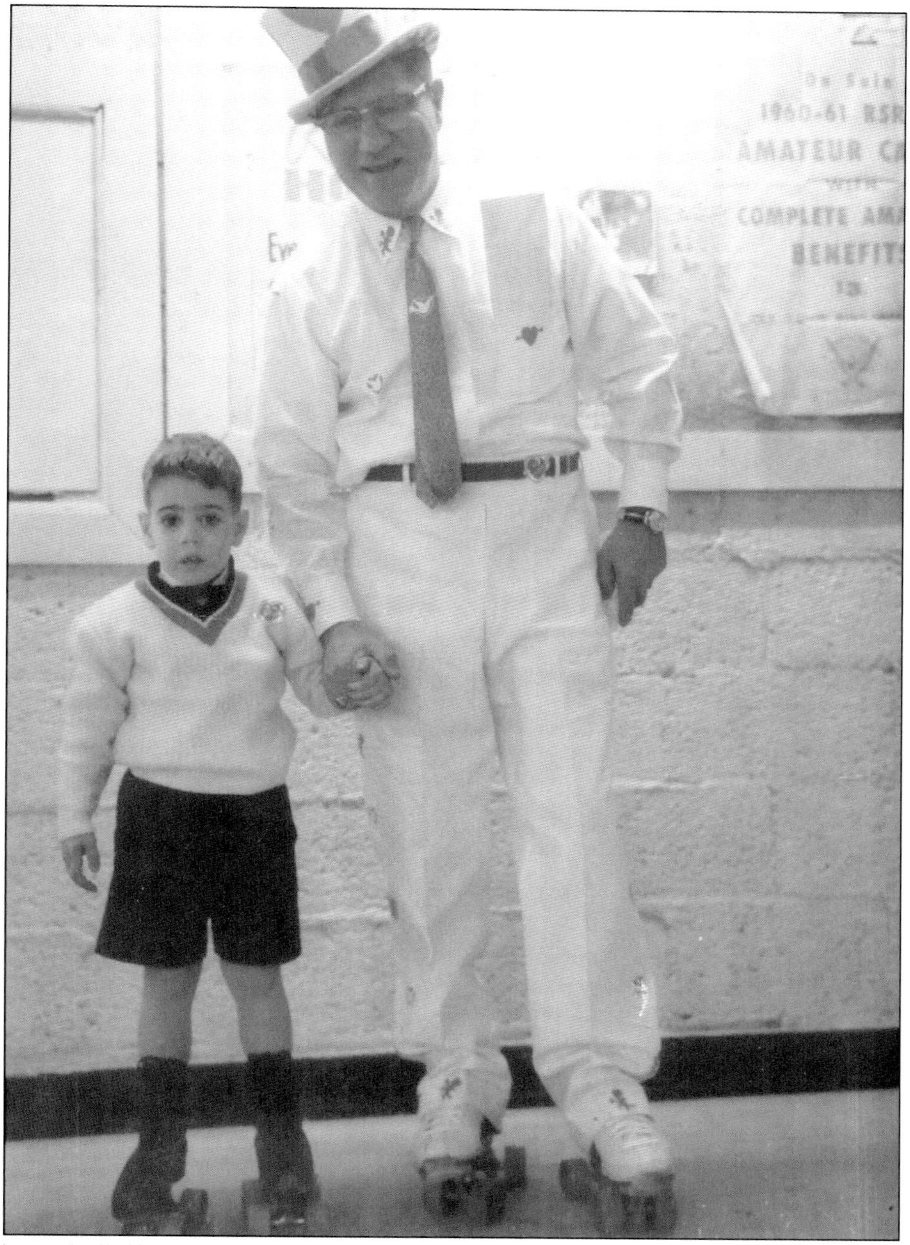


David Maiolo (left) poses with his father, Frank Maiolo, at Riverside Rollaway Heart Fund Night on February 14, 1961. After the elder Maiolo's death in 1966, his widow, Susan, operated the rink; eventually, David joined her in the family business. Frank was known for his hats as much as his stunts. In 1953, he sent a telegram to newly sworn in Vice Pres. Richard Nixon offering to purchase the $35 silk top hat worn at the inauguration for $50 when he learned that Nixon would have preferred a homburg. Maiolo's intention was to make wearing a top hat a practice down at the rink and to pass the hat among spectators to collect money that, along with a percentage of the gate, would go to the March of Dimes. Rose Mary Woods, Nixon's secretary, responded by letter: "The vice president greatly appreciates your offer to buy his top hat, but he is going to keep it as there will undoubtedly be occasions when he will have to wear it." Maiolo had already donated the $50 to the March of Dimes. (Courtesy of Susan and David Maiolo.)

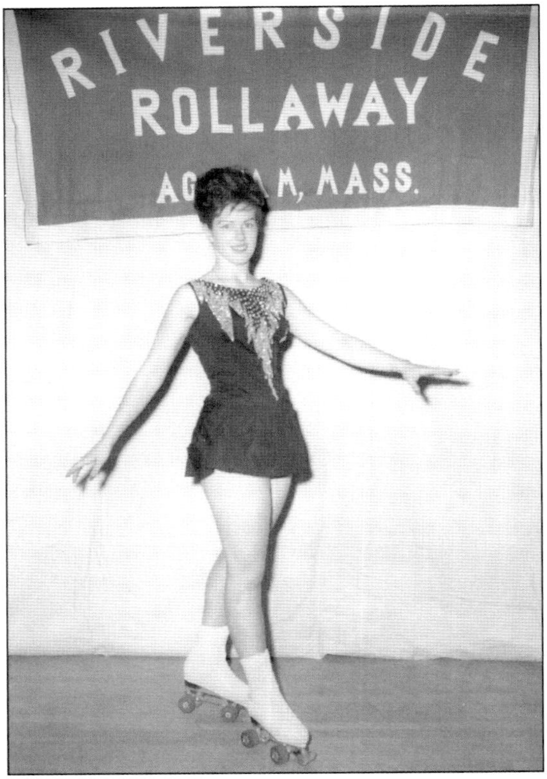


*Sports Illustrated* reported in its August 10, 1959, issue that "Sylvia Haffke, graceful 19-year-old secretary from Chicopee Falls, Mass., representing Agawam Skating Club, rolled off with Senior Ladies crown in American Amateur Roller-Skating Championships, Boston." Known for the "strength of her jumps, the speed of her spins, and the beauty of her carriage," Haffke was North American champion in 1959, 1963, 1964, and 1965. (Courtesy of Susan and David Maiolo.)

Charity benefits continued after Frank Maiolo's death. Pictured are friends and employees gathered at the Rollaway's Cancer Fund Night in 1967. Identified on the back of the photograph are, from left to right, (first row) Ann Lucier, a Mrs. Connors, Karen D'Amato, Irven Veto, and James Maiolo; (second row) Paul Lucier, Frank Kanop, Roland D'Amato, "Hot Dog" Mazzie, Gay Maiolo, a Dr. Curtiss, and a Mrs. Cross. (Courtesy of Susan and David Maiolo.)

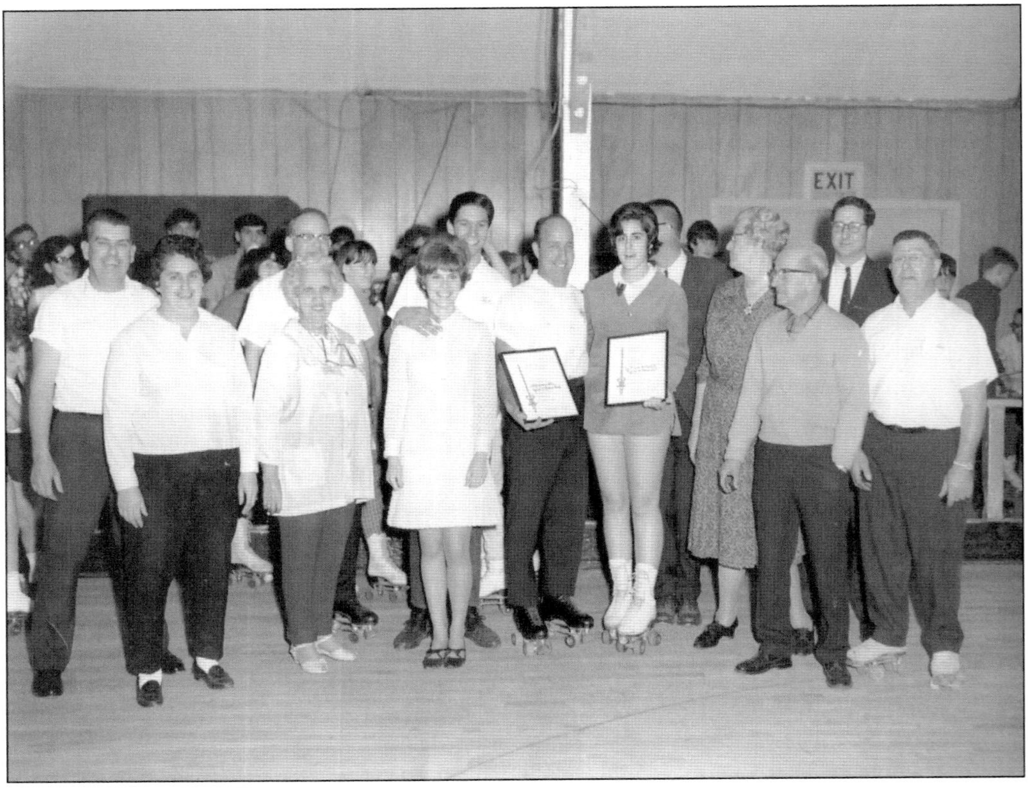

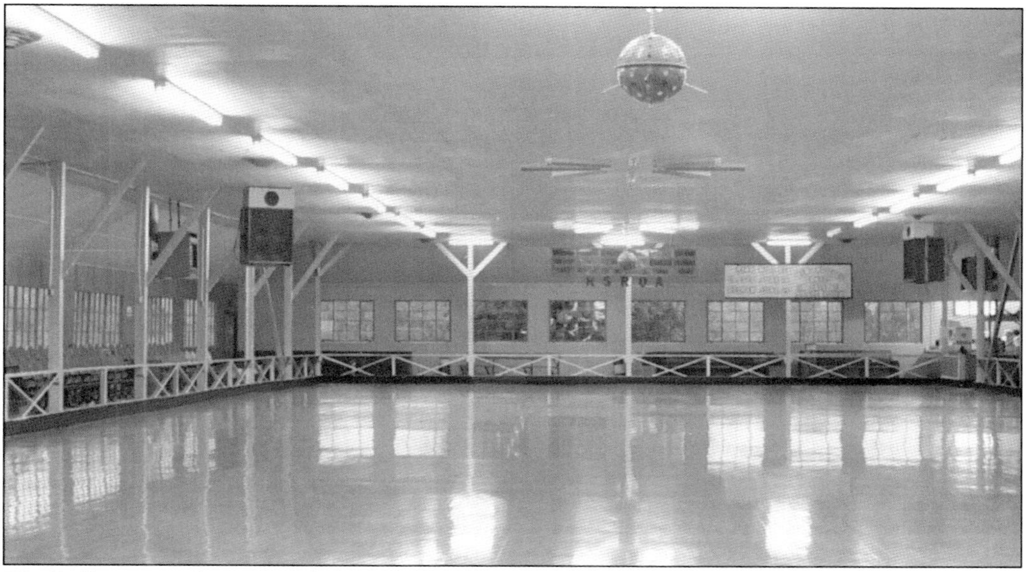

The Rollaway was known as the Rink of Discipline for many years. A 1957 notice read, "Any skater showing any implications of bad sportsmanship, such as arguing amongst themselves, making a spectacle of themselves, no respect for manager, 'pro' this rink or any other rink, will be released from club activities immediately and a possible suspension of your amateur status." The floor at the Rollaway was given a plastic coating in the 1970s. (Courtesy of Susan and David Maiolo.)

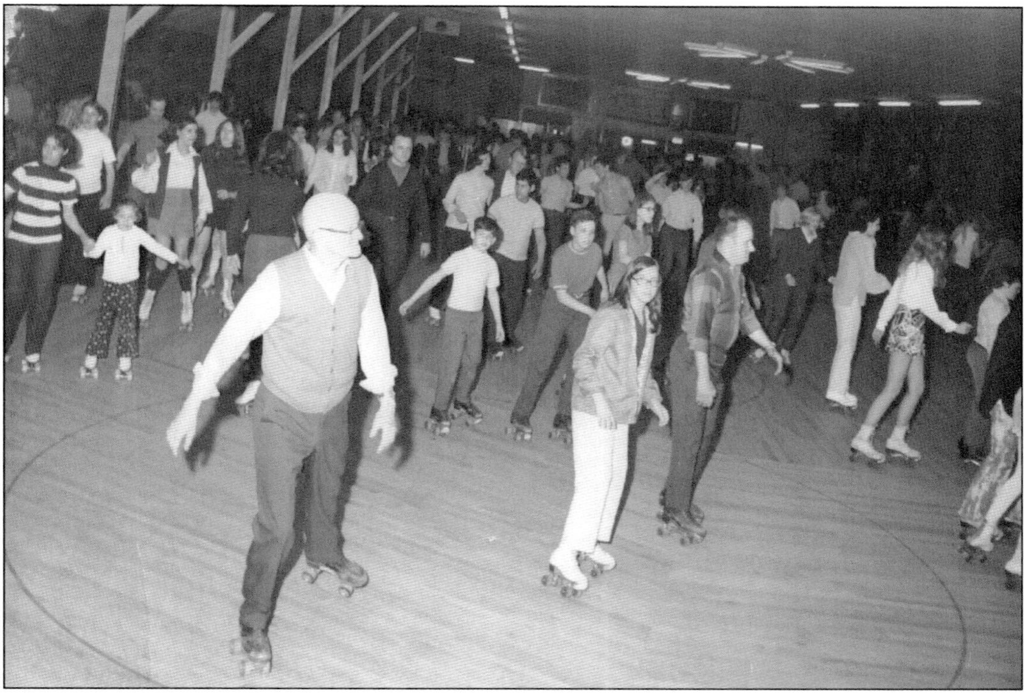

Time was running out for the Rollaway as Jack Shea (foreground, at left) joined skaters on this crowded night. The rink floor guard and a popular fixture, Shea was known as a jovial prankster. Although a 1974 letter from Ed Carroll Sr. curtly read, "As per our conversation of August 1, 1974, I will demolish the rink starting December 1, 1974," actual demolition did not take place until April 1978. (Courtesy of Susan and David Maiolo.)

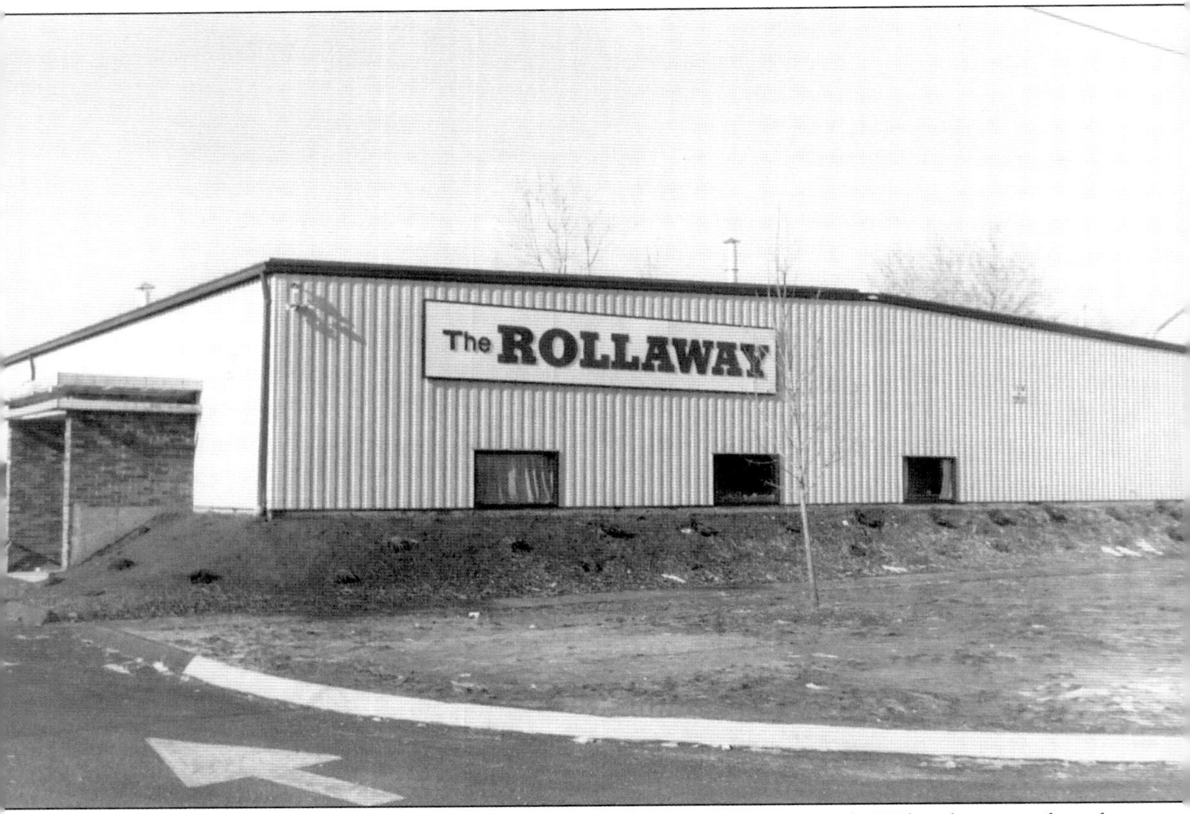


Ed Carroll Jr. demolished the old rink to add parking. He commented, "What happened to the roller-skating business is that the skateboard came into popularity." He added that skating was somewhat dated, "but that's only my opinion." Regardless of those sentiments, Susan and David Maiolo opened the new Rollaway (pictured) 200 yards away at 1756 Main Street on Friday, October 13, 1978. The 9,000-square-foot rink featured a $20,000 lighting and sound system and offered 1,000 pairs of rental skates. The new interior was nearly identical to the original. The operation was also a family affair, with help from Susan's daughter Gay, her mother, Viola Cross, and brother-in-law Jimmy Maiolo. The Rollaway was especially popular throughout the 1980s and operated for two more decades, closing in 1998. The Maiolo generosity was especially evident (and appreciated) when the author met with Susan and David while researching this book. Having just met, they handed over their entire archive of photographs and news clippings and said, "Use whatever you like." (Courtesy of Susan and David Maiolo.)

# *Nine*

# The Speedway

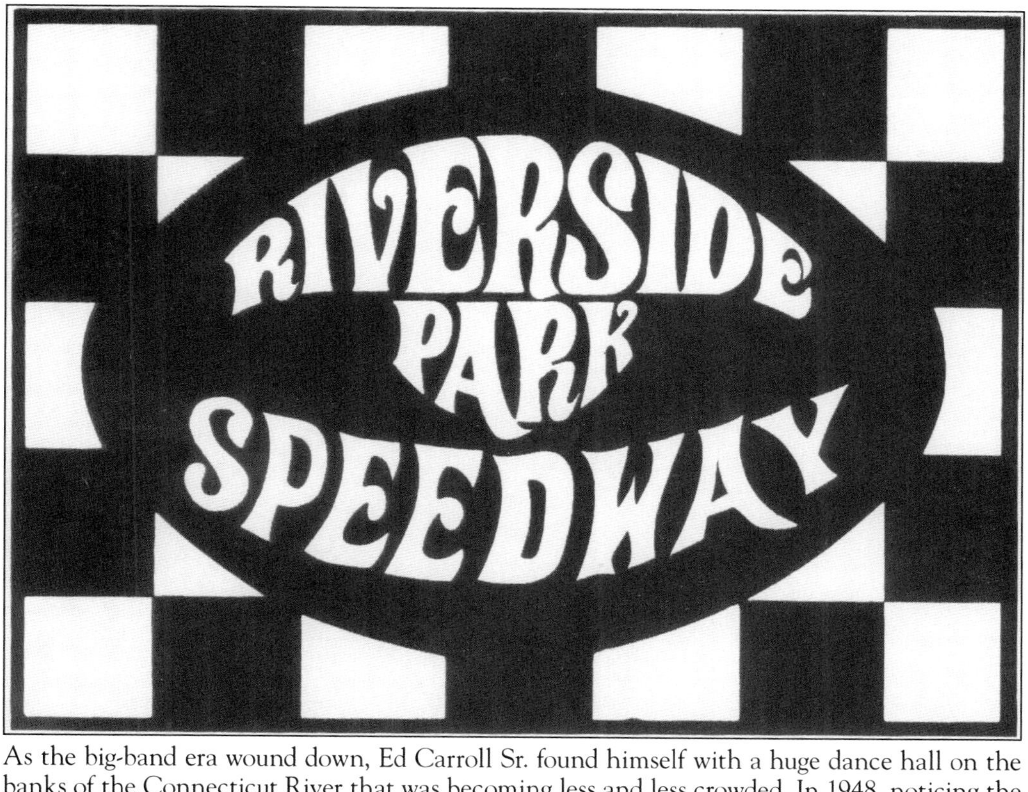


As the big-band era wound down, Ed Carroll Sr. found himself with a huge dance hall on the banks of the Connecticut River that was becoming less and less crowded. In 1948, noticing the rising popularity of auto racing, Carroll demolished the former Crystal Ballroom and constructed a flat, one-fifth-mile dirt track in its place. The bleachers were replaced with stadium seating in 1965. In 1972, the turns were banked and the track extended to a one-quarter-mile length.

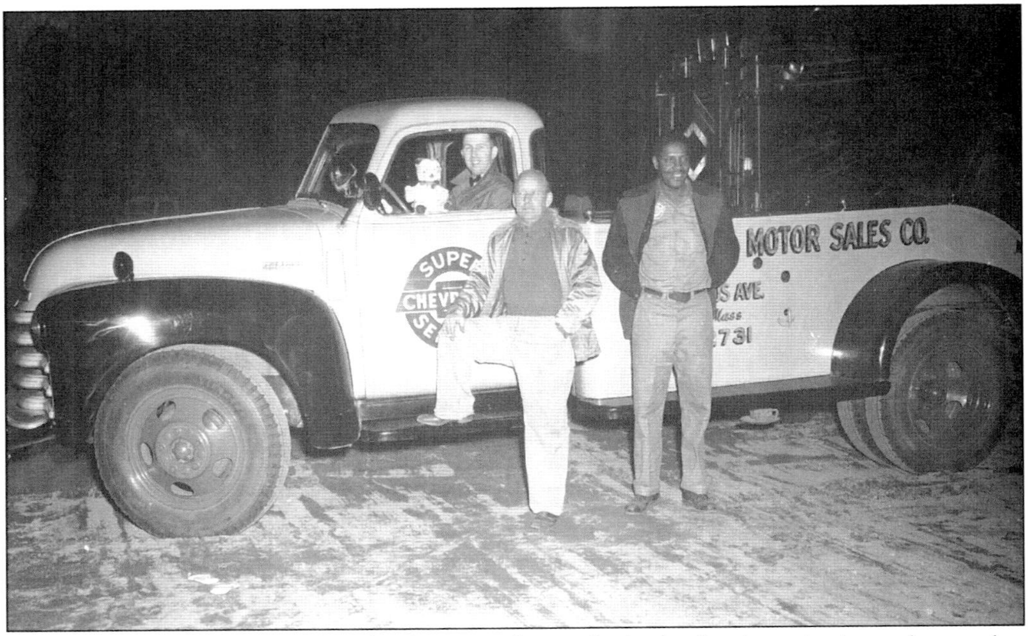


Robert F. Balise, pictured at the wheel sporting his workaday leather bow tie, drove the wrecker at the Riverside Speedway during its early years. At the time, Balise Motor Sales had the only wrecker in the area with a power boom (most were hand cranked), and track owner Ed Carroll wanted track wrecks cleared quickly. Later, Balise would drive the ambulance at the track for decades. (Courtesy of Robert P. Balise.)

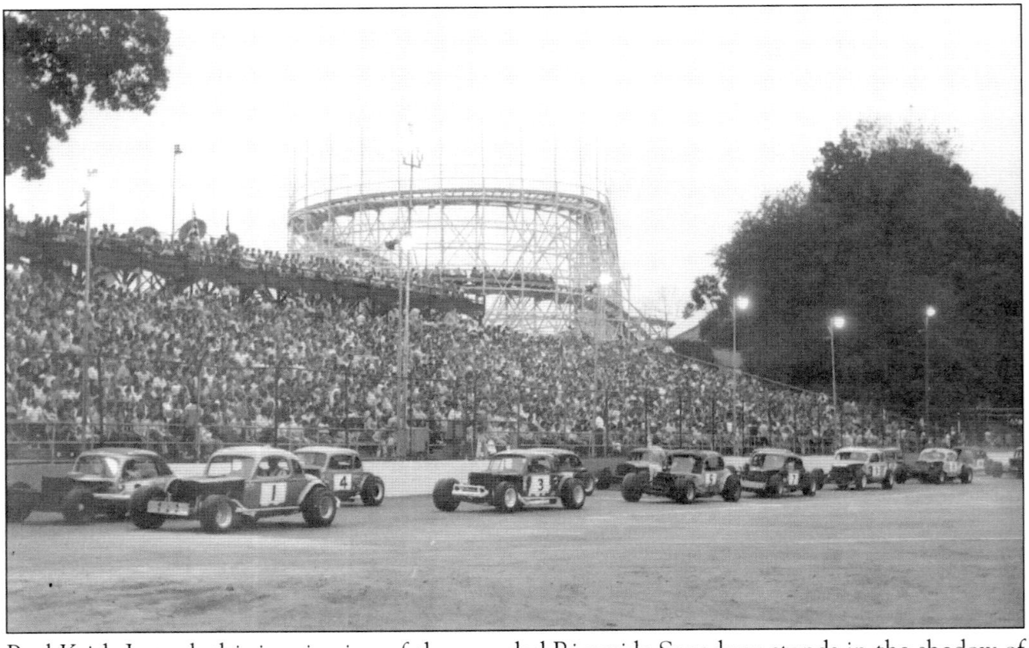

Paul Krish Jr. took this iconic view of the crowded Riverside Speedway stands in the shadow of the Thunderbolt roller coaster. This was the preferred setting for portraits of drivers in their cars. From this angle, the looming roller coaster was a landmark that immediately identified the track as Riverside. The Riverside Speedway was a popular Saturday night destination until the track was closed at the end of the 1999 season, ending more than 50 years of auto racing at Riverside.

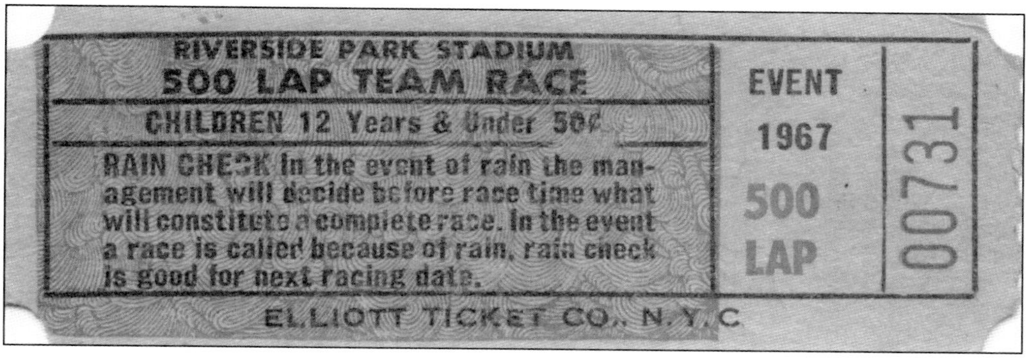


Pictured are tickets from the 500-lap team race in 1967 (above) and a standard stock-car race from 1971 (below). The new 7,000-seat Riverside Stadium opened on June 2, 1948, with a parade of dignitaries riding in convertibles. Led by the Major John J. Leonard VFW Color Guard & Drum Corps, Agawam selectmen E.L. Talmadge, Giles Hallady, Henry L. McGowan, Agawam police chief Perley J. Hewey, Springfield mayor Daniel B. Brunton, and Springfield Chamber of Commerce representative Robert D. Fuller joined Riverside Park owner Edward J. Carroll, park publicity director Harry Storin, and 5,000 race fans to witness a 25-lap midget car race, which was won by Dick Shuebruk. Although midget racing was very popular, modified stock cars soon became the featured event. In the 1960s, races were run under the sanction of the United Stock Car Racing Club. The first NASCAR-sanctioned event was held in 1976. (Below, courtesy of John Lazazzera.)

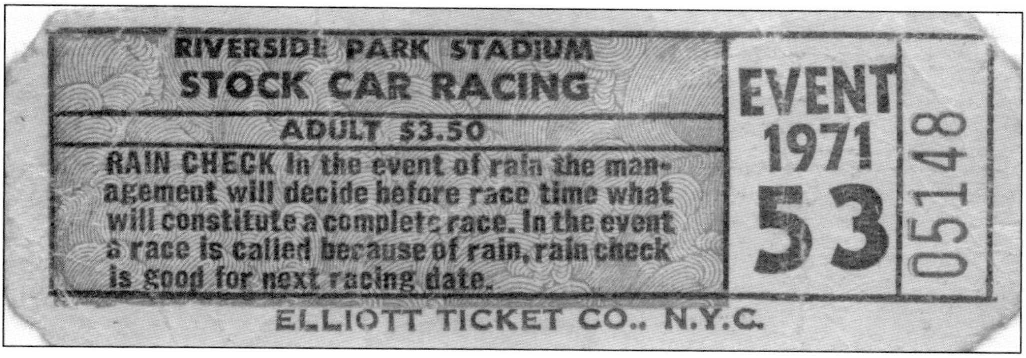

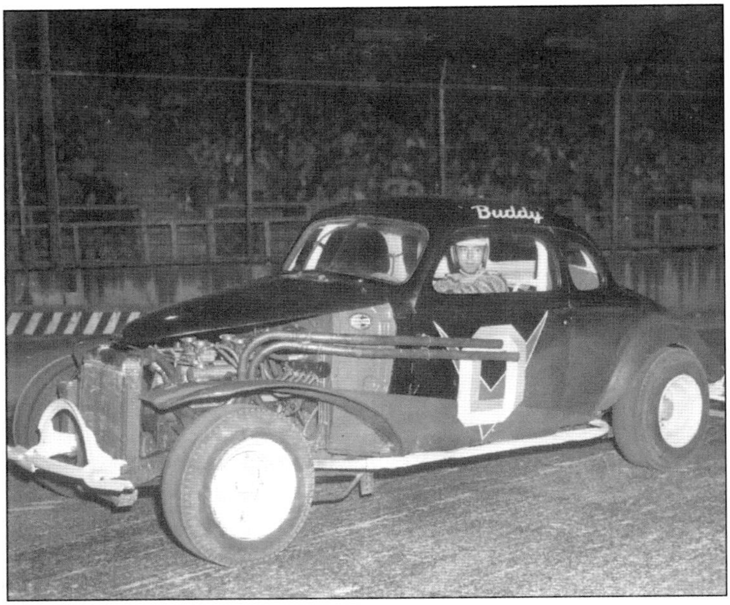


Charles "Buddy" Krebs considered Riverside his home track for most of his 21-year career from 1951 to 1972. Krebs posted 43 victories over 19 winning seasons and is third on the all-time Riverside wins list. In his first year at Riverside, he won 37 races, including the Riverside 500, a feat no other driver has duplicated. Krebs, who retired in 1974, is a member of the Riverside Park Speedway Hall of Fame. He died in 2006. (Courtesy of Robert P. Balise.)

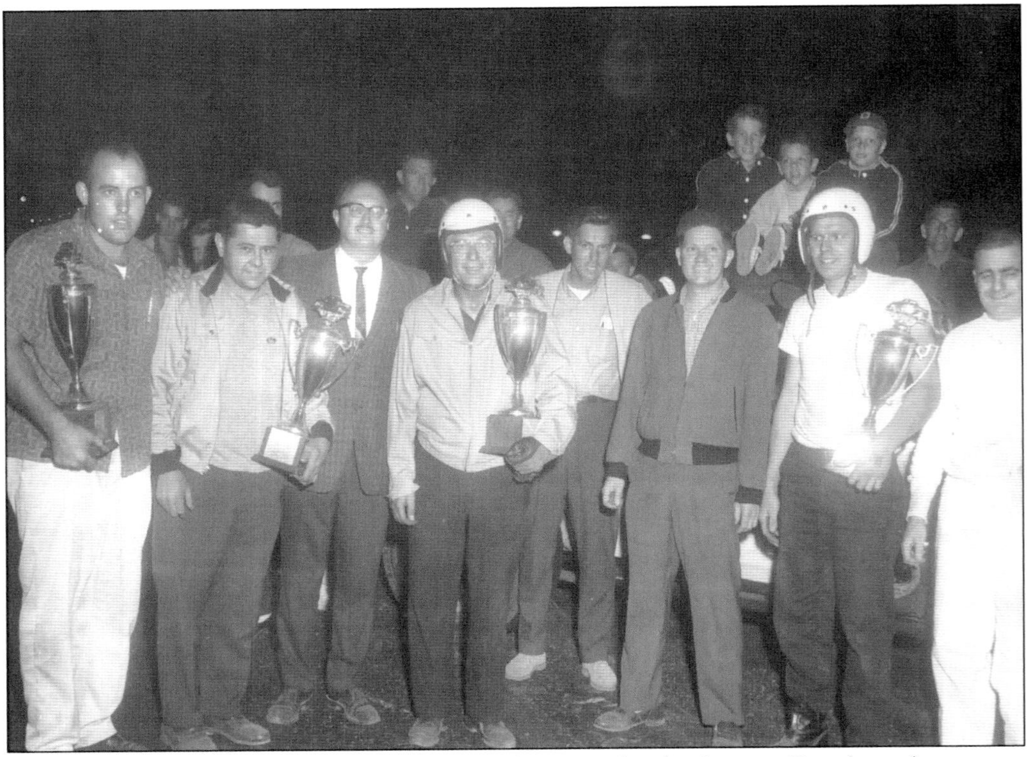

Chauncey "Jocko" Maggiacomo (center, in helmet) was another fan favorite. Here, he and teammate Bobby Bishop (right) gather after winning the 1964 Riverside 500, a 500-lap, 125-mile tag-team race that was held from 1951 to 1977. Maggiacomo was the speedway champion in 1952, 1953, and 1955, and he is eighth on the all-time Riverside wins list with 31 victories. A member of the Riverside Park Speedway Hall of Fame, he retired from racing in 1965 and died in 1998. (Courtesy of April Brunelle.)

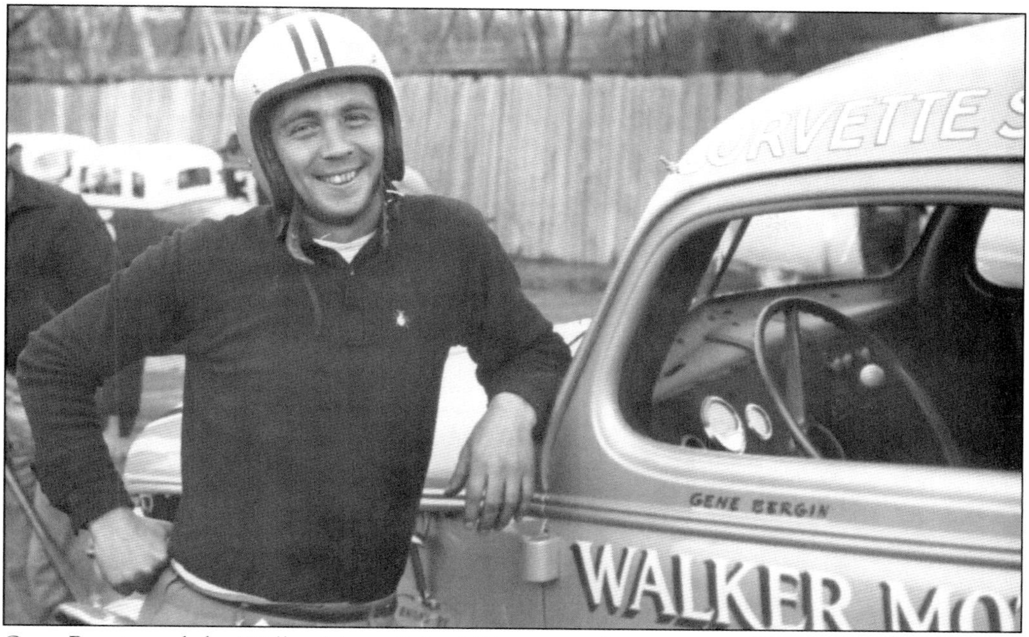


Gene Bergin and the Walker Motor Sales M6 car, seen here, were well known at the Riverside Speedway. Bergin won 16 features at Riverside between 1955 and 1963, including, with Buddy Krebs, the 1960 Riverside 500. His 16 wins and seven winning seasons tie him for 17th place on the Riverside all-time wins list, along with Benny Germano and Charlie Glazier. Bergin is a member of the Riverside Park Speedway Hall of Fame. (Courtesy of Robert P. Balise.)

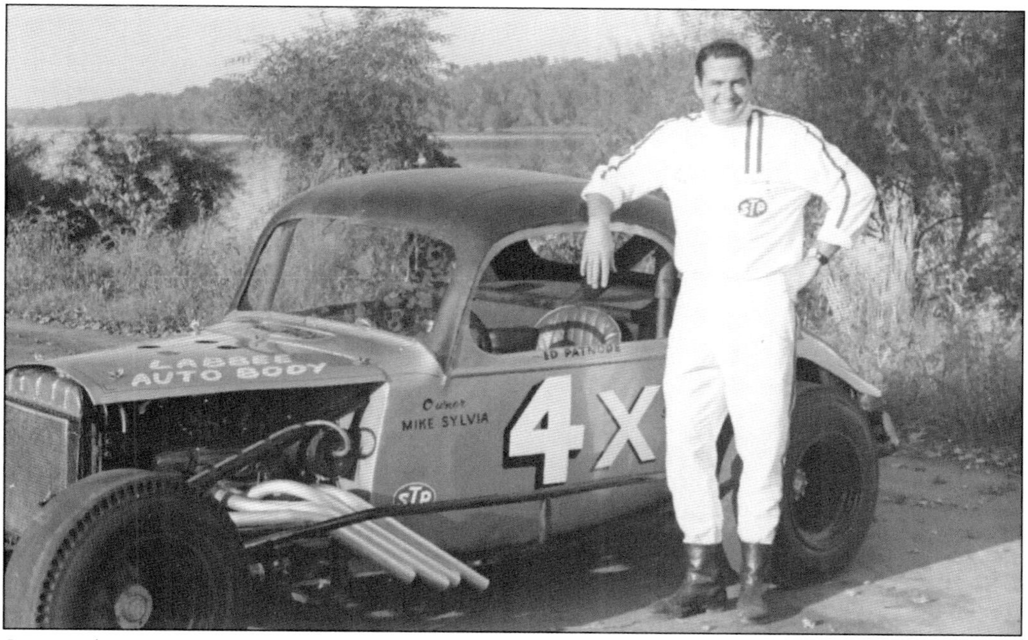


Seen at the Riverside pits in 1968, six-foot-five-inch "Big Ed" Patnode literally filled the car. Patnode won the Riverside 500 with teammate Buddy Krebs in 1963 and is ninth on the all-time Riverside wins list with 27 victories and 12 winning seasons. Patnode, whose racing career spanned from the 1950s into the 1970s, is a member of the Riverside Park Speedway Hall of Fame. He died in 1993. (Courtesy of Debi [Patnode] Harper.)

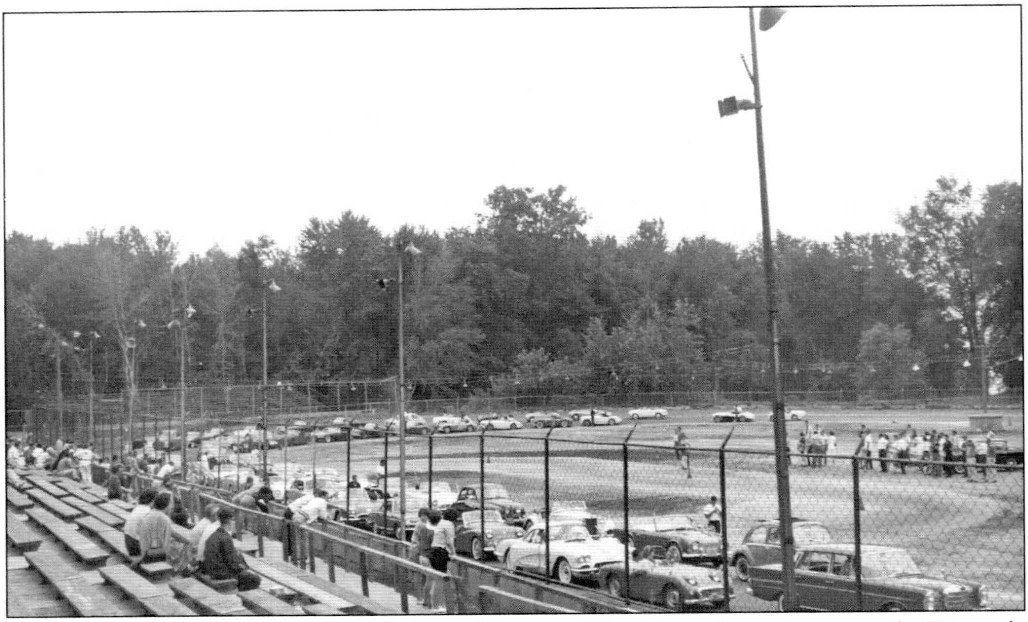

In addition to the regular Saturday night modifieds and Tuesday night novice races, the Riverside Speedway hosted other automotive events, such as truck races, demolition derbies, and rallies; it also held a number of concerts. Ron Sanders photographed one sports-car rally, which was held on a Sunday afternoon in the summer of 1962. Being led by a Mercedes sedan, the starting lineup (above) includes Chevrolet Corvettes, various MG and Triumph models, Volkswagens, an Austin-Healey, and even a Saab. The rally course started in the backstretch of the racetrack, turned into the infield where drivers made a hard right turn around one cone, weaved through two more cones before reentering the track, and ended with a sprint to the finish line. Below, a relatively new Jaguar XKE speeds through the course. The model had just been introduced in 1961. (Both, courtesy of Ron Sanders.)

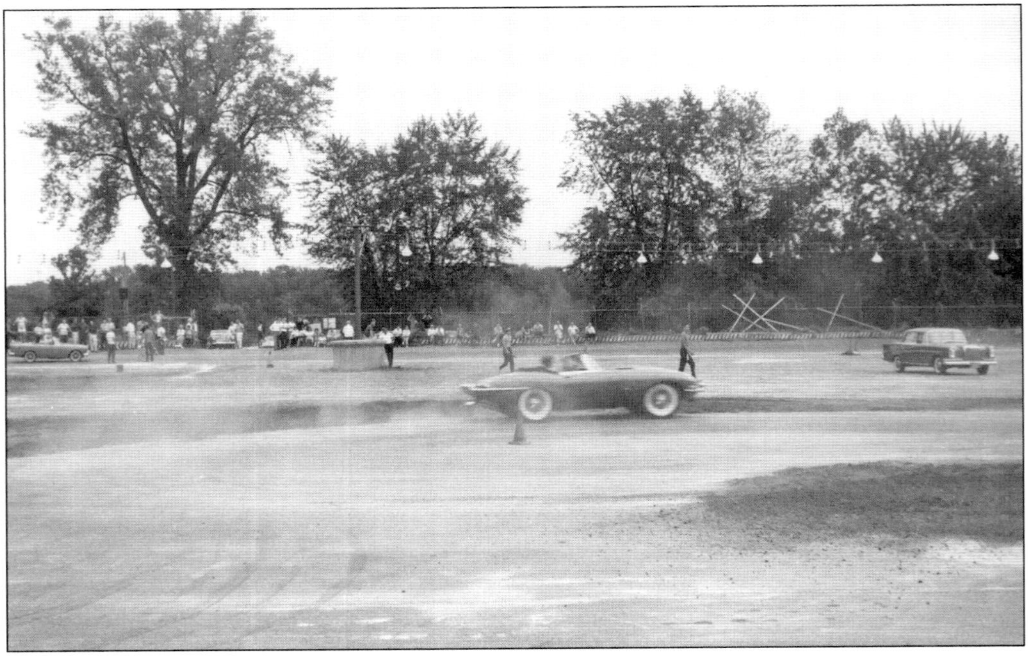

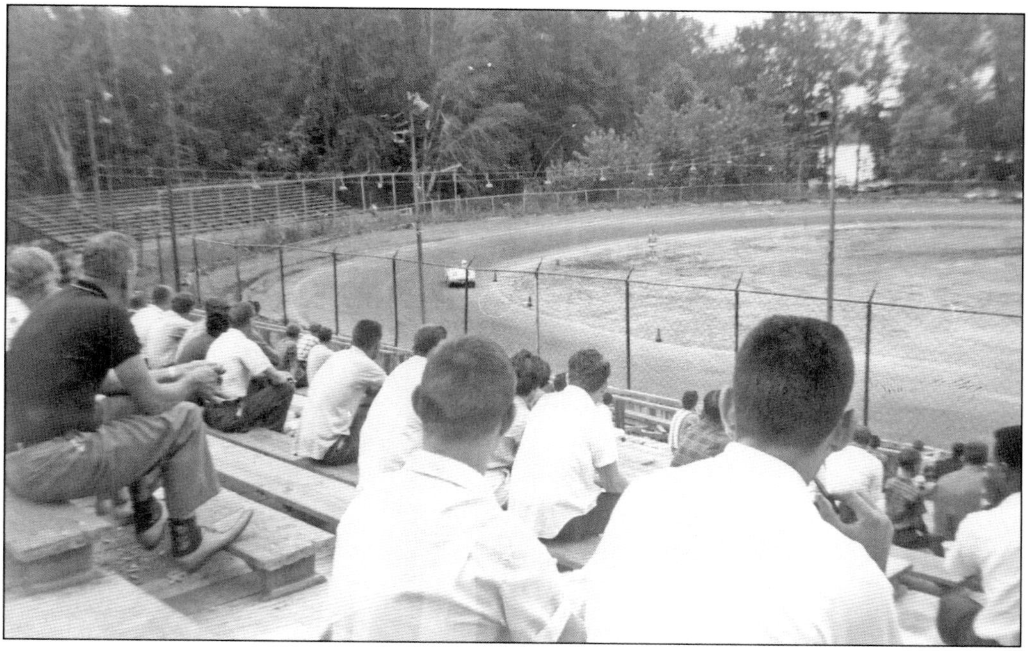

These two views of the same 1962 sports-car rally, with the Connecticut River visible in the background, clearly show just how close the track was to the water. The only thing between the track and the shore was the speedway pits. As anyone in the area remembers, when the races were run the sound would travel mightily across the river, much to the annoyance of residents of neighboring Longmeadow, Massachusetts. The roar of the cars could be heard throughout Agawam and as far away as Springfield's Winchester Square, almost seven miles away. (Both, courtesy of Ron Sanders.)

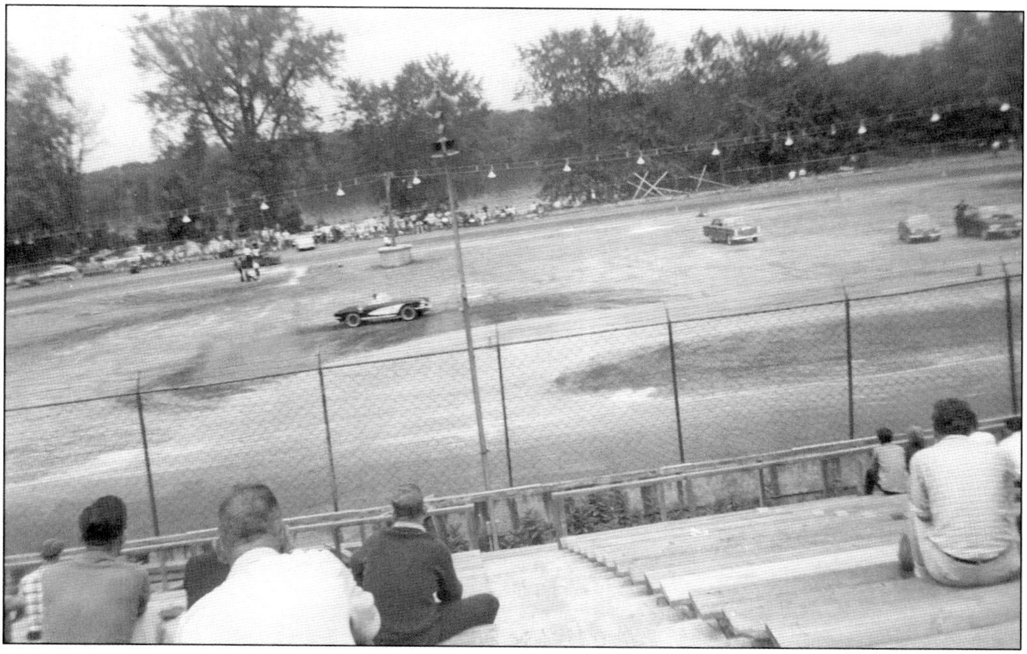

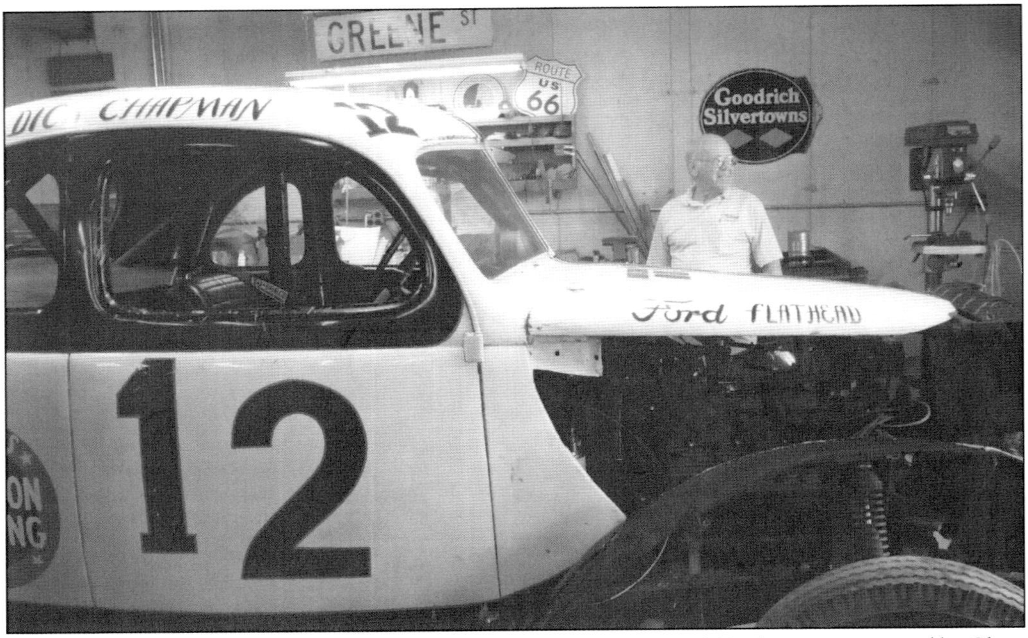


Dick Chapman was reunited with the last of his three No. 12 cars in 2008 after it was restored by Chris Sedlmayr of East Chatham, New York. Chapman, of Agawam, Massachusetts, raced at Riverside from 1951 to 1978. The 1937 Ford flathead coupe had spent 15 years in an Upstate New York chicken coop before it was found and restored by Sedlmayr. Chapman, in his 80s, is the oldest licensed NASCAR driver in the country and races the car at nostalgia events. (Courtesy of Dick Chapman.)

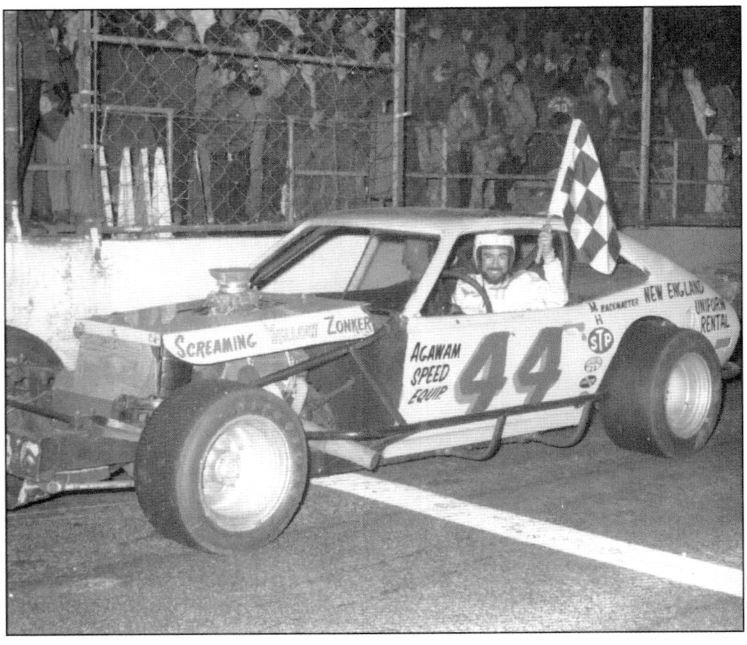


A member of the Riverside Park Speedway Hall of Fame, Gary Colturi was a talented and well-liked 12-year racing veteran when the 29-year-old died in June 1973 from injuries sustained in a motorcycle accident. This happened just months after the death of his 26-year-old wife. His five wins and four winning seasons place him in a 14-way tie for 46th place on the all-time Riverside wins list.

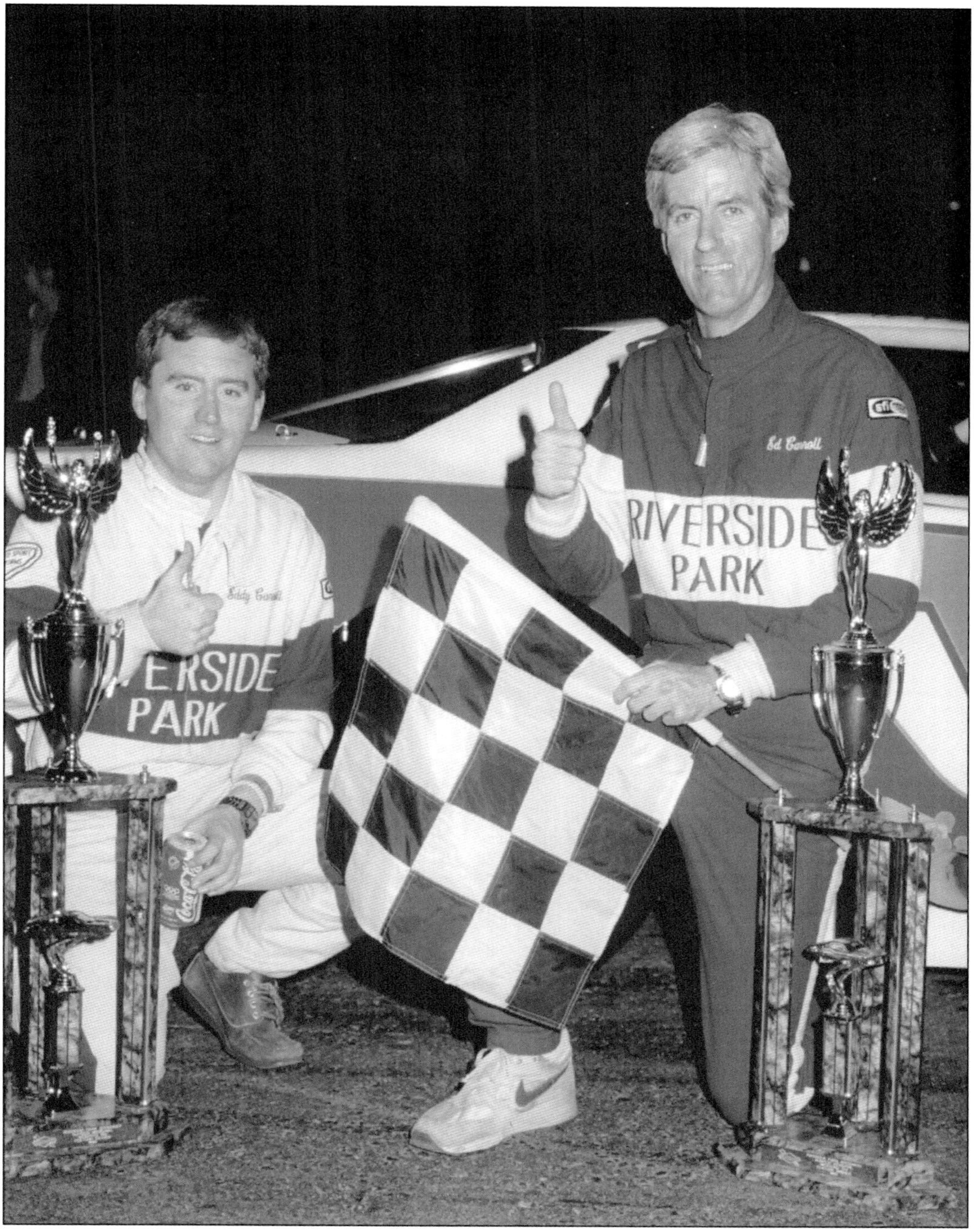


Ed Carroll Jr. got into stock-car racing after his son Billy took an interest in the sport. Billy drove Strictly Stock for a short time, then decided to abandon the sport in order to attend college after his father bought two Pro Stock cars. With openings for two drivers, Ed decided to drive one and offered the second to his other son, Eddy. At the time, Ed Jr. was one of the few, if not the only, track owner/promoter/drivers in the country. He finished his 10-year career with 10 wins. Eddy would go on to win many races at the speedway, including an unprecedented four Pro Stock Champion titles from 1996 to 1999, the last year the track was in operation. Here, Eddy Carroll (left) and Ed Carroll Jr. give thumbs-ups after winning the 1992 Riverside Park Speedway Sunoco Memorial Weekend 100. (Courtesy of Edward J. Carroll Jr.)

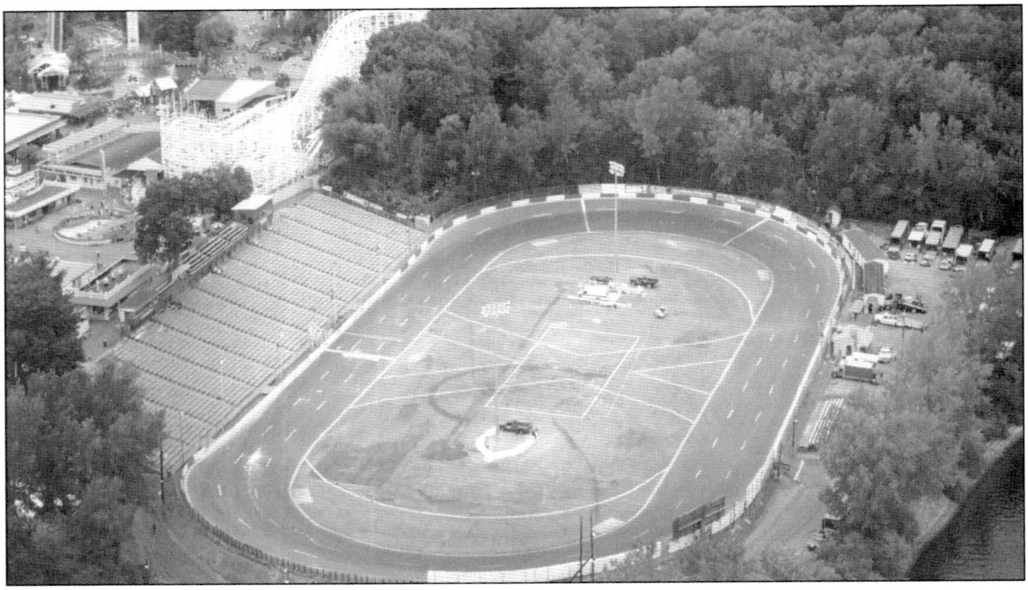

The Riverside Park Speedway is shown in 1999 nestled between the Thunderbolt roller coaster and the Connecticut River as it had been for over half a century (above). The same view, taken in 2000, is shown after the demolition of the speedway and construction of the Superman Ride of Steel roller coaster (below). Race fans have never forgiven the management of Six Flags for shutting down the speedway, which ended the rich legacy of stock-car racing that had been built over many decades by track owner Edward Carroll Sr., racing director Harvey Tattersall, Jr., and drivers such as Gordon Casey, Jerry Humiston, Bob Stefanik, John Rosati, Bob Polverari, Reggie Ruggiero, and others mentioned here. (Both, Aerials by Don Couture, courtesy of Mike Donahue.)

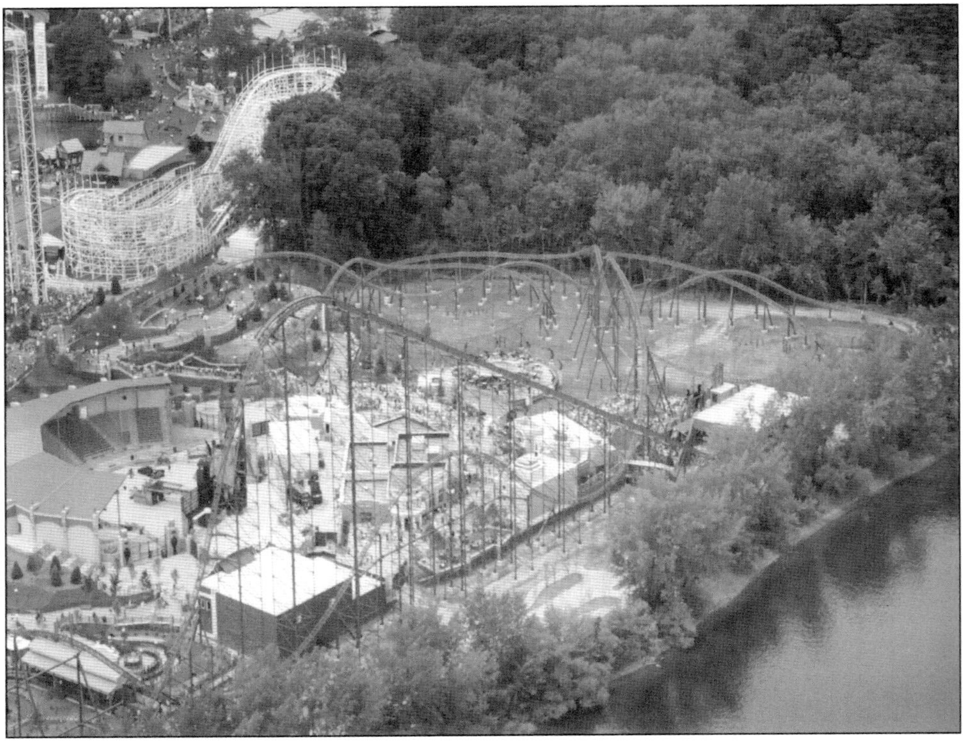

# *Ten*

# A New Era

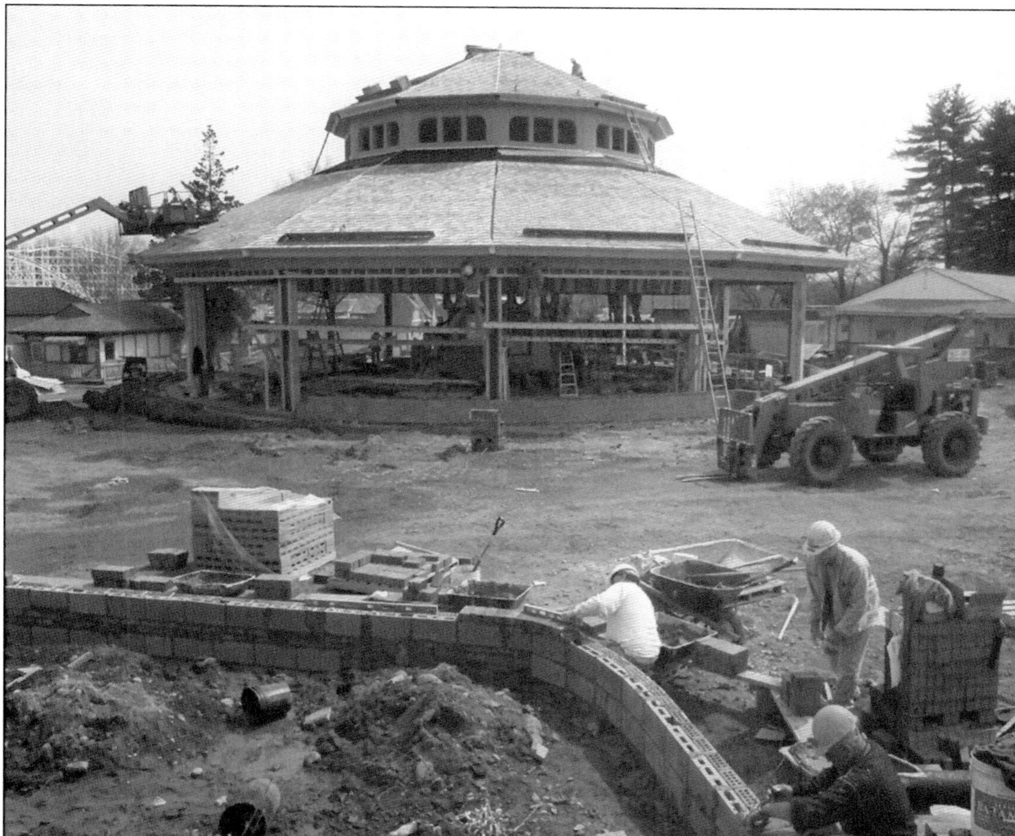

After the 1996 purchase of Riverside by Premier Parks, $20 million in improvements began, including the relocation of the carousel to a Victorian-style building near the park entrance. The $10 million Mind Eraser roller coaster was the main attraction when the park opened in 1997 as Riverside The Great Escape. That same year, Premier Parks bought Six Flags Corporation. (Photograph by Don Treeger, courtesy of *The Republican*, Springfield, Massachusetts.)

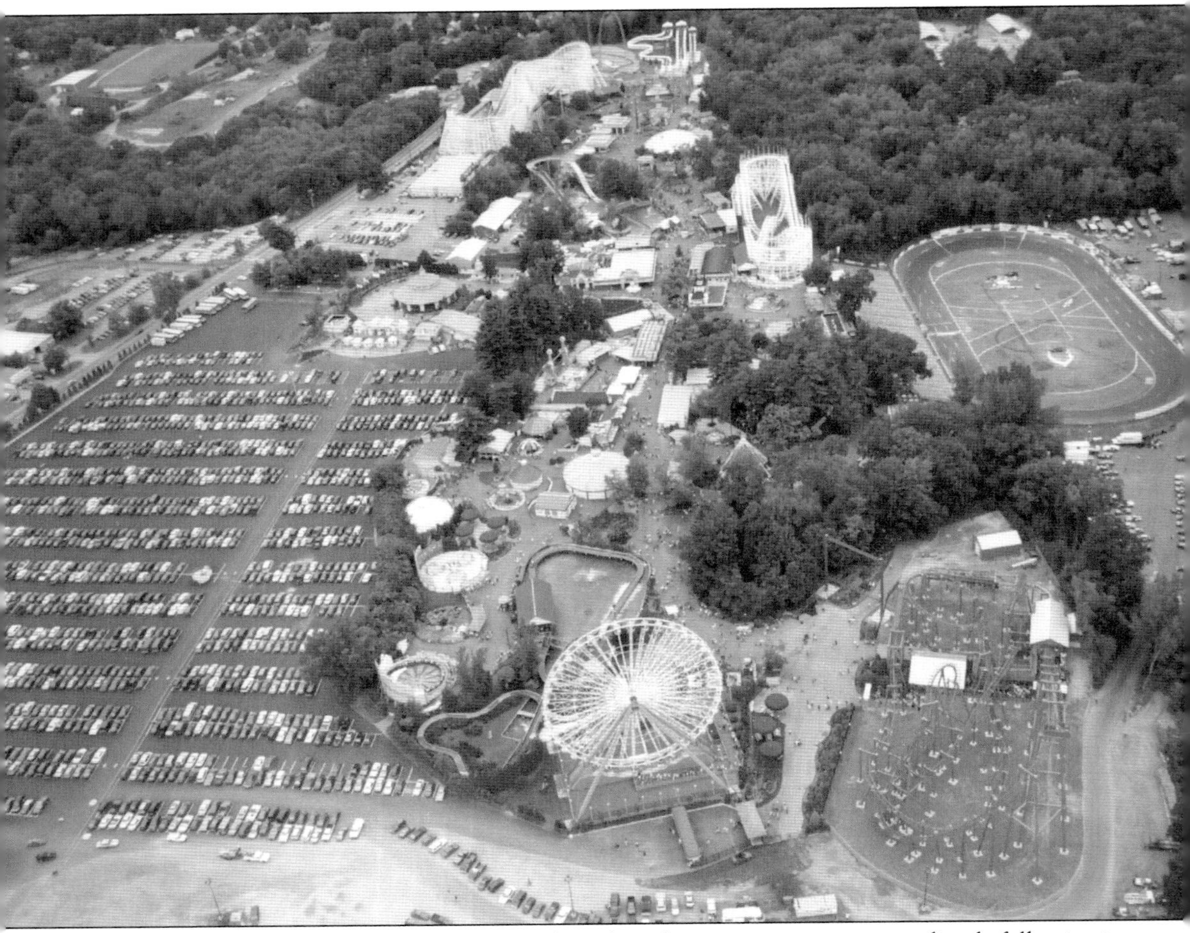

This photograph from 1998 shows Riverside Park in the transition years immediately following its sale to Premier Parks. The speedway can be seen (top right), the new Mind Eraser roller coaster (bottom right), and the new carousel building (just below the Cyclone roller coaster at top, center). A $30 million improvement project took place for the 1998 season, with the addition of the 185-foot Hellevator drop tower, the $12.6 million Island Kingdom water park, a $4 million children's park with three new rides, a 1950s Main Street, additional bumper cars, and updated models of the Spider and Scrambler rides. The park also added more than 60 acres of parking to meet the increase in visitors. In May 1998, a Latin American Festival that attracted nearly 20,000 people to the park caused a six-hour traffic jam on Main Street. As a result, Riverside management canceled five concerts scheduled for the remainder of the season and announced plans to build a pedestrian bridge over Main Street so visitors could walk from the parking lot to the park without stopping traffic on Main Street. (Aerials by Don Couture, courtesy of Mike Donahue.)

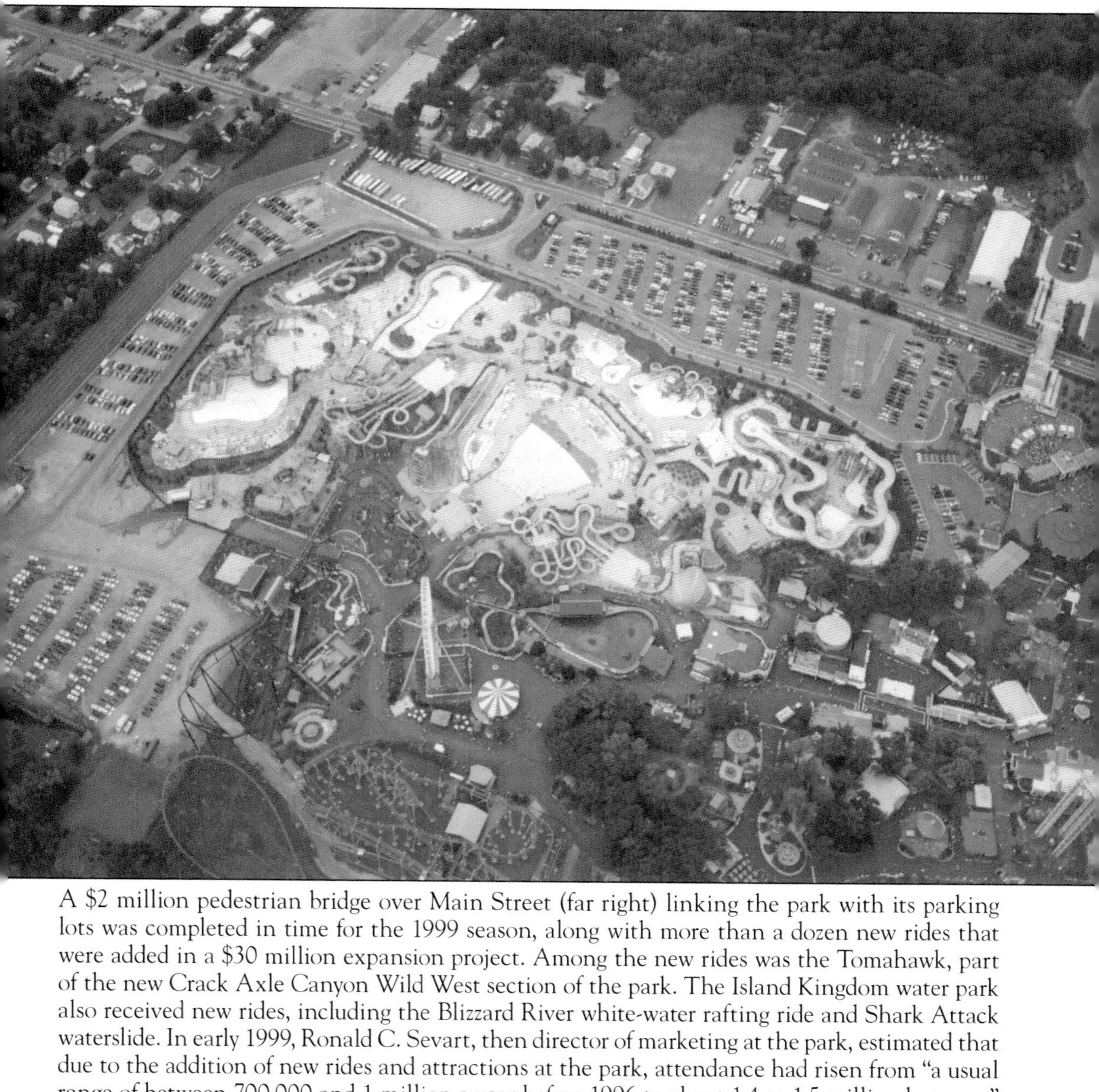

A $2 million pedestrian bridge over Main Street (far right) linking the park with its parking lots was completed in time for the 1999 season, along with more than a dozen new rides that were added in a $30 million expansion project. Among the new rides was the Tomahawk, part of the new Crack Axle Canyon Wild West section of the park. The Island Kingdom water park also received new rides, including the Blizzard River white-water rafting ride and Shark Attack waterslide. In early 1999, Ronald C. Sevart, then director of marketing at the park, estimated that due to the addition of new rides and attractions at the park, attendance had risen from "a usual range of between 700,000 and 1 million a year before 1996 to about 1.4 to 1.5 million last year." At the end of the 1999 season, it was announced that Riverside would open in May 2000 as Six Flags New England. The closing of the Riverside Speedway after 51 years was also announced. (Aerials by Don Couture, courtesy of Mike Donahue.)

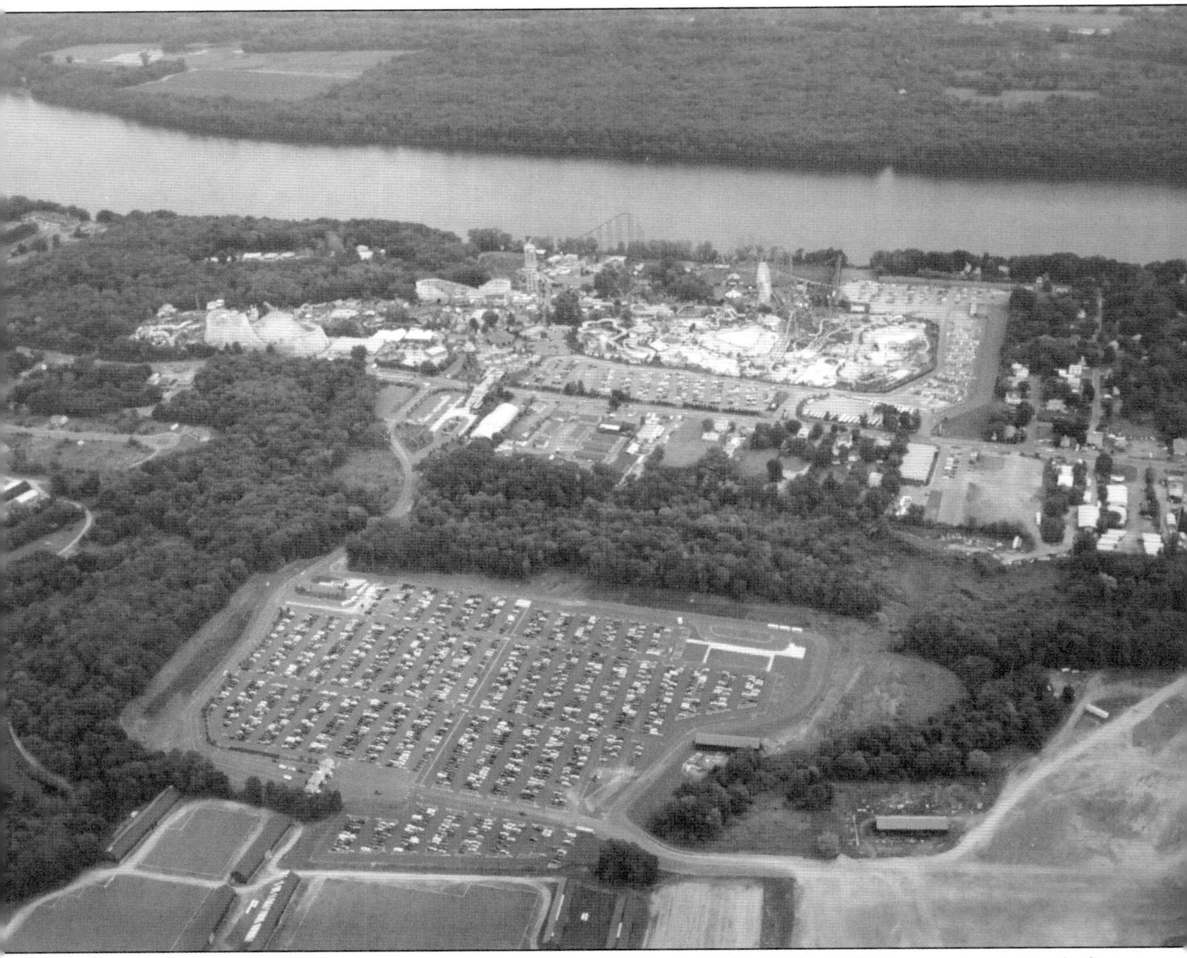

Six Flags New England opened in May 2000 with another $40 million of improvements, including the new Superman Ride of Steel roller coaster, which was named Best Coaster on the Planet for two years running by *Park World* magazine. By this time, more than $100 million had been invested in park improvements. Assessed at just $6 million in 1996, the park's valuation had risen to nearly $26 million in 1998, and by 2010, it was set at just over $81 million. The $2.1 million in taxes paid in 2010 qualified Six Flags New England as Agawam's second-highest taxpayer. This aerial view from 2003 includes the huge parking lot on the west side of Main Street at the bottom of the photograph, the park, and the Connecticut River beyond. The 235-acre park has continued to grow and add rides and attractions. The Superman roller coaster was re-themed in 2009 and reopened as Bizarro. Considered by many to be the world's best, the 5,400-foot coaster reaches speeds of 77 miles per hour. In 2011, the park opened with yet another new attraction, the Gotham City Gauntlet Escape from Arkham Asylum roller coaster. Somewhere, Henry J. Perkins and Ed Carroll are smiling. (Aerials by Don Couture, courtesy of Mike Donahue.)

# BIBLIOGRAPHY

*75th Anniversary Booklet*. Agawam, MA: Town of Agawam, 1930.
*Agawam, Massachusetts: Over the Span of a Century, 1855–1955*. Centennial souvenir booklet, 1955.
Archives of the Agawam Historical Association, Edith LaFrancis Collection, Agawam, MA.
Archives of the Lyman and Merrie Wood Museum of Springfield History, Springfield, MA.
Cecchi, David. *Agawam and Feeding Hills*. Charleston, SC: Arcadia Publishing, 2000.
———. *Agawam and Feeding Hills Revisited*. Charleston, SC: Arcadia Publishing, 2005.
Historic Racing website. www.historicracing.com.
LaFrancis, Edith. *Agawam, Massachusetts*. Agawam, MA: Town of Agawam, 1980.
McHugh, Jim. "The Ed Carroll Story." *Amusement Business* 83, no. 26 (July 3, 1971).
Orsucci, Jolece. "Riverside remains 'biggest show in town.' " *Agawam High School Mirror*, April 1986.
Quinn, William. *The Origin and Development of St. John the Evangelist Parish of Agawam, Massachusetts*. Westfield, MA: *Historical Journal of Western Massachusetts*, 1975.
*The Republican* Archives, Springfield, MA.
"Riverside Park." *Western New England Magazine*, July 1913.
Riverside Park Collection. Private collection of David Cecchi.
*Riverside Park Employee Newsletter*, various issues, 1977–1981.
Riverside Park Speedway Collection. Private collection of Bob Balise.
*Riverside's Thunderbolt Times*, April 1988.
The *Springfield Republican* Historical Archive, 1844–1946. www.newsbank.com.